COUNTRY OF ASH

A Jewish Doctor in Poland

1939–1945

COUNTRY OF ASH

A Jewish Doctor in Poland
1939–1945

EDWARD REICHER

Translated from the French edition by
Magda Bogin,

based on Jessica Taylor-Kucia's
English version of the original Polish

BELLEVUE LITERARY PRESS
NEW YORK

First Published in the United States in 2013 by
Bellevue Literary Press, New York

FOR INFORMATION CONTACT:
Bellevue Literary Press
NYU School of Medicine
550 First Avenue
OBV A612
New York, NY 10016

Library of Congress Cataloging-in-Publication Data
Reicher, Edward, 1900–1975, author.
[W ostrym swietle dnia. English]
Country of ash : a Jewish doctor in Poland, 1939–1945 / Edward Reicher ;
translated from the French edition by Magda Bogin, based on Jessica Taylor-
Kucia's English version of the original Polish. — First edition.
pages cm
Includes bibliographical references and index.
ISBN 978-1-934137-45-1 (alk. paper)
1. Reicher, Edward, 1900–1975. 2. Jews—Poland—Lødz—Biography.
3. Jewish physicians—Poland—Lødz—Biography. 4. Jewish
physicians—Poland—Warsaw—Biography. 5. Holocaust, Jewish
(1939–1945)—Poland—Lødz—Personal narratives. 6. Holocaust, Jewish
(1939–1945)—Poland—Warsaw—Personal narratives. 7. World War, 1939–
1945—Poland—Personal narratives, Jewish. 8. Lødz (Poland)—Biography.
I. Title.
DS134.72.R44413 A3 2013
940.53'18092--dc23
[B]
2012046157

Bellevue Literary Press would like to thank all its generous
donors—individuals and foundations—for their support.

Book design and composition by Mulberry Tree Press, Inc.
Manufactured in the United States of America.
first edition

1 3 5 7 9 8 6 4 2
ISBN 978-1-934137-45-1

A true coward is one who fears his own memories.
—Elias Canetti

Translator's Foreword

Magda Bogin

That Edward Reicher, a Jewish doctor from Lodz, should have lived through the Nazi occupation of Poland and the ghettos of both Lodz and Warsaw, from which more than 500,000 Jews were sent to their deaths or killed during World War II, is remarkable. The odds were entirely against him. That he should have done so with his young wife and small daughter—and without ever leaving Warsaw—is astounding. The story of this book parallels the improbable arc of their survival.

Dr. Reicher's account, which he began to write in 1944, was lost in the last days of the war as he and his family played a deadly game of cat-and-mouse with the Gestapo and Polish informers. Under assumed names and in separate hiding places on the Polish side of Warsaw, to which they had fled in a vegetable cart after three years in the ghetto, they lived in unrelenting terror for nearly three more years, moving constantly in a series of close calls, wrenching decisions and daredevil escapes.

Reicher reconstructed his story in the early 1960s, many years after the events he describes. His intent was simple and without literary pretense: to leave behind a record of what he and his family had endured, in the hope that future generations would choose humanism over savagery.

Despite his modest aim, what he produced reads like a novel. *Country of Ash* is a vivid canvas of life in the ghettos from which hardly anyone emerged alive, an almost photographic record of the suffering, cruelty, heroism, ingenuity, despair, chance encounters and, in the end, the unexpected kindness of strangers that spelled the difference between death and life for Reicher, his wife Pola and their little daughter.

But this is far more than the story of a single family. Reicher peopled his manuscript with dozens of characters whose lives intersected in a world of unprecedented evil and transcendent grace. Some of them, like Herman Höfle, the cherub-faced Nazi commander who oversaw the liquidation of the Warsaw ghetto and, years later, unrepentant, hung himself while awaiting trial after the war, are well-known to historians, as is Chaim Rumkowski, the delusional self-proclaimed King of the Jews, Reicher's former neighbor, who ran the Lodz ghetto for the Germans before allegedly being burned alive by fellow inmates at Auschwitz. Then there is Janusz Korczak, the head of the Jewish orphanage in the Warsaw ghetto, who accompanied his charges to Treblinka, refusing to save himself and abandon them alone to their fate. Others belong to the ranks of workers, doctors, thieves, swindlers, aristocrats, musicians and nuns—some heroes, some villains, but all inmates of the prison that was Poland under Nazi rule. Unforgettable are Toni Schmidt, the German conscript from the Sudetenland who fell in love with Reicher's young sister-in-law Alina and risked his life to supply the hidden family with food; Yola Glicenstein, the beautiful teenager who became a ghetto cause célèbre for stealing bread to save her starving parents; Leon Kac, the Jewish barber to the Gestapo, who believed to the end that he and his family would retire to the Riviera after the war; and Roza Chmielewska, the Warsaw prostitute who led Reicher to her home just as a Polish crowd prepared to turn him in to the Gestapo.

Finally, there are the thousands of Jews trapped in the shrinking ghetto, whom Reicher portrays from the vantage points of the rooftops or cellars where his family had taken momentary refuge: the daily columns of Jews being marched to Treblinka, "growing smaller and smaller, as at the end of a film" and the hundreds of young Jewish fighters, many exuberantly marrying as they prepare to die in the uprising of 1943 (after one such wedding, Reicher and his wife are smuggled back to their basement hideout in a hearse, riding in two coffins side by side.)

Reicher's portrait of wartime Warsaw through Jewish eyes, first from within the ghetto and then from the Polish side, gives us a twentieth century vision of hell —a view that evokes the teeming paintings of Brueghel but whose understated grief pays tribute to the doomed characters he so hauntingly describes, including his own father.

Edward Reicher died before his work was published. In 1989, fourteen years after his death, his original version was published by a Polish exile press in London at the behest of his daughter Elisabeth.

Seen first in these pages as a toddler asleep in her crib while German planes strafed Lodz, then as a four-year old learning to dance in the Warsaw ghetto and finally as a six-year old who was given a false name, delivered to a Warsaw convent and separated from her parents at the height of the war, Elisabeth Reicher eventually settled in France, where she became a psychoanalyst specializing in the effects of trauma.

Twice married to non-Jews and diligent in her profession, Elisabeth Reicher is in a way the heroine of her father's story, which she rescued from oblivion just as her father once rescued her from death. In 1990 she and Jacques Greif, a friend and colleague of her father's, translated Edward Reicher's book from Polish to French.

It is hardly surprising that the hidden child who knew that her own and her parents' lives depended on her ability to conceal her true identity should have struggled to define herself or that she should have chosen psychology as a profession. In her preface to the French edition, Reicher alludes to the pain of growing up after the war in a drastically diminished family—one in which the living had to take the place of the dead. "For a long time," she writes, "I did not enjoy hearing my father's stories or remembering my own; I even denied their importance."

Only after her father's death, reading the manuscript he had left behind, did she come to appreciate her parents' "acrobatic" efforts to survive and to understand, as she puts it, "that I could not shortchange the past." In subsequent scholarly articles, she explored the shadows of the Holocaust in more dispassionate prose. "Assimilation may overlap with an effort to adapt in order to survive," she wrote in the psychoanalytic journal *Controverses*. "But pain left unexpressed is a mute witness, like a burning ember ready to flare up again. That witness, like a transfusion, is transmitted from parents to children." Was she describing herself?

We can only guess. But facing her own death from cancer in 2006, Elisabeth Reicher asked that a Star of David be placed on her coffin.

Now, like a time capsule or a scrapbook miraculously salvaged from beneath the floorboards of a bombed-out ruin, *Country of Ash* appears in English fifty years after it was written, thanks to a small group of French survivors who believed that it deserved a wider audience.

There is an entire literature of the Shoah, yet here is a book that tells a story unlike any other. Unlike Primo Levi or Elie Wiesel, Paul Celan, André Schwarz-Bart, Ida Fink or Nellie Sachs or so many other survivors whose works have stirred millions, Edward Reicher was not a writer. Though we might disagree, he considered himself an ordinary man. After the war, when Herman Höfle was finally brought to trial for war crimes, Reicher was asked to testify against the man who had been his patient when he was forced to join the Gestapo's team of Jewish doctors. "I went," he writes, "as the representative of all those who had been gassed and incinerated in Treblinka, killed in the ghetto or suffocated to death in the cattle cars carrying them to the concentration camps."

In Polish, in French and now in English, Edward Reicher's testimony continues to speak for the dead. Many people, both Jews and Christians, some knowingly risking their lives, others unwittingly tipping the balance in his favor, helped him and his family survive the Shoah. The story of this translation has been yet another instance in which many hands and much detective work have played a role. Among them I would like in particular to thank the writer Renata Jablonska of Tel Aviv, Elisabeth Reicher's closest friend, who shared with me what she could about the Reichers' lives after the war. I would also like to thank my sister, Nina Bogin, who first brought this work to my attention. Translating from the French version of the book, it has been an honor for me to be one of the links in the chain that preserves this story for posterity.

FOREWORD

My father was not a talkative man. He used few words when he spoke about the far-from-ordinary experiences he had lived through. Still, certain facts always recurred. I don't think my parents could have forgotten them. They said they had become "other," or perhaps gone a bit mad. For my father to write all this down meant to bear witness, but above all to be less haunted, less inhabited. It was also to forgive.

His original manuscript, written as events unfolded, was destroyed in the ruins of Warsaw following the uprising of 1944. He rewrote it from memory after liberation and completed it with testimony from other witnesses—Roza, for example, the prostitute who saved his life, when she came to collect her promised reward, or Hermann Höfle, the coordinator of Operation Reinhard, whom my father was forced to treat while he was in the Warsaw ghetto. How could my father have known that he would one day encounter him again before a tribunal in Salzburg, where Höfle would deny having ordered the deportation of hundreds of thousands of Jews?

My father wanted his memoir to be published. Yet in Germany, where he had settled, no one was interested for years. To be more exact, everything having to do with the Holocaust was purged, and this meant in history books, too. Things have changed now. Today, the history books are no longer silent, but now people say there have been books enough on the subject. And so, when my father died in 1975, his manuscript was still unpublished.

I will not speak about the events my father recounts in this book, but rather of their resonance in me and in others who lived through the same experience. Among the Jews of the Diaspora, so-called

11

blood ties were often painful. Things were extremely difficult for the survivors, but they were even more so for their children, shut within such sharply reduced families. None of those who perished had died a natural death. All the deaths had been barbaric. In certain cases, people had had to abandon their loved ones in order to save themselves. And there were no graves. Those who remained had no choice but to continue living. They also had to take the place of the dead.

People can emerge from such a situation with the determination to do everything and achieve success, but they often carry a secret bitterness. Their true feelings have been frozen, with no hope of ever thawing.

I did not enjoy hearing my father's stories; nor did I like to think back on my own. For a long time, I even denied their importance. I was afraid of memory's clarifying power. This fear was not unfounded. Alongside the reality of the Nazis, there were also betrayals, which that reality brought to light. Had not a cousin of my father's, one of the Jewish "dignitaries" of the Warsaw ghetto (later exterminated like everybody else), offered my father a deal? He was willing to arrange for my father to escape but without my mother and myself . . .

Can one die again and again? In those times, it was not impossible. I was afraid that the absurdity unleashed by memory would uproot all rational thought and deprive everything of meaning.

In a sense, I was correct. Later, I came to understand that I could not shortchange the past. Alongside the absence of meaning, there was also meaning to be found.

The life force is astounding. It enables one to find acrobatic solutions, to withstand being stripped bare like someone who has suffered critical burns, or to become a virtuoso of intuition and possibility in order to remain a part of this world. When help came from outside, it was sometimes not from those on whom one had counted, nor for the reasons one expected. Reading through my father's notebooks, filled with line after line of his regular, slanted handwriting, I pushed away the thorns of nonsense and sloughed off the scales of my own useless, bitter rebellion. In the process

I discovered in my parents two human beings with unsuspected strengths that had enabled them to escape that country of ash.

More than anything, I realized as I read that life could finally be acceptable.

—Elisabeth Bizouard-Reicher
Paris, September 1990

COUNTRY OF ASH

A Jewish Doctor in Poland

1939–1945

INTRODUCTION

I did not write this book from a desire for revenge; nor was it my intent not to forgive. I have been too overwhelmed by the generosity of certain men and subjected to too many acts of injustice and too much suffering by others.

It isn't hard to die, but it is hard to live while fighting evil. I have forgiven those I met after the war who dealt me the fiercest blows during that lawless time. To this day, some of them still walk freely in the world. If I forgave, it was at the request of sincere Christians, those who saved me. They all had faith in another justice that would one day punish the criminals.

This book has no literary pretensions. It is the description of the life of a Jewish doctor who survived the worst years, from the beginning to the end of our persecution.

If it contains no accusations and expresses no desire for revenge, it is because a man who has traveled through hell can no longer feel such things. All his feelings are dead.

Nor does one find here the hatred that poisons men's hearts and destroys all hope of cooperation and peace among them. The man who has written this memoir has aged; his hopes no longer belong to him. He has entrusted them to the next generation, for only they can attempt to overcome the vile actions of the past.

Only the young can choose to do what whole generations of their forebears failed to do: embark on the path of a true and just humanism.

1962–1963

PART I

OUR WANDERING BEGINS

THE LODZ GHETTO

1

I will never forget September 1, 1939, the day our calvary began.

Autumn was coming but it was still very hot. We had not had such a beautiful summer in years. My wife and I had retired late the night before, wanting to enjoy the evening as long as possible. The powerful scent of flowers filled the interior of our house in Ruda Pabianicka.* As things turned out, that was to be our last evening of peace.

The outbreak of war caught me entirely by surprise. Perhaps my work as a doctor had kept me removed from current politics. In any case, I didn't believe there would actually be a war, although you could feel it in the air.

We slept with the windows open. At five o'clock in the morning we were awakened by a series of loud explosions. I ran to the window. The sky was blood-red. Enemy planes had attacked the military airfield in Ruda Pabianicka. Polish planes were fighting off the invaders, supported by antiaircraft defense. My wife joined me at the window and we watched the strange scene before us as if it were a film. Planes that had been hit fell to the ground in flames. "It's the Germans," Pola whispered.

We continued standing by the window, unable to tear ourselves away, even though we could not yet comprehend the full horror of the scene. In my wildest dreams I could not have imagined that my young, graceful wife, whom I had surrounded with wealth and wrapped in a life of ease, would display such strength and character during the war. It was she who kept my spirits going at times of unbearable exhaustion. We had been married for only four years.

---

* The suburb of Lodz where the author lived; also the location of the military airfield.

I had married her out of pure love, and it was the best decision of my life.

Our little Elzunia was not awakened by the bombs. She was fast asleep in her small bed, deep in a child's peaceful slumber.

When day broke, the airfield was just a smoking pile of rubble. We were sitting in the dining room having breakfast. I turned on the radio and heard that the Germans had attacked Poland. I still didn't realize the extreme magnitude of the event.

2

After a few days, the war had us in its grip.

3

Early on the morning of September 6, my eighty-two-year-old father telephoned from Lodz and asked me to come over right away. He was very ill and all alone. I had been to see him two days before, when he had been feeling relatively well. My wife didn't want me to leave Ruda. The trams had stopped running, so I had to go on foot. I found the old man seated on the coping of the well in the courtyard of his house. His face was streaked with tears, and he was praying. My father was a deeply religious man. He sought consolation in his conversations with God.

"Good morning, Papa," I said. "It took me rather a long time. There was no public transportation, so I had to walk."

"Thank you for coming," he answered in a trembling voice. "Forgive me, but I couldn't find a doctor." All his modesty, an entire lifetime devoted to doing good deeds, was contained in that one sentence. My father was a stooped old man with snow-white hair and a gray goatee. Extremely near-sighted and frail, he was exceptionally kind. I asked what ailed him and set straight to work. He had not been able to urinate for the past forty-eight hours. His enlarged prostate was causing him unbearable pain. I found two men to help me carry him inside. I inserted a catheter to empty his bladder. When I left the room he was praying ardently.

A few hours later, all the men in Lodz were ordered to leave the city and walk to Warsaw. It was feared that we would fall into the hands of the Germans. What was I to do? I couldn't abandon my sick father, my wife, my young child. I ran through all the options in my mind, but was unable to decide. I wanted to return to Ruda, but by that point the road had been cut off. I approached an officer on the street.

"An order's an order and you are no exception," he replied. "An order's an order" rang in my ears. Devastated, I dialed our phone number in Ruda. The line had been disconnected, yet just that morning I had called my father from my house. What had happened to my family? I went back inside to see my father.

"I'm too old and sick to go with you," he said in a tired voice. "May God bless you. He alone knows what is right, and human life is insufficient to comprehend him." He could see what I was feeling, but said no more and gave me his blessing. His kind eyes comforted me. I left the room. My father's loud praying could be heard throughout the house.

I joined the human procession headed northeast out of Lodz. We passed a military hospital and I stopped to ask the director for work as a doctor, but he refused. I was furious, but a few days later I learned that his refusal had probably saved my life. Despite their Red Cross signs, the hospital vehicles had been strafed by German planes and destroyed. Almost all the doctors had been killed.

Evening was coming. I was in the midst of a river of people who had set off from Lodz. It was warm and beautiful, and the red sunset foretold that the beautiful weather would continue. The mass of people filled the width of the road. They were mostly men, but there were also whole families—men, women, and children—weighed down by heavy bundles. I thought of my wife and child, and reproached myself for having left them.

4

Outside Lodz, on the road to Brzeziny, the German planes began their murderous work: they aimed their machine guns onto the crowd, and people began to fall under the bullets. The beautiful red sunset heard the groans and cries of the wounded. Whenever the drone of the planes became audible overhead, people would dive into the fields, throwing themselves flat among the potato plants. In the chaos, many lost their possessions, broke arms or legs, even suffered heart attacks. But the crowd was merciless, everyone mindful only of himself. The farther we walked, the more corpses we saw. Thousands of flies beset the bodies.

After a long walk along roads under constant bombardment, I reached Żyrardów. When I learned that Lodz had been occupied, I had no choice but to stay, and found work in a local hospital.

Soon after, the Germans arrived and occupied Żyrardów. The next morning, they ordered all Jewish men out into the streets and drove us from the town. There were more than a thousand of us. Women and children were allowed to remain at home. I regretted being thirty-nine instead of nine. . . . But maybe, I told myself, the situation for my wife and daughter won't be so bad. And won't my father be able to hide in his big house in Lodz if conditions there are the same?

A man I knew well, Hubel, was walking next to me.

One of the officers, a dark, strapping, handsome young man, stopped alongside us.

"Could you please tell me what's going on here?" I asked naively.

"All the Jews are going to be shot. They asked for it when they fired surreptitiously on the soldiers who were entering Żyrardów," he replied.

"But I'm a doctor," I said. "I need to go to the hospital to do my job."

"Are you a Jew?"

"Yes."

I felt his leather crop strike my face. I tried to stanch the blood flowing from my nose with my handkerchief. That was my first German slap. Later, countless others were to follow. But this was a lesson for me: never ask a Nazi anything, and never speak to one.

We were forced to run four abreast out of the city. Those unable to keep up, primarily the old and the infirm, were shot. When we reached the last building in town, Hubel walked away from the group and dove into an open doorway. He had lost all self-control. An officer ran after him. He checked to make sure he had no weapons on him, ordered him to turn toward the wall, and finished him off with a bullet to the back of the neck.

I can't be sure of this, but Żyrardów may have been the first concentration camp for Jews in Poland.

Despite our tragic position, I couldn't help but admire the Germans' superb organization. We were forced to build our own fence, with metal stakes and barbed wire that were swiftly supplied. The field was barely larger than an acre, so things were rather cramped. We were surrounded by German sentries with their submachine guns aimed straight at us.

A strange system of order prevailed. We were given no food, but women from the town brought it to us.

"That is forbidden!" the soldiers screamed, chasing them away from the barbed wire with their whips, but the women continued to bring us food. They even smuggled quilts and rugs into the camp. The field was damp, which was detrimental to many people's health. Fortunately, the beautiful weather held, and problems caused by the damp were relieved by the warm rays of the sun. Nevertheless, there were cases of serious illness, even deaths.

Two elderly people died of pneumonia. One of them was a friend of my father's, Aaron Reibenbach. I will never forget his feverish eyes burning with hatred at the German guards. When we asked the officers for medical assistance, they answered, "We don't care about the sick. At last you dirty Jews can croak. Jews caused the war and deserve no pity." Conditions in the camp deteriorated. There were no lavatories. Everyone's physiological needs had to be taken care of in one corner of the field. The stench was terrible.

All strata of society were represented in that camp: intellectuals and those barely able to read; Orthodox Jews in long black caftans with sidelocks and beards; liberal Jews and agnostics; a small group of social outcasts; criminals; cripples, blind people, deaf-mutes; and here and there the occasional mentally unbalanced. . . . But there were also many courageous, noble, wise people, including highly educated rabbis. We all lived together in that field, under the open sky. We struck up friendships, played cards and chess, and told war jokes—some old and some brand-new.

Some of the young people played soccer and other sports or performed circus tricks. Naturally, various cliques and groups formed. The rabbis and devout Jews prayed, and they demanded that the other Jews pray, too. They spoke of the sins of the Jews and foretold the imminent arrival of the Messiah.

Twice a day, generally beginning at 5:00 A.M., the Nazis organized what they called "gymnastics." We had to stand up and fall to the ground scores of times. In the hands of the Nazis we were like marionettes children play with to amuse themselves by pulling a string. This so-called exercise was exhausting for the old and infirm, who were beaten mercilessly with whips. Cases of heart failure were increasingly frequent among them. Their situation grew hopeless. We constantly tried to figure out what we could do, but we could change nothing. Our future was uncertain; we had no idea what they intended to do with us.

One day, a large number of young Poles appeared at the fence. We could see that the Germans had taken pains to include as many social outcasts as possible among them. We were ordered to form one long line and strip to our underwear—we even had to remove our shoes. We were soon to learn what all this meant. Displaced Jews were known to have gold, money, jewelry, and foreign currency sewn into their clothes. Everything of any value was hidden in their clothes; some people had even concealed things in the heels of their shoes.

We were given the Poles' rags, and they received ours. Had the situation not been so dramatic, we might have found it funny. Thin people got fat people's clothes. A young Pole had to put on a caftan, and a rabbi, a peasant's smock. I, too, forfeited my clothes, and with them my stethoscope. All I received in return was a pair of trousers, for my Pole had been cunning enough to come without a jacket. But the Poles were deceived too. Beyond the fence, their new Jewish clothes were taken from them and they were given overalls. In this way, our valuables fell into the hands of the Germans.

The next day the officers brought in several pairs of barbers' shears. Every Jew with a beard had it cut off; not even the rabbis were exempt. But the more cunning had an idea. They tied scarves around their chins, claiming toothaches; strangely, they managed to keep their beards.

I had been in the camp for seven days when suddenly my name was called out by the Germans. I was terrified, but I knew I had no choice—I was in their hands. I reported to the officer who had come for me. He ordered me to retrieve all my belongings and follow him. I had nothing to bring. My comrades in misfortune looked after me with pity. I felt like a condemned man, and I was thinking of Hubel and his fate.

5

I was escorted out by two officers. We left the camp and headed for the center of the town.

On the main street in Żyrardów, people stared at me as if I were a criminal; indeed, in my dirty shirt and torn trousers, I must have looked like one. I was taken to the German police station. I had to stay in the waiting room. My guards smoked cigars and talked, casting fierce glances at me from time to time. At last, the door of the municipal police chief's office opened and an adjutant appeared. The officers stood to attention and moved aside. The adjutant led me into the office of his superior. Older and taller, with graying temples and a severe face, he belonged to an earlier generation and had doubtless fought in World War I.

Despite his enmity, there was something humane and just in his gaze. My first impressions rarely failed me, although there were exceptions. Later I would meet unspeakably cruel sadists with the faces of innocent children. One well-known forensic physician wrote in his memoir: "The majority of young murderers have the faces of angels." But my intuition proved true to form in the case of the town commandant.

"Are you Dr. Edward Reicher?" he asked in a deep voice.

"Yes."

"How can you prove it?"

What was going on? Had my family bought me out, did someone want to do me in? My time in the camp had taught me that my torturers had many different methods.

"Speak!"

"The Poles took my jacket with my papers in it," I said calmly. "I can give you no more than my word of honor. But Dr. Jankowski from the hospital here knows me and can confirm my identity."

"It is he who needs you," said the officer. He ordered the adjutant to connect me to the hospital. A moment later I heard Dr. Jankowski's voice on the other end of the receiver. My Polish colleague, whom I knew from the hospital in Żyrardów, had done all he could to get me out of the camp, and he was pleased with the results of his efforts.

After we spoke, the police chief took the receiver from me and with German precision demanded confirmation that I was the correct Dr. Reicher. Then I was free to leave the police station. Free! I ran to the hospital. I already felt as though the camp was a receding nightmare. The world and life became real to me once more.

Dr. Jankowski was waiting for me in his office. His long face lit up.

"It is good you are back, my friend. I need your help. We have a lot to do." He shook my hand firmly. I thanked him for freeing me. "First and foremost, you must have something to wear," he said, pointing to my rags. He brought me some of his own clothes, but they were huge on me, so he lent me some money and I bought myself a suit. Then I returned to my Żyrardów quarters. My assistant prepared me a wonderful lunch and did everything she could to help me forget the horrors of the camp.

Once news of my release began to spread, the house filled up with guests. My patients came, and so did the mothers, wives, sisters, and children of men interned in the camp. The women wept and despaired, and I attempted to comfort them, saying that others would soon be free, as I was.

As I continued working hard at the hospital, I came to realize what a truly wonderful man and friend Dr. Jankowski was. He was without a doubt one of those "aristocrats of the spirit"; a faultless man, always prepared to make sacrifices and to fight for the truth. He thought nothing of expending effort or time for those around him. He was a true Christian. There were few people like him, but I later understood that among the Poles there were others like him, prepared to risk their lives to save the persecuted Jews.

A few days later I learned that the inmates at the camp were at risk of typhus, that terrible lice-borne plague. Lice infestation was widespread among the men due to the poor sanitary conditions. I told Dr. Jankowski about the people in the field. He contacted the municipal police chief and arranged to meet him.

I was sure that when the Germans heard about the infestation they would understand the gravity of the situation. Typhus was not a danger just to Jews; an epidemic could break out at any time.

Dr. Jankowski did not return until evening. The trials of a difficult day were visible on his face.

"As you know," he said, "I went to see the town commandant and put the facts before him. At first he wouldn't hear of anything. Then he called in a German military physician. The two Germans deliberated on the situation without me. Finally, they announced that the camp is to be closed." And that is exactly what happened. After being thoroughly bathed, and their lice-infested clothing disinfected, the Jews were sent back to their families. A typhus epidemic was averted.

Had this situation occurred three years later, we would all, men and lice together, have perished in the gas chambers. . . . Be that as it may, I am almost certain that of all the former prisoners of the camp in Żyrardów, I am the only one who survived the war.

6

In those early days of autumn 1939, those of us who had been interned in the camp resolved to return to our own towns and villages. The war between Germany and Poland was over and the occupying authorities had no objections.

The group from Lodz, to which I belonged, had even agreed on our return date. I had to bid my friends farewell. Good Dr. Jankowski had changed. The furrows on his face had deepened and the puffiness beneath his eyes had spread unhealthily.

"You want to leave, and I am to stay here alone with my patients."

"I owe you a great deal. You freed me from the camp, and you saved the other Jews who were imprisoned there. You became personally involved in a situation that could have harmed you. Thank you again in the name of all those you saved."

The old man lifted his hands in a gesture of defense. "Any decent man would have done the same in my position. I was merely doing my duty."

I took my leave and never saw Dr. Jankowski again.

I made my way to the meeting point for the Lodz refugees. There were about thirty of us all together, including women and children. We set off on foot toward Lodz, which lay about fifty-five miles away. Though the weather was still beautiful and warm, the early mornings were cold now. But the sun dispersed the morning mists and warmed my chilled bones. By noon it was always hot. We walked mostly on side roads, avoiding towns. The landscape in that region is totally flat. We made a point of walking through forests. The peasants let us sleep in their barns, and by and large they were fairly well disposed toward us. At night we set up watch wherever we stayed, with a change of guard every three hours. We were stopped many times by German police and military personnel. We told our story truthfully and they allowed us to proceed. At long last we reached Lodz.

7

My wife was seated by the same well of our house on Poludniowa Street where my father had been waiting for me a few weeks earlier. I was dirty and tired. She wept with joy.

"I'm so happy you're back. We'll never be apart again," she said over and over again. We sat on the sofa in our room with Elzunia asleep in her cot. She was smiling in her sleep, her balled hands tucked under her chin. The poor thing had no idea what awaited her. We spoke in low voices.

"Day and night I stood by the window, or I waited for you downstairs in the courtyard. I never slept. All I did was wait."

Her voice broke. Her beautiful face was pale and tired. The sleepless nights had carved deep shadows underneath her eyes.

"I thought you were dead. I couldn't go back to Ruda. The neighbors were threatening me, saying that a Jewess had no business living in their midst, and in such luxury. The Germans requisitioned our house. I had to leave everything behind. And here the Germans often force me to do hard labor."

That evening, we all gathered in my father's apartment to celebrate my return. My two brothers, who had fled to Warsaw with their families, joined us, along with a few of our close friends.

I learned about the unbearable situation of the Jews in Lodz. If things were already this bad, what was to come? New anti-Jewish ordinances were being issued every day. Jews could keep only a small amount of money. Jews were forbidden to have gold. Jews were not allowed to conduct commercial transactions with Aryans. Jews could not own commercial or industrial businesses. The curfew for Jews was 6:00 P.M. Jews were not allowed to walk along Piotrkowska, Lodz's main thoroughfare, now renamed Adolf Hitler Strasse.

Jews were not allowed to travel by train. All Jewish real estate, factories and commercial businesses were either confiscated or handed over to Aryan trustees. Jewish bank accounts were frozen. Jewish safe deposit vaults were opened and emptied. Jewish physicians were not allowed to treat Aryan patients. All infractions were subject to draconian measures. The death penalty was a daily occurrence.

Every hour was a struggle, every day a new battlefield. There were many casualties. Shouting SS men and Gestapo officers would arrive at people's houses first thing in the morning. They would haul the Jews off to forced labor and help themselves to the contents of their wardrobes. Possession of jewelry or furs was forbidden; this was the pretext for arbitrary searches and for looting all possessions. One day, a German soldier showed up with his mistress and made off with Pola's best dresses and furs. Jew hunts were staged on the streets. Jews were easy prey, because they wore yellow stars both front and back. They were beaten, forced to do the hardest work, and robbed. They were killed. To resist was useless; it brought only death threats.

Evening raids proceeded as follows: a few Germans would enter the home of well-off Jews. Within moments, the Jews were forced out. They were allowed to take nothing but absolute necessities, and only what they could hold in their two hands. The victors scrutinized hands, necks, and ears for valuables. If they noticed anything they immediately seized it without mercy. And so in an instant all possessions, the fruit of generations of hard work, were irrevocably lost. The apartment and everything in it would be occupied by Germans from the Reich, the Baltic states, or Volhynia. Such had been the tragic toll of the preceding days.

8

The very next day after my return from Żyrardów I ran into trouble. Someone rang the doorbell very loud. A small, slight man with red swastikas on his sleeves stood before me. Without a word of greeting and in total silence, he pressed his way into the house. He was young, no more than nineteen years of age. He wore very thick glasses and gave the impression of being a clumsy, awkward youth. His thick spectacles indicated severe myopia. He did not remove his cap, and still said nothing. He walked from room to room. When he came to the living room he stopped before the bookcase, a handsome specimen of late eighteenth-century furniture. Inside it were volume after volume of valuable leather-bound editions of almost all the German classics: Goethe, Schiller, Lessing, Klopstock, Wieland, and many others. It was my father's treasure; he had studied in Germany.

The young man perused everything carefully with his nearsighted eyes. Only after a quarter of an hour did he speak his first words:

"What is this?" he asked, pointing to the works of Heinrich Heine.

"It's the work of the German poet Heinrich Heine."

The man from the Security Service was smaller than me. He stood on tiptoe and punched me in the face. I had never imagined I could bear such a strong punch. I lost my three front teeth and was bleeding profusely from my mouth. I spat the three broken teeth out with my blood.

"You should be ashamed of yourself, young man; this does you no honor . . ." His response was another punch. Without a word, he goose-stepped out of the apartment. I rinsed my mouth and iodized my wounds.

As time went on, the Jews were treated worse and worse. To avoid forced labor and other unpleasantries, we hid in cellars or attics.

Very early one morning two Gestapo officers arrived. I didn't have time to hide in the cellar. They asked for Dr. Reicher. There could be no doubt they intended to take me away. They escorted me to 75 Narutowicz Street, headquarters of the Gestapo at the time. There, I was forced to spend the whole day carrying a heavy wardrobe on my back all the way from the lobby up to the top floor, over and over again. Ten hours without a break.

I was so tired that I had trouble breathing. I was drenched in sweat. Whenever I tried to stop, a Nazi officer was on top of me with his whip, which he used more than once.

Not until a few days later did I learn whom I had to thank for that murderous labor. A Gestapo officer who knew me and had consulted me as a physician let me know that a colleague, Dr. S., a Volksdeutscher*, worked for the Gestapo, and had personally ordered that I be singled out for that absurd work. I have no idea why, nor did I ever learn the full truth about that incident.

I would have never expected such malice of him. We had known each other from before the war; he had a degree from a Polish university. We had been on good professional terms, I had never done him any wrong, and I had never noticed the least trace of anti-Semitism in him.

Could he have changed so? Dr. S. was shot for unknown reasons during the war by his own countrymen, the German authorities.

By this time, Jews had to wear a yellow star sewn front and back onto their clothes. There was thus no way of concealing one's Jewish identity. One day, Pola was in the city park with our daughter when some soldiers ordered her to follow them, supposedly to do forced labor. She resisted, saying that she could not leave her child unsupervised. She lay down on the grass and held onto a tree. They beat her to separate her from the child. Elzunia was left alone in the park. My wife was three months pregnant. Even so, they forced her to carry heavy furniture. She tired easily and had to take frequent breaks.

---

* Citizen of occupied Poland, but of ethnic German origin.

This enraged one of the Nazis, who threw his rifle to the ground and kicked her in the abdomen with his big boots. When she began to bleed they released her. The doctors confirmed a miscarriage. From then on, my wife never recovered her full health.

Fortunately, as we were well known in Lodz, people found Elzunia and brought her home.

The pain of this event caused me a terrible mental shock. I had to come up with a way for us to escape such suffering. I needed some connection with the German authorities. I thought of Pastor L., the director and chaplain of the Protestant hospital in Lodz. A good, wise, handsome man with an open face, high forehead, and expressive eyes, he would empathize with our misfortune.

For several years I had been the Protestant hospital's consultant in my field, and had enjoyed an excellent relationship with Pastor L. I was certain he could help me. Now that the Germans had invaded Lodz, the Deaconow Hospital had become the German military hospital, but Pastor L. had retained his post. I placed all my hopes in him.

I called him in the morning and he offered me an appointment at the hospital at 4:00 P.M. This in itself surprised me somewhat, for I had always been able to see him at any time. He had always been genuinely well-disposed toward me. Full of hope, I went to Północna Street, walking through beautiful Helenow Park, where I had spent my childhood and youth. My whole life passed before my eyes as in a film. I arrived at the entrance to the hospital. The bizarre look in the eyes of the German soldier in the sentry box brought me back to the present. He saw my yellow star, but let me through when I told him whom I had come to see.

Pastor L. made me wait half an hour. I stepped inside his office. As if he were my closest friend, I told him about my situation and about my recent dire experiences.

I explained that I had a wife, a small child, and an elderly father, that every day there were new humiliations, that we had no freedom of movement. I asked him for a letter from the hospital certifying that I was a doctor. Such a document would change my life entirely, and with a modicum of good will he could provide one. I had been a consultant at the Protestant hospital for so many years. But I proved to be badly mistaken.

He glared at me.

"You are a Jew, and the Jews caused this war. The Jews are to blame for everything. I can do nothing for you, because you are a Jew." This was a terrible blow. Only now can I judge this man, whom I had considered a Christian and a humanitarian. It made no difference to me whether he had succumbed to Nazi propaganda or had simply undergone a change. What an immense difference there was between Dr. Jankowski and Pastor L.! I have no idea if Pastor L. is still alive. Were he to read these words, would he blush with shame?

But not everyone was like him. I had an elderly German colleague, Dr. Ekert, whom I knew only very superficially. Along with everything else, I had financial problems, because my bank account and safe deposit box had been blocked. I had lost a lot of money at Żyrardów when we were forced to exchange our clothes for Polish rags. I phoned Dr. Ekert and offered to sell him all the medicine in my office. As it happened, foreseeing a possible shortage of drugs if war broke out, I had stocked up on supplies in August.

Dr. Ekert was nearing sixty, blond with a lot of gray. He paid me for the medications; he also offered me a loan. He helped me again later, and when my father was left alone in the ghetto, he tried to help him materially as long as was possible.

The war changed everything. We were able to tell good men from bad with absolute precision. And sometimes, just as we reached the very limits of despair, we would encounter people like Dr. Jankowski, Dr. Ekert, and others, such as Toni, of whom I will speak later on. . . .

9

Warsaw had fallen. After the German-Soviet pact, the Russians occupied the eastern part of Poland. Poland was vanquished. The lands that had been granted to Poland under the Treaty of Versailles, and the lands along the river Warta, were annexed by the German Reich. The remaining territory occupied by the Germans was called the General Government, and its capital was Kraków.

Dr. Hans Frank, a lawyer, pedantic bureaucrat, and murderer, was appointed head of the General Government.

We were then living in an apartment in my father's large house. We shared our quarters with my wife's eighteen-year old sister, Alina, a pretty, charming girl with a mane of jet-black hair, green eyes, and a beautiful bronzed complexion. She was very intelligent. She never lost her cheerful disposition, laughing and singing all day long, and doing everything possible to dissipate our sadness. This delightful creature helped us always and in everything, and her ease, gaiety, jokes, and playfulness lifted our spirit. At that point we were spending our days in a hiding place down in the cellar; we had electric light there, so we could read. We felt safe there; the Nazis would not find us and haul us off to do forced labor, such as carrying heavy wardrobes up and down long flights of stairs.

My medical office was in the same building; all my equipment and machines were still intact. I hadn't removed my doctor's sign, although I no longer saw patients, for I was afraid I would be taken away for hard labor if I did. Whenever I dared to go to my office, I was very quiet, and never opened the door if the bell rang. My father's house was very large, with thirteen windows overlooking the street. Some of it was rented out to tenants, although my father, my brothers, and I occupied a good number of the apartments.

One day, the concierge came to see me and whispered that a German policeman had been looking for me for the past several days. He had brought this man a bottle of vodka and assured him that his intentions were honorable, but he urgently needed a medical consultation. He said he would be back the next day at 7:00 P.M. I said I would need time to reflect before agreeing to see him, but the concierge was so reassuring and persuasive that at the appointed time I went into my office.

The doorbell rang at exactly seven o'clock. I opened the door, prepared for the worst. Before me stood a tall young man in the uniform of a German policeman. He was well nourished and had a smiling, pleasant face. He might have been around twenty-five and appeared to be a full-blooded Aryan. Nevertheless, his green uniform, his swastika, and the pistol at his side unnerved me. "Are you Dr. Reicher?" he asked quietly, in German.

"Yes. Please come in." He entered the hallway. I glanced at the stairwell; it was empty. On the second floor, there was only one door, which led into my office. I closed it and threw the bolt.

"What brings you here?"

"A strange malady," he began, uncertainly. "For many years, since my childhood, I have had a skin disease that torments me terribly. The itching is the worst part. I don't know how I've managed to take it for so long. People here in Lodz said you were a very good specialist. I have a feeling, a kind of deep intuition, that you will help me. I've been to see all manner of dermatologists in Germany, Austria, and the Sudeten-land, my homeland. None of them gave me any relief."

He looked pleadingly at me. I scrutinized him closely. Looking into those honest blue eyes, I began to trust him. But could I believe a Nazi policeman? I was afraid of him, for my previous experiences had been too bitter.

"Sir, as a policeman and a soldier you surely know I am a Jew, and that I am not allowed to treat Aryan patients, on pain of death. Besides, you're a German in uniform. I even wonder if it's not a risk for you to seek treatment from me."

"I've already thought that through, Doctor. I shall certainly not betray you, even if you don't help me, or even if my condition worsens. But I firmly believe that you will help me."

Was there nothing sinister behind these assurances? Had Dr. S. come up with something else to bring me down?

I asked myself all sorts of questions, and I had my doubts—the instinctive self-preservation of a victim. But this man inspired my trust.

"Please don't be surprised that I'm hesitant to treat you. There is something surprising about the fact a German policeman seeks me out at such a terrible time for me. I'm sure you understand. Experience has taught me to be extremely cautious."

"Trust me, Doctor. All I want is your medical help; please examine me," Antoni Schmidt asked. "I will never forget this. You may be sure of my gratitude."

He had convinced me. I gave him a thorough examination. He had a chronic skin disease, *neurodermatitis circumscripta*, an illness that causes terrible itching and often leads to acute suffering and sleep disturbances. Now I understood his insistence.

"Come back to see me tomorrow at the same time," I told the young man. "I will treat you."

He took his leave, and his face was radiant. He shook my hand firmly, looking fully into my eyes. This farewell dispersed the last of my scruples, of course.

I went back down to our hideout in the cellar, and told Pola and Alina of this curious development. Pola had reservations; she was afraid for me. Alina, however, that cheerful optimist, was very moved by my account. She was on the side of the unknown policeman.

"He's a good man," she said with conviction. "He will do us no harm." And she turned out to be right.

In my office, I had an excellent Siemens x-ray machine. I retrieved the Roentgen lamp from where I had hidden it so that the whole device would not be looted. Equipment from doctors' offices was already being confiscated. Without its lamp my machine was useless, and would not be attractive to Nazi plunderers.

The next day I treated Schmidt's skin with radiation. I repeated the treatment one week later. The effect was extraordinary. Within three weeks his disease was under control and at least partly, if not entirely, cured. From then on, Antoni Schmidt, a Sudeten German, was our close friend. We already called him Toni. He was truly grateful, which he showed us at every opportunity. He brought us food, and gave my little daughter presents of chocolate, candy, oranges and other southern fruits. He also became our pillar of support during our journey through hell, which had only just begun.

10

Our little family had grown. Toni was our newest member. At our request, under extremely difficult conditions, he traveled to a small town near Poznan to see my father-in-law, who gave him gold coins worth twenty dollars each that he concealed in his holster. Those dollars in gold helped us survive the subsequent years. Toni became my life-and-death friend.

One evening we were eating supper in the kitchen. Toni had brought us a large sausage. This was an event worthy of due celebration. Given the circumstances, we had set out a veritable feast. Pola, Alina, and I were all conversing, along with Toni, of course, who was playing with Elzunia. Suddenly, the pleasant atmosphere was broken.

"Open up!" someone barked in German. We quickly cleared all traces of our meal from the table. Toni turned pale. I rushed him to the kitchen stairs, which led down to a second doorway that opened out onto the garden. He fled. He was afraid there might be a guard posted at the bottom. If he had been caught, he would have been arrested, and then . . .

Meanwhile, Pola opened the door. She was shoved aside by three SS men with death faces and whips.

"Gold, money, diamonds!" they shouted. The plunderers had to content themselves with an Astrakhan fur coat, my wife's last. Annoyed, they finally left. We were unable to calm down for several hours.

Toni returned the next day. He had expected the worst and was relieved it had all ended with a coat.

Toni fell in love with Alina.

The feeling was mutual. This was love between a German policeman and a young Jewish girl, between a representative of extermination and the person he was supposed to destroy. They loved each other tenderly even in those merciless times.

11

Our situation was becoming more and more critical. We no longer knew what to do. We couldn't go out on the street. The yellow star was an invitation to humiliation and torment. The Star of David, symbol of our people, our religion, and tradition, had been transformed by the Nazi regime into a sign of debasement. We could be beaten and treated like pack animals. We had no rights. We were beyond the law.

Lodz was renamed Litzmannstadt; it had been subsumed into the Reich. Anyone who could escaped to Warsaw or better still to Russia. Good and evil ceased to exist. For many, life became unbearable.

The most valuable people committed suicide, among them many of my friends and colleagues, the best and noblest of people: Dr. Liege, Dr. Kurianska, Dr. Frenkelrat, and many others. Friends I loved, colleagues I respected for their vast knowledge. Each loss wounded us more deeply.

There were two Jewish cafés in Lodz. The best-known one was owned by Bernheim. It was on Adolf Hitler Strasse and was called the Astoria. The entrance was on a side street, which meant that Jews could still frequent that café, because Adolf Hitler Strasse was off-limits. People went there to drink tea or coffee and play chess.

One day, a police raid shattered the calm of the café. They entered, frisked all the patrons, and seized everyone's identity cards. They ordered everyone to report to police headquarters the next day to retrieve their cards. Those who did so were never seen again: they were shot in the woods beyond Zgierz. Those who suspected a trap were lucky. They surreptitiously changed address, though they need not have. The police never even looked for them.

They were killing Jews like rabbits on a hunt. Or slaughtering them like chickens in a coop. One removes one or several chickens, kills them, and leaves the rest in reserve, to wring their necks another day.

One day, German police came to our neighbors' house and to ours, demanding that we hand over our rugs. They refused to give us receipts. One of our neighbors, also a Jew, notified the local police. The officers were recalled, but at six o'clock the next morning an SS unit appeared. They announced that we were to be punished for denouncing the Germans. Each of us had to take a heavy rug on our backs and carry it to a monastery six miles away. It was raining. The ground was muddy and slippery, and we trudged along in the mud. The SS men drove their car alongside us, goading us with their whips. Dead tired, we reached the monastery, where the SS quarters were.

That was the beginning of our via crucis. We were made to carry heavy blocks of stone up a spiral staircase and back down again, over

and over. This torture lasted for six hours. But the worst was to follow. We were led into the courtyard of the cloister. Before our eyes,
they drove nails into planks of wood. Then they began to chase us.
The nails tore our clothes and struck us in the face. We all lost blood.
I received a serious head injury. A Polish middleman was sent to our
wives with a demand for a ransom. If they didn't pay, we would be
killed. Securing our freedom cost a fortune. We were freed that night.
I lay exhausted for ten days while my wounds healed. My brothers
were subjected to similar abuse, even worse, but they drew the correct conclusion. For a large sum of money, they obtained Bolivian
residency visas and genuine Italian transit visas; then, for a vast sum,
they obtained passports from General Governor Frank. They emi-
grated and saved their lives. They never had to live through the hell
that was my fate until 1945. They escaped Hitler's realm in early 1940.
I didn't, because I didn't want to leave my old sick father.

12

In February 1940, in the city of Litzmannstadt, formerly Lodz, the
first ghetto opened its doors. Many Jews had been waiting for this
moment. They imagined that life there would be more bearable. Perhaps at last they would be left in peace in their own district. How
deluded they were! For Hitler, the ghetto was simply a more efficient
way to exterminate the Jews. Nazi propaganda nonetheless offered
the following justification for keeping us in isolation: Jews need to
be confined to ghettos because they attack and loot. They are carriers of contagious diseases such as typhus and typhoid. They must be
isolated to prevent epidemics. It is they who bring disruption and
problems into the National Socialist system for the distribution of
consumer goods. In the ghetto, it will be easier to keep an eye on Jewish merchants. Jews do not like work. They are lazy. In the ghetto they
will learn what their hands are for.

The ghetto was located in Baluty, the poorest district of Lodz. Until then, Baluty had been home to the poorest of the poor, the unemployed and criminals. Before the war, it was dangerous to go there at
night. The habitués of its dark taverns were thieves, pimps, prostitutes

and bandits. Attacks on passersby were common, and one could even expect to be knifed. This was where the Jews of Lodz were parked.

Some two hundred thousand people were supposed to move into an area that could barely hold thirty thousand. The houses in this district had no sewage systems, and only a few had running water. Baluty was crisscrossed by foul sewage canals and small tributaries of the river Lodka from which Lodz derives its name.

The resettlement began, starting in the south of the city and gradually moving north toward Baluty.

Ordinances were issued daily listing the streets the Jews were forced to leave. Their apartments were occupied by Poles and Germans. The best Jewish apartments, obviously, were given to Volksdeutsche. Every day I saw thousands of Jews trudging toward Baluty, toward the ghetto, with suitcases and bundles on their backs. Mostly they carried pillows, eiderdowns, cooking pots, and clothes stands. Sometimes the transports were accompanied by canaries and goats. But most of the Jews took only what they could hold in their hands or carry on their backs. Only rarely did one see horses or carriages. The most highly prized conveyance was a baby carriage. People were the beasts of burden. Parents pulled the carriages and children pushed them from behind. Policemen goaded them with whips. We also saw sick and injured Jews. We did not live far from Baluty, so we had a little time. But our turn came too.

13

Toni helped us, as always. He brought food and candy for the little one, and was attentive to Alina. He had already begun to speak of marrying her. But the day of our resettlement approached.

Martin Klein, a Volksdeutscher, came to see me. Klein was a short man with a large trembling head and thin arms and legs. He screwed up his eyes suspiciously whenever he peered at people or things. He looked like a spider. A quarter-century earlier we had been classmates for three years. We had shared a desk and been inseparable. While I was in medical school, Klein took an apprenticeship in a factory. Later, whenever we ran into each other, we would go to a bar and reminisce about our school days over a good meal washed down with drinks. Because I was better off, I always footed the bill. From time to time he would borrow money from me. He never repaid me, and I never reminded him.

This same Martin was now standing before me. He greeted me heartily and sat down, tactfully, in an armchair.

"My dear Edward," he began. "Your father has a big house, like all Jews. You and your father will soon be exterminated. But you are my friend from school . . . So tell your father to leave me his house." He rocked back and forth in the chair and looked around with a proprietary air, as if everything belonged to him now.

I wanted to throw him out. Martin smiled. I gritted my teeth.

"I will give you an answer tomorrow. I have to ask my father," I answered with difficulty.

He rose to his feet with the allure of a lord, which didn't go at all with his diminutive silhouette. He surveyed everything around him, and as we made our way out of the house a Swiss watch disappeared into his coat pocket.

"In any case, you won't be needing it anymore." Those were his parting words to me.

How could I have spent time with this man over many decades without ever really knowing him? I could never have imagined that he would be the person he revealed himself to be. How can a man keep his true character hidden for so long? Or had this historical moment perverted his soul? Was there no other way for things to be? Only evil people react this way. But then, must there be a true catastrophe for evil instincts to prevail?

The next day, Klein showed up with a horse-drawn cart. He pulled out an official document issued by the mayor of the city of Litzmannstadt, naming him the administrator of our house. But first he wanted to know what my father had decided. As I hesitated with my answer, he put his cards on the table. His deceit knew no bounds. His documents notwithstanding, we hadn't made him the owner of the property. That enraged him, and he began to plunder the apartment. My rosewood living room set found its way onto his cart.

"You pulled off a nice heist," I told him. He smiled.

As soon as he left, I went to see my trusted Polish and German patients. I asked them to accept the contents of my apartment and doctor's office. By that evening, we were almost done. When Klein showed up the next day, the house was empty. He was so greedy for my furniture that he forgot himself entirely and exploded with rage.

"Why didn't you leave everything for me? And I'm your friend! You Jews will all die in any case!" He looked helplessly around him, flailing his arms. Now it was my turn to smile, albeit with bitterness. Klein ferreted out a few more odds and ends, and left. But what he said about the extermination of our people proved correct. He already knew this, whereas we did not remotely suspect what lay ahead.

Before we entered the ghetto, one difficult mission remained. The synagogue my father had founded possessed some liturgical silver dating from the sixteenth, seventeenth and eighteenth centuries— priceless museum pieces my father had collected in Poland and abroad. The fate of that silver now gave him no peace. Day and night he worried about how to keep those sacred objects safe. It was a question of his faith and conscience.

Goering had ordered all Jewish assets to be confiscated. However, since he knew perfectly well that Jews would attempt to hide their wealth, special institutions had been set up to prevent this. Known as *Sonderkommando*, these bodies carried out raids and used torture to obtain information.

We could no longer afford to wait. One night, we secretly brought the silver into our apartment, where a trusted, devout old Jewish artisan concealed the treasure in a specially constructed wall in the larder. He did a masterful job. Now my father could move to the ghetto in peace.

That dark November day came. Rain poured from the gray sky. The empty rooms of our apartment were grim. We were freezing. This was the day of our move, the start of a new phase of our lives. If up to then we had had any hope, it was snatched from us now.

Ghetto . . . what a strange word! Just six letters . . . Word of unknown origin, synonym of anguish, death, misery, illness.

Ghetto . . . It means hell!

As we were moving out, Martin Klein paid us the honor of a visit. He searched every piece of our clothing to make sure there were no items of jewelry or dollars sewn into the linings. He took the better pots and all my better clothes. It occurred to me then that one might kill a man like Klein. His informer was the concierge, Matusiak, who kept Klein abreast of our every move. Klein and Matusiak looted all the apartments in my father's house. Then, in 1945, Matusiak looted all the Germans who had lived in the house, who were trying to escape. At last, after Klein's search, our suitcases were closed.

My father was seriously ill. He had a high fever and his eyes were deeply sunken. We carried him out to the carriage, slipped a few pillows under him, and covered him with a rug.

The old man looked sadly at his house. His beard, always neat, was unkempt.

"I built this house," he began, and his gaze passed over the long row of the building's high windows. "Fifty years I lived here, fifty years of my life. Four children were born to me here. For all those years I ran my business here." Tears streamed down his furrowed face. "My beloved wife died in this house. Here I built my synagogue, a place of peace and faith, to honor His name. Here I raised my sons to respect life and love people. And now, at eighty-three, I must leave my house and move to the ghetto, to live in bondage." The old man raised his head, cast a tragic glance at his house, and broke into bitter sobs. The horse shook itself and the carriage slowly pulled away.

14

The tired horse pulled the carriage to the ghetto. We stopped on the corner of Zgierska Street, where the Temporary Ghetto Housing Office was quartered in a small police station. Father moaned in the carriage. He was in unbearable pain because of the urinary retention caused by his enlarged prostate. I couldn't help him. Where could I have done anything for him?

I went to see Chaim Rumkowski, the head of the Jewish Council. He was surrounded by a throng of people. Everybody needed help. And Rumkowski was all-powerful. He was the lord of the ghetto, second only to God. I told him my problem. I needed an apartment right away for my ailing father. I knew Rumkowski because I had treated several of the children in his care. He sent me to a young official who knew me personally. I should add that for some time I had been a member of Rumkowski's advisory board, and as such had a certain role in the "self-government" of the Jews of Lodz. I was also one of the directors of the Council's health division.

"I will try to find you something good," the young official assured me. We rode down Zgierska Street to an attractive house that had belonged to a rich Jewish businessman. At this point, the ghetto had not yet been sealed. Later, both sidewalks of Zgierska Street were cordoned off with barbed wire and only Aryans were allowed to use the street.

We were assigned two rooms, one for my father, and one for us. We were lucky. Some families were squeezed eight or ten to a room. A separate room adjoining my father's was allocated to his nurse, Frania, and her parents.

We were just settling my father into bed when Rumkowski burst in shouting.

"Out!" he screamed. "This is too good for the Reichers. I need this house for other people." His whole body was shaking with rage. "The Reichers will not stay another minute here. We have a place for you on Pfeifer Street."

"But Mr. Rumkowski, for pity's sake, my father is gravely ill. He needs to be in bed. And our carriage has already left. Where will I find another?"

"What is pity to me? Does anyone have pity on me? Go to Pfeifer Street. You'll find a carriage. I'm not going to repeat myself! Yes, even Dr. Reicher must obey my orders. . . ."

Rumkowski went out. The young official was rigid with fear. I didn't want to rile Rumkowski further, so I asked the young man to find a carriage. After some time he returned. We put my father in the carriage and set off for Pfeifer Street. There, everything was dirty and desolate. The streets were narrow and the houses poor, small and ugly, made of wood, not stone. This was the worst part of the worst district of Lodz. Garbage and refuse from the houses flowed into the gutters, which stank, poisoning the air. It was difficult to breathe. Enormous rats stared curiously at our carriage. They didn't run away. I was nauseated.

People with careworn faces were scurrying in all directions along the narrow, winding streets. Pale, undernourished children played above the gutters, floating small paper boats on the fetid water.

At last we reached our destination. It was a wooden house set apart from all the others. We had been assigned a large, dark room. Nurse Frania and her family were given another. The house was old and damp. There were four rooms in all and a kitchen.

We were lucky to have decent fellow residents. They were elderly, educated people: the brother, uncles, and aunt of the famous pianist Arthur Rubinstein. The young housing official bade us an embarrassed farewell. But he was in no way at fault for the way Rumkowski had treated me, the same Rumkowski who had once assured me of his gratitude and promised that he would look out for me forever.

15

Rumkowski played a major role in my life in the Lodz ghetto. It began with him, and ended with him.

Before the war, Chaim Rumkowski had been our neighbor. He lived at 26 Poludniowa Street, and I at 28. Initially, we were no more than acquaintances. He was a small factory owner and worked hard. He was also the volunteer director of the Jewish orphange in Helenowka, just outside Lodz. This made him greatly respected in the Jewish community, for there were few who sacrificed their precious time to orphans.

One day, Rumkowski called me and asked me to examine a little girl from the orphanage. I gave him an appointment and he came to see me. I see him standing there before me to this day. He was tall, handsome, and around fifty-five, with white hair and light blue eyes. With him was an eight-year-old girl in tattered clothes. He looked upset and worried.

The little girl had gonorrhea. This was no rarity among small girls at the time; in the poorer strata of society, where the whole family shared a single bed, women, unaware of their disease, infected their daughters. But only their daughters. Boys were not infected in this way. At that time, when there were no sulfa drugs or antibiotics, the disease was hard to treat. With luck, a specialist might manage to cure a patient over a period of months. It was a significant burden on the physician, as he had to repeat the treatment every day. Above all, such treatment took its toll on the sick child.

I explained that the girl could infect her fellow orphans through her sheets, towels, use of the same toilets, and so on. Rumkowski was scared. I suppose he hadn't imagined the matter to be that serious. He asked me to go at once to Helenowka and examine all the children. I suggested hospitalizing all the sick children, but he wouldn't hear of that. Perhaps he feared the loss of his position, which was so important to him. He could have been accused of not attending to his duties. Some time later, I learned from the mothers of some of the girls (not all of them were full orphans) that Rumkowski suffered from a certain perversion. If that had become known, he would certainly have been removed from his position and would have faced a criminal trial.

Rumkowski justified his unwillingness to have the children hospitalized by saying that he had a good nurse in the orphanage who would do everything I told her to. With tears in his eyes he promised his gratitude if I could eradicate the disease. But who would want Chaim Rumkowski's gratitude? (I was to experience the true nature of his gratitude some years later.)

I went to Helenowka the next day. Three small girls had gonorrhea. Nevertheless, I marveled at the cleanliness and order in the orphanage: a lot of good was done for the orphans there. A pretty, young nurse helped me with the examinations and treatments. I visited Helenowka twice a week. The sick children were isolated, and a few months later they were well. Rumkowski wanted to pay me, but I would not accept any money.

During my visits to Helenowka I became familiar with the life and customs there. They had around twelve acres of arable land. Rumkowski was trying to ensure that the boys and girls learned how to farm. The idea was that they should emigrate and put their agricultural knowledge into practice. Rumkowski was an ardent Zionist.

Even then I noted in him a character trait that I would later come to fear: Rumkowski was a tyrant. Later, in the ghetto, this caused many tragedies. In the orphanage, he was an unfettered despot; perhaps that was why he feared for his position. He made it rain and he made the sun shine.

This position of authority suited him well. In the orphanage he did as he pleased; he was subject to virtually no control. But those appearances were deceptive. Rumkowski was unhappy with himself and his environment. He even complained about this on his frequent visits to me. His sexual habits had led him to bankruptcy.

People said he had been blackmailed by the mothers of the little girls who had fallen prey to his lust. They had extracted large sums of money from him in exchange for silence. That was a criminal offense, and although he was never officially charged, the payments he made to those women may explain why he went bankrupt.

After that he became an insurance broker, which undermined his position in the orphanage. He was no longer so well trusted. Indeed, he was a failure not only in business but also in his personal life. He lost two wives, although he had never wanted children.

By 1937, Polish anti-Semitism had intensified because of the rise of Nazism in Germany. Rumkowski and I often spoke about this. He believed that Hitler would solve the Jewish question. He even made the astonishing prediction that racial persecution would ultimately lead to the creation of an independent Jewish state.

I often asked myself why Rumkowski never made a career in the El Dorado that was Lodz. He came from an Orthodox Jewish family in Lithuania and had barely ever set foot in a regular school, although he had attended heder, Jewish religious school. He spoke no language well. He never mastered German, and spoke only broken Polish and Russian. The only language he spoke well, albeit with a strong Lithuanian accent, was Yiddish.

Long before the war, Rumkowski told me that he was closely related to Alfred Rosenberg, the famous Nazi ideologist and author of *The Myth of the Twentieth Century*. He even claimed to have an ongoing correspondence with him. Later, when Rumkowski became the absolute ruler of the ghetto of Litzmannstadt, I often thought back on that connection. When Rumkowski went bankrupt, he moved away from Poludniowa Street, because he could no longer pay his rent. He rarely came to see me after that. But we still saw each other occasionally, right up to the outbreak of the war.

16

A few days after the German army invaded Lodz in September 1939, some German officers paid a visit to the Jewish community. Rumkowski happened to be there at the time. The officers asked no questions; they just observed the men. Then one of them told Rumkowski he would be the chairman of the Jewish Senate. I often wondered whether it was a calculated move or a mere twist of fate that made this lunatic the dictator of the Lodz ghetto. A more perfect delegate for Hitler's regime would have been hard to find. Did Rosenberg really know him? If so, did he know that Rumkowski suffered from megalomania and a persecution complex?

To this day I don't know the real story. Perhaps the officers had simply been having fun; perhaps nothing had been planned in advance. Perhaps Rumkowski's graying, patriarchal head with its blue Aryan eyes had won them over. Who knows? In any case, they made a perfect choice. Rumkowski must have been at least sixty years old. He had a formidable amount of energy and a real gift for organization. In that respect, he was practically a genius.

This uneducated man was absolutely convinced that he would outwit the Germans. He thought that with their help he would be able to create an independent Jewish state. And he was convinced that the labor of his workers would suffice to pay for it. He was sure the Germans wouldn't ask for more.

So he threw himself with zeal into organizing the ghetto work force for the Germans.

He behaved as if he had always known that in 1939 the Germans would come and say: "You will be the president of the Jewish Council." Rumkowski made sure all the Nazis' orders were carried out. At their behest he would send thousands of people to their deaths. But in order to rule his grotesque Jewish state, he had to have a "government." He proclaimed an auxiliary council.

Many intelligent, honest, cultured people were members of this council, including scientists and specialists from a wide range of professions. But Rumkowski was jealous of them. Everything had to be done in his name. It was his government, his hospitals, his post office, his workshops, even his money.

The money was truly a joke. There were two denominations: the *Chaimka* and the *Rumka*. This money had no value except within the ghetto. Everyone was forced to exchange their old money for *Chaimkas* and *Rumkas*. With this, he prevented many people from escaping; without money, they had no way of supporting themselves on the Polish side. This is exactly what he wanted to accomplish. He was actually quite pleased with himself.

The whole thing was sheer madness. If I remember right, on one side of each bill was a drawing that depicted people throwing chains from their raised wrists as they gazed toward the sun with enraptured faces; on the other side, there was Rumkowski's head. He was the absolute ruler of the ghetto, just as he had been the ruler in Helenowka before the war. He was a despot. This was not a ghetto, but the Jewish state of King Rumkowski.

Court sentences were issued in his name. He ordered judges to issue death sentences. They refused.

"Let him issue death sentences himself," they said. And in the synagogues, where prayers were always said for the head of state, prayers were now offered for the success of Rumkowski, president of the Litzmannstadt ghetto.

Based on my conversations with Rumkowski before the war, I would have thought he wanted to improve things for the Jews. But power robbed him of his senses and drove him mad. When things didn't go his way, he would lose his mind entirely, shouting and screaming in his high-pitched voice. I had occasion to be on the receiving end of his explosions of rage. One such event remains engraved in my memory.

17

Rumkowski's council did not last long. One day, his ministers were arrested by the Germans and shot in the woods. Why? No one knows. The victims included some good friends and colleagues of mine. Not long afterwards, I received a personal letter nominating me as "minister"—in other words, a member—of the Jewish Council. It was signed by Rumkowski. Instead, I paid him an unofficial visit that same evening.

He lived outside the ghetto, on Kilinski Street. His apartment was modestly furnished. Rumkowski pointed me toward a chair.

"Please be seated, Doctor."

"Thank you. I received your nomination to the Jewish Council, and I've come to thank you."

"It is good you came, Doctor. You will be assured of a career with me. I shall now be the king or, if you will, the president of the first Jewish state in two thousand years. I have been charged by the supreme German authorities with establishing a model ghetto. And I intend to make it an independent, modern state! It will be unique and perfect! My councillors must offer me their solid support. We will enter the annals of Jewish history. As to you, I am appointing you my Minister of Health. I shall make a jewel of this ghetto."

I studied the man carefully. His beautiful blue eyes sparkled. He was carried away. His splendid white hair floated about his head. There was something spectral, almost ghostly about him. He looked exactly as I imagined our prophets must have looked.

I suddenly realized that I was sitting across from a madman, and I had no idea how to respond. His personal dynamism and the aura that emanated from this mediocre character made me uneasy. I felt myself go pale.

"What's wrong?" he asked. "Are you ill?"

His voice, as it became slightly more human, restored my equilibrium, and I steadied myself. At that moment, I realized I had to do everything possible to not become a "minister." The fate of that first council passed before my eyes. I did not want to end up with a bullet in my head as one of Rumkowski's "ministers." But what would happen if I asked this lunatic to release me from this dubious honor? I summoned up the preceding years.

"My dear Rumkowski, do you remember the time you assured me of your gratitude, and said you would repay me and help me to the best of your ability?"

"I am at your service."

"Mr. Rumkowski, you know that I am an experienced physician, but I have no talent for organization. I would make a very poor minister of health. I would like to continue my work as an ordinary physician, treating the sick, and in this way be of use. I must work to support my aged father and my family. Please allow me to decline this honor, a distinction which I duly appreciate."

I immediately rued my words. Rumkowski's face turned red. He stood up and foam appeared at the corners of his mouth.

"What can you possibly be thinking, you idiot? Do you really believe you may do as you please?" he squealed in his terrifying falsetto. "There is a war going on here, and we are like soldiers—we must follow orders, obey unconditionally and perform our duties, or die! If you do not do what I say as president of the Jewish Council, I shall crush you like an ant. You shameless worm! If you ever again have the nerve to refer to our acquaintance at the orphanage, you shall go to the place from which no one returns alive!"

Rumkowski jumped. He stood before me, massive and threatening. Madness gleamed in his eyes. I held my tongue.

"Not a word more!" he screamed. "Tomorrow morning Dr. Reicher takes over the Department for Combatting Infectious Diseases. This office does not yet exist. It must be organized. Dr. Reicher shall no longer be minister of health. He is too cowardly. And in his new office he will be answerable only to the German authorities."

I said a few more words in the hope of calming him down, like a psychiatrist addressing a patient. But there was nothing to be done. Rumkowski showed me the door.

18

Early the next morning I set off for the Jewish Council's Department of Health to begin setting up my office. At that time almost everyone in the ghetto was still unemployed, so I quickly put together a staff. In consultation with my colleagues at the Department of Health, I established that every case of infectious disease accompanied by a high fever had to be reported, and that all those deemed ill had to be hospitalized.

The ghetto was a perfect breeding ground for epidemics of all kinds. Large numbers of people crowded into a small space, the total absence of sewers, hunger, almost no soap—all that conspired together. And what weapons did I have? Rumkowski knew perfectly well what he was doing when he gave me such a heavy burden as a punishment for insubordination. I went to his office and explained the situation. He issued me a pass.

With an attorney as my adviser, I went out to the Polish side to meet the German authorities and put the situation to them. This was just at the point when the ghetto was being fenced in. The attorney and I had to wear two yellow stars each, one on our chest and one on our back. On Adolf Hitler Strasse people stared at us as if we were wild animals that had just escaped our cage. Every police officer we passed checked our papers. At the German health office on Eighth Army Street, we presented our woes with great seriousness. They laughed in our faces.

"Let disease destroy the Jews," they told us. We barely escaped the furious dogs that were set upon us, and were lucky to return to the ghetto in one piece.

But the next day I had to return to the Polish side. The German authorities were preparing a complaint against me. A young physician, Dr. Rozowski, had treated a woman with typhus and failed to report it. Someone had reported him, and he had been arrested and taken to a German jail. He was facing a death sentence. Dr. Rozowski was young and had mistaken typhoid fever for influenza. Rumkowski considered me to be at fault. He wanted to have me destroyed for reasons we both knew. I knew too much about his perversion and his past.

Once again I stood before him in his office.

"I hate you. I will show you what I am capable of," he said. On the wall hung a portrait by Mojsze Szwarc, the ghetto painter. It showed the sleeping ghetto at night. A light revealed the Church of the Blessed Virgin Mary and the bridge over Zgierska Street. A lone German soldier stood watch over the empty street. Everyone was asleep except Rumkowski. He was brooding over the fate of those he had to help: starving mothers whose dried-up breasts had no milk for their babies, the sick, the dying, the beggars, those lost in prayer. . . . He was depicted as an angel. Poor, starving artists painted such pictures for a loaf of bread. . . .

No, I thought, Rumkowski does not sleep, oh no. . . . He is not hungry and he is not suffering. In the house where we were to have lived, he had established a harem for himself: beautiful new women, with replacements brought in from time to time. It was officially called a sanatorium or rest home, but everybody knew the truth, though no one dared to say it openly. The women there did not go hungry. They were happy to be able to eat and support their families.

"You know that you're answerable to me for every case of typhus. Let nothing like that incident with Dr. Rozowski ever be repeated," Rumkowski said.

I resolved to do everything possible to save my younger colleague. I had a good friend on the Polish side, a Dr. Bigler. He was not a physician, but a doctor of philosophy. Dr. Bigler lived at 36 Magistracka Street, in a house occupied by German judges and prosecutors. He often visited them, and they him. His father, Rudolf Bigler, came from a fine, worthy German family in Lodz; he was also a friend of my father's. I called Dr. Bigler and we arranged to meet on the Polish side.

Once I left the ghetto, I carefully removed my yellow stars to be less conspicuous, although that could have cost me my life. Dr. Rozowski's life was at stake. Dr. Bigler received me cordially. He was very moved by Dr. Rozowski's story, and promised to do all he could. Over dinner and a glass of good wine, he spoke with the lead prosecutor in the case. Rozowski was acquitted. My joy was immense. I thought that this would change Rumkowski's opinion of me for the better. But I was wrong. Rumkowski still wanted to get rid of me.

My wife had been closely following my battle with the king of the ghetto.

"We are young and we have a child. We need to save her," she said. "We can't just stay here and watch our own destruction. We have to escape."

But I couldn't abandon my sick father without providing for his care. We decided that I would stay, while Pola and the child would flee to Warsaw. At the time, that was still possible. Our parting was extremely painful, but in the end I agreed. There was no other way.

19

Epidemics were raging in the ghetto. It was inevitable that many cases went unreported. I would return home to my father exhausted and starving after a long day of draining work. One evening, Dr. Miller came to see me. Like me, he headed one of the offices of the Department of Health. We had known each other for years. He was worried and out of breath, and told us of a conversation Rumkowski had had with the chief of the Jewish police, which he had learned about by chance.

"Dr. Reicher must be brought to justice. He has not reported a number of cases of typhoid fever," was the drift of the exchange. I understood that Rumkowski wanted to get rid of me once and for all. What should I do?

"Your only chance is to flee at once," Miller advised me. I had stayed in Lodz because of my father. I could not take my elderly, invalid father with me. But in prison I would be of no help to him. Much less as a cadaver.

Should I stay, or go? That was the hardest decision of my life.

I had to escape from Lodz, escape from Rumkowski, from the death threat that now hung over me. From Warsaw, I would still be able to help my father, but here in Lodz I no longer could. I asked Dr. Rozowski to look after my father. His good nurse, Frania, would stay with him. I took little food or money with me. My father and I both cried as I took my leave. My father had raised three sons. He had given all three of us a university education, and now all three of us had abandoned him.

My father died on the first day of Hanukkah. Frania wrote me in Warsaw to inform me. He was buried alongside my mother in the Jewish cemetery, his head on a pillow of earth I had brought back from Rachel's grave in Palestine in 1932. Did he die of illness or of hunger? That thought haunted me for years. Frania died in Auschwitz in 1944. Dr. Rozowski was also murdered there.

Rumkowski, "King of the Ghetto of Litzmannstadt," carried out all the Germans' orders and dispatched a vast number of his subjects to their deaths in Chelmno and Auschwitz. But his turn would come. One day, he too was sent to Auschwitz. The Jews there apparently burned him alive in the crematorium as soon as he arrived.

20

The night was dark. Not a star in the sky. Thick clouds concealed the moon. A piercing wind chilled me to the bone; it was a few degrees below freezing. I was in the Jewish cemetery in Lodz, by the family tomb of the Poznanskis, the richest Jewish family in Lodz, waiting for the smuggler who was to take me across the border between the Reich and the General Government. I had to wait from eight in the evening until five in the morning. The pre-arranged signal was three whistles. It was one of the longest nights of my life, and one that worked both for and against me.

My warm fur coat, fur-lined boots, woolen underwear, and warm scarf should have shielded me from the cold. And yet, standing motionless, my mind was seething. Had I done the right thing? Would Rumkowski come looking for me in the Warsaw ghetto? Would I ever see my father again? What if something happened to Pola and Elzunia? Would I cross the border safely? Would my guide keep his word? He had already received an advance, but would he be honest?

I dozed off on the steps of the tomb. I was awakened by strange noises. Luckily, it was not Nazis. A man and a woman were digging with a shovel. I realized why: they were burying their valuables. It was common now. The cellars of houses had become unsafe ever since the

Germans had begun to dig trenches into them a meter deep in search of Jewish treasures.

It was three o'clock in the morning. I could no longer sleep. All at once, I began to scratch myself. I itched as if a thousand bedbugs and fleas were biting me. I scratched myself as best I could in my thick clothes, and this helped me forget my worries. I had been scratching for an hour, when suddenly I heard a soft whistle. My guide! I drew close to the grave of one Isidore Finkelstein right by the cemetery wall, exactly as planned.

"I'm here, Doctor. Are you ready?"

"Yes," I answered.

"Good. Move away from the wall now. I'm going to throw you a ladder."

I moved a short distance from the wall. A small wooden ladder flew over it and landed between the graves, its fall muffled by the snow. I stood the ladder against the wall and with limbs stiff from the cold pulled myself up. I saw barbed wire. How could I get over it?

"Don't be afraid. Here are some rags to wrap around the wire." I caught the rags and bound up the wires as best I could.

"Hurry up!" the smuggler shouted.

At that moment I saw two shadows approaching the wall. I panicked. Was it the couple that had been burying their valuables? I shouted: "Beat it, if you value your life!" It must indeed have been the same couple, for the shadows obediently withdrew and vanished among the gravestones. I was standing on top of the cemetery wall. The guide handed me an old quilt that I also lay across the barbed wire. I threw the ladder over the wall. Despite all my precautions, my pants were torn in many places. I picked up the rags and quilt so as not to leave a trace. I was out of the ghetto. . . . The smuggler was a tall, broad-shouldered Polish farmer in a sheepskin coat, high boots and a wide hat.

We departed quickly in a wagon pulled by two strong horses, taking the less traveled roads toward Głowno. Day was breaking and the sky was tinged with pink. It was lighter now, and we could make out the world around us. It was a typical Polish landscape, with flat fields, forests, and villages with thatched-roof wooden cottages. The smuggler lived on the border. Some of his fields were in the Reich and the rest in the General Government, so he had the right to cross the border in both directions. I, of course, could not. I parted company with my "travel agent" in a village inn.

He gave me a few tips for the crossing. I was to meet up with him again at an appointed place on the other side. The border cut through the small town of Głowno. To cross the border one had to cross a small river about sixteen feet wide that looked completely frozen. To be safe, I tried out the ice closest to shore. It held. I continued out across the ice with confidence. But just when I had almost reached the other shore, the ice gave way and I found myself up to my waist in gelid water. My clothes filled with water and became unbearably heavy. Luckily, the river wasn't deep, and the surrounding ice was strong. Once I managed to remove my fur coat, I was able to scramble out.

Now what? I couldn't call for help. I climbed onto the river bank and sat down exhausted beneath a solitary tree, a blue spruce. I was completely frozen. I had to take off all my underwear and clothes to wring the water out. It was in this unfortunate and ridiculous situation that two German border guards, both middle-aged, appeared out of nowhere. By this point, I couldn't have cared less. I was completely resigned to everything.

"Great way to stay healthy," one of them said. "You certainly set an example, swimming in the middle of winter." They both laughed, pleased with themselves.

I had to put my wet clothes back on. They weighed a ton. As I was doing so, I managed to put on the white armband with the blue star that Jews in the General Government wore on their sleeve. Luckily, the soldiers failed to notice this maneuver, and I suddenly realized how I could deceive them. In fact, I had heard of this trick back in Lodz.

The border post was more than a mile further on. There, my personal effects were searched, but they found nothing suspicious on me.

"We see that you live in the General Government. You are not allowed to cross the border. There are severe punishments for this. But as you are a physician and have already punished yourself by falling into the river you shall only pay a fine," the sergeant said. I paid a large sum, but of course was given no receipt.

"Now return where you came from. Do not attempt to cross the border again, or your punishment will be more severe."

"I came from Warsaw and I would like to go to Lodz, where I have family," I answered quickly. "You saw my papers from Lodz. I must get back to my family in Lodz."

"That is impossible. Return to Warsaw." They took the bait. I wanted to wait until my clothes were dry, but I realized that staying on the border was not without danger. I proceeded to the place where I was to meet my guide, and he took me to Lowicz.

My wife had relatives in Lowicz: Uncle Reichenberg, Aunt Szajna, and their three beautiful daughters. They were appalled when they saw me in such a pitiful state. I had to go straight to bed, and they sent for a doctor, Dr. Brokman. I was shivering, and I had a high fever, a cough, and very achy bones. The diagnosis was pneumonia. I was lovingly and wonderfully cared for in Lowicz. Dr. Brokman came twice a day to see me, and two weeks later I felt almost well—strong enough, at least, to continue on to Warsaw.

I thanked my relatives profusely for their superb care, and Dr. Brokman for his efficacious treatment. Jews were not allowed to travel. They were not allowed to change their place of residence. I rode the bus to Warsaw as an Aryan. The owner of the bus was a good friend of my relatives.

I was on my way to join my family once more.

Part II

IN THE WARSAW GHETTO

1

I entered the ghetto via Tlomackie Street. The gate was guarded by a German gendarme and a Jewish officer; nearby stood a Polish policeman in dark blue. I headed onto Leszno Street, the main street of the ghetto. I was completely stricken by what I saw. What a difference between the free, Polish side of Warsaw and the Jewish ghetto! On the Polish side there were open spaces, beautiful parks, trees, flowers, stores well-stocked despite the war; there were calm, well-dressed people strolling past happy embracing couples walking arm in arm . . . People smiling almost as if they were in Western Europe. But here . . . it was a different world.

A world that could only have taken root in the mind of a medieval inquisitor. Filthy, narrow, dark streets. Swarms of children, a huge tattered crowd. Leszno Street led straight to hell. There were market stalls along both sides, one after the other, selling cheap, shoddy merchandise. Their owners were among the ten thousand chosen of the ghetto . . .. Next to them were poorer traders whose tables were spread with spools, thread, ribbons, lace, pins, or nails. In the ghetto, these were treasures that could prevent death by starvation. There were peddlers too, with all their wares on their back—bric-a-brac, clothes, often even dirty laundry.

The sidewalks were dotted with hundreds, even thousands, of beggars pleading for a piece of bread. *Hot rachmunes, yidishe menshen, gibs a shtikele broyt!* "Have pity, fellow Jews, give us a morsel of bread!" they cried. Most of them were so weak that they could no longer sit up. Some were lying on the ground. I will never forget those silhouettes and those emaciated faces already marked by death.

"Even just a piece of crust. Have pity, Jews. I'm hungry, I'm dying. . . . Help me, in the name of the Almighty!" Many could no longer even speak. Their voices were broken. They could only moan. Their legs and faces were pitifully swollen.

And in all this desolation there was music. Whole orchestras and soloists, some of them famous virtuosos, even celebrities, before the war, were playing for bread. Bread was everything. Bread was life. They asked for nothing more. Only to live, to live and to survive. Some artists tried to scrape together a living another way. They didn't beg on the street. They put on their last fine clothes, sometimes even a whole tuxedo, and went from courtyard to courtyard, playing as if possessed. They forgot themselves, forgot the times, and the dank courtyards were transformed into concert halls.

It was heartbreaking to see graying virtuoso violinists dressed in dark clothes, their pants perfectly pressed, their white shirts spotless, and their neckties knotted in the Wagnerian fashion, playing Mendelssohn and Schubert . . . Tragic melodies that stirred the strings of our lives.

This was the ghetto.

It tore at the heart to see the scrawny fingers of small children reaching for a crust of bread. They pleaded with their eyes and cried out to us, but what could we do? We were often hungry ourselves. We had nothing to put in the pot. I had always been moved by Hans Christian Andersen's tale "The Little Match Girl." I would never have believed that children could suffer so!

Women with no milk for their babies sat on the sidewalks. Bodies covered with paper lay along the walls. Everyone averted their eyes. The employees of Pinkiert, the owner of a large funeral parlor, took them away.

There may have been no bigger funeral business in the history of mankind than that of Mr. Pinkiert, who believed that by burying others he would escape being buried himself. And indeed, he was spared that fate. He was burned in the crematorium in Treblinka, his ashes scattered by the wind.

There were also "grabbers," or "snatchers," on the streets. They were entirely a product of the times. They were mostly men, mostly young, and they waited for their victims outside bakeries. When a woman, older man, or child came out onto the street, the grabber would throw himself at his victim and tear the bread from their hands. He would then leap a few paces away and devour the bread on the spot, even as he made his escape. By the time he was caught, the bread would be in his stomach. If a grabber fell into the hands of passersby, he would be beaten horribly. Thus trapped, the grabber would moan, cry, and bleed under the blows. But he had survived.

There was no remedy for them; no punishment that could deter them. As hunger spread in the ghetto, there were more and more of them. There was a whole army of them. I saw all this and felt its effects myself.

Each city in the world has its accomplishments. Warsaw had the biggest ghetto in Europe, maybe even in the history of mankind.

I took all this in within the space of a few minutes as I crossed the ghetto toward our apartment.

Our lodgings were on Leszno Street, one flight up. The apartment belonged to an elderly couple, the Nowiks, who rented us a tiny room. To reach it, I had to cross through another, which was occupied by a family of six. My wife, bent over a steaming basin, was doing the laundry. Our daughter was lying in the only bed in the room.

My wife embraced me tenderly. "It's a miracle to see you here. We must never separate again."

She searched my overcoat, my vest, my pants, and my underwear for lice, paying special attention to my shirt and collar. She had to. A terrible epidemic of typhus was raging in the ghetto, and tens of thousands of people were sick. Typhus is transmitted by body lice. From then on I had to submit to these examinations several times a day.

In the meantime I took a look around at my new home. It was so small it felt as though there was not enough air for all of us.

My wife, obsessed with cleanliness, aired the sheets and beat the mattresses every day. Hygiene was essential for survival. I stared at her. What had happened to one of the most beautiful, elegant women in Lodz? She had grown haggard, aged, and depressed. She noticed my searching gaze.

"All this will pass," she said. "I feel like a caged bird. The bird grows sad, its feathers lose their sheen, and one day it dies. The same thing is happening with me. I'm worn out, I'm exhausted, but that is because you were not with me." I pulled her close.

"We must be inseparable, Pola. But if we have to, we must have the strength to separate again."

I stroked her silky black hair. Could I have survived without Pola's love?

We had enough to eat, thanks to the jewelry and the gold dollar coins Toni had brought us from my father-in-law in Debie. We sold one coin after another, and lived off that.

My in-laws no longer replied to our letters. My wife was very worried. Maybe they had had to move; they hadn't had time to let us know. Perhaps they were far away . . . There was no way to find out. I had no idea what to say, so I said nothing. I had a strange premonition that they were no longer alive.

Pola still had hope. We didn't discuss it. A few months later we learned that her parents had been gassed at Chelmno, near Kolo.

2

I registered as a physician with the Jewish Council's Department of Health. This meant that I instantly and automatically became a staff physician. I was allocated five large houses on Pawia Street, where I had to oversee the general hygiene, examine the occupants to prevent the spread of any contagious diseases and, above all, make sure no cases of typhus were being covered up. These tasks were ordained by German decrees.

I began to search for an office space. I found one at 5 Solna Street, in the home of a violin teacher named Frenkel. In the mornings I made my rounds and in the afternoons I saw patients.

I was assisted in my work by Koprowski. He had once been one of the great Lodz industrialists, a millionaire, but now he was a pauper. He was pleasant to deal with, fifty-five years old, and a great lady's man. Before the war he had written to Winston Churchill warning him to deal with Nazism. "A large block requires a big ax," he had written. Koprowski had a psychopathic fear of the Germans. One day, when a German entered his apartment, Koprowski hid in the bathroom and flushed his gold dentures down the toilet. He was afraid that the German would pull his dentures out and kill him.

Gradually, my life in the Warsaw ghetto began to stabilize. But I could not get used to the conditions. Almost half a million people lived there, as if they were in a prison. Even within the ghetto walls, freedom to move around was restricted, and that freedom came at a high price.

The smugglers were the best off. Everything possible was smuggled in from the Polish side. Every day, truckloads of food arrived. Cows, geese, chickens, flour, sugar, chocolate, wine, vodka—even flowers, since there were several florists in our midst. Even though smuggling was punishable by death, business thrived. It was the small-scale, retail smugglers who got caught. The big fish, the capitalists, could buy their way out. It was from them that the German, Polish, and Jewish police all took a cut. Everything functioned smoothly; to quote a popular phrase, "the cupboard looked the other way." Sometimes in the course of things a few Jewish policemen lost their lives, but that never stood in the way of business. New policemen appeared, and the cupboard looked the other way.

Many workshops and private factories (shoes, textiles, brushes) smuggled their wares out to the Polish side. In addition, there was business licensed by the Germans. "Petty thieves hang while the big ones go free," the saying goes, and that's exactly how it was.

Small children smuggling loaves of bread to keep their families from starving were cruelly punished. Those children were heroes, keeping whole families alive for months. Some German policemen allowed children to go out onto the Polish side to bring back bread, but there were also vile murderers who turned it all into a joke, and who took pot-shots at the children. The most brutal one was known as Frankenstein. He was short, deformed, and ugly, with spindly legs, but he was an elite marksman. His fanatical hatred led him to murder children. Every day, young heroes perished near the wall. Without a trial. It was rumored that Frankenstein had five children of his own of whom he was very proud, of whom he even spoke with touching tenderness.

The people I visited as a public health physician in the houses on Pawia Street lived in terrible squalor. I inspected all the houses every day, apartment by apartment. Few families were living in humane conditions—only those who were still earning any money. The rest, around 90 percent, were dying of starvation and typhus. Every day I reported cases of the disease. I had to do this in order to prevent the spread of the epidemic, but I didn't find it easy, because the sick would be forcibly taken from their families and isolated in the hospital. Parents refused to hand over their children. People feared—correctly—that they would never see their brothers, sisters, children, or parents again. The buildings where cases of typhus had been confirmed were quarantined, apartments and clothes disinfected, and the houses sealed; no one could leave such a house. The poor victims tried to bribe me into not reporting the disease, but I had to do my job.

But hunger was an even greater evil than sickness. In order to conserve energy, the hungry did not leave their beds. They grew thinner and thinner, then swelled with the edema of starvation and died. To avoid funeral costs, and to keep their food rations for as long as possible, families would not register the deaths. The dead would be carried out under cover of darkness and placed by the walls, covered in newspaper. The next morning, Pinkiert's employees would cart them away on rickshaws. A rickshaw meant for two would hold twenty corpses, even more, stacked one atop the other, head to toe. Hundreds of unidentified corpses were buried in mass graves. This was life on Pawia Street, where I was a public health physician.

But it was not like that everywhere. In one of "my" houses lived a highly educated teacher, Samuel Glicenstein, with his wife and only daughter, Yola, a beautiful girl. Yola was a victim of one of the ghetto's most tragic and most moving stories.

3

Yola Glicenstein was a beautiful, elegant, graceful, slender girl with an oval face and large, expressive eyes. She was eighteen years old. Her parents had been unable to find work, and the family was in danger of starving to death. Prostitution was the only way out, but Yola had too much integrity. What could she do to save her parents and herself? Become a smuggler! She would slip through to the

Polish side and bring back food. Looks and beauty can help in life, but beautiful people also attract attention. . . . Her charm, her lovely smile, and her grace had won over the policemen, who let her in and out through the ghetto gates without bribes. She was young and full of life and heedless of the dangers. Polish informers lay in wait for people who left the ghetto without authorization. If their victims did not give them money, they reported them to the Germans, in return for a reward. Sometimes the informers could be appeased with vodka or homemade brandy. Some informers were as young as eight or ten years old. For a while, Yola's forays over to the Polish side were successful. She was proud of that. She used to remove her white armband with the Star of David as she left the ghetto. But there was a slip.

One day, on the Polish side, she was accosted by a young man.

"Step into this doorway, young lady."

She followed him, although she was afraid. "You're Jewish," he said.

"No, I'm not. How could you think such a thing, you good-for-nothing?" she replied.

"Don't bother lying. I saw you leave the ghetto."

"So what? I had business there."

"Really, my sweet? Then why did you take off your armband and put it in your left jacket pocket?" the boy asked scornfully. Yola was too wise to continue lying.

"Well, so now you know. But let me go," she begged.

"Oh no, you're too pretty for that. You can go *afterwards*." The young man was not a informer. He didn't want money from Yola, he wanted something else. . . .

"I can't, I'm engaged. Please understand," Yola pleaded.

"You come with me now."

Yola wavered. She noticed an officer standing by the doorway. The policemen at the gate were laughing at the young Pole who was now gripping her arm. All she could come up with was "Let me think about it . . . I'll let you know. . . ." Unwillingly, the boy let go. Yola fled back into the ghetto.

"Under no circumstances must you let Yola out onto the Polish side again," I pressed her father, who told me the story when I went to inspect their apartment. "I understand your position, but Yola mustn't leave again. It's too dangerous." Yola wasn't there at the time. She had gone to see her fiancé, Dr. Konigstein. Maybe he could help her.

"You're right, Doctor, but you know Yola."

I only learned what happened next several days later. Yola's parents forbade her to smuggle again, and for a few days she stopped. But she would not ask her fiancé for money, because he had his own parents to support. She couldn't bear to see her own parents slowly starving to death on watery soup.

One day, she slipped out in secret. She wanted to bring back a few potatoes, some bread, and some vegetables. At first everything went well, and she made it out onto the Polish side. But she made the mistake of going out through the same gate as before. The young man was lying in wait. He had been waiting for days. Suddenly, he was there at her side. She was frightened, and tried to escape, but he held her tight.

"Come, my precious. It appears you've finally decided to make me happy," he said.

"No! No!" Yola pleaded.

"Nothing will happen to you. We'll just go to my place."

"No!"

"Well, in that case we'll go to Szucha Avenue."

Szucha Avenue was home to the Gestapo headquarters. In a rage, Yola began punching him, but he gripped her tighter and she couldn't move. She cried out in pain. A crowd formed around them.

"What's going on?"

"Leave her alone, pervert!" people shouted.

A German policeman arrived on the scene.

"What's all this?" he asked.

"I had an argument with my girl," the young Pole attempted to save the situation.

"Maybe she's a Jew. She looks like one," came a woman's voice from the crowd.

The German looked at Yola.

"Come with me," he ordered. The young pair went with him.

"You can see she's a Jew," the same woman piped up. The crowd dispersed. The young Pole may have loved Yola; in any case, he wasn't out for money.

At the police station he assured the officers that Yola was his fiancée, but they found her Jewish armband and Jewish identity card in her jacket pocket. The despondent young man tried his best to save her, but in vain. Yola was arrested. The boy dissolved in tears and was set free. Yola was taken to a Polish jail and locked up with thieves, traffickers, and prostitutes.

The next morning she was transferred to the Gestapo on Szucha Avenue. Under cross-examination, she admitted going out onto the Polish side without authorization because she wanted to take a piece of bread back to her starving parents.

This was punishable by death. Escorted by two German policemen, Yola was taken to the Jewish prison on Gesia Street.

When she failed to return home, her parents panicked. They informed her fiancé, Dr. Konigstein, and me. I advised them to wait until the following day, and then to go to see Kohn and Heller. I knew them both from Lodz, where they had both been unremarkable Jewish merchants. In the Warsaw ghetto, however, they had grown wealthy and influential. In association with the German officials in charge of the ghetto, they ran a major smuggling ring. Even though they were Jews, they were on the best of terms with the Gestapo. . . .

They also had the license for the horse-drawn shuttle buses that ran between the small ghetto and the large one. These were heavy wooden wagons pulled by old, tired horses, which could carry twenty to thirty people.

The next morning, at the very moment when Yola was being interrogated on Szucha Avenue, we went to see Kohn and Heller. They held court in their offices on Leszno Street.

Glicenstein and his wife went in to see them. I waited outside with Konigstein, who was in an extreme state of anxiety. At last Yola's parents came out. While they told us the details of their meeting, Heller stepped into an adjoining room, where we could hear him on the phone. He returned after quite a while and told Yola's parents that their daughter was under arrest and that she was facing the death penalty for leaving the ghetto without a pass.

In this respect the Germans were merciless. There was no room for appeal in cases where their orders had been contravened, especially where Jews were concerned. But the mighty Kohn and Heller assured the Glicensteins that they would do everything possible to save their daughter, although there was no guarantee they would succeed.

Yola's parents were unconsolable. We accompanied them home, discussing what to do next.

"I belong to an underground Zionist youth organization," Konigstein said. "I'm going to take them Yola's case. Maybe they can help."

We parted, and the battle to save Yola Glicenstein's life began. She and her fiancé were well known in the Zionist youth organization that was later to produce the Jewish insurgents of April 1943. The young people wanted to attack the prison, free Yola, and then hide her. This was possible, but at what price? How many innocent victims would the German reprisals claim?

It was decided to buy off the mistress of Dr. Auerswald, the head of the ghetto administration. Kohn and Heller were put in charge. They needed to come up with a diamond ring for the mistress of the German master of the ghetto. Diamonds were very expensive, but that was what we had to procure. We needed a large sum of money to free Yola. We began to fundraise.

The young people moved mountains. House committees organized their own collections, with lists of the amount given by each tenant. Money was also collected in larger stores and cafés. I chose the Café des Arts, where I used to go with another doctor. Lots of people went to that café, even if they could not afford to eat there, just to breathe in the atmosphere. When we walked in, Diana Blumenfeld was singing our ghetto song, "*Aheym*" ("Home Again"). I asked everyone to make a contribution to save Yola. Only a handful of people knew about the diamond.

Plays were staged, too, with the proceeds going toward rescuing Yola. We even raised money in the synagogue, and there were all kinds of amateur events, including a play for children in which my own small daughter danced (and was much applauded). The smugglers collected money among themselves. With all this, we had to be careful to avoid suspicious types who could have been Gestapo moles. But at last the necessary sum was amassed, and a beautiful, pure, blue-white diamond was purchased.

Kohn was to present this priceless gem in a ring to Dr. Auerswald's lover. Kohn's wife claimed that the woman had promised to help. No one can say with any certainty today what really happened. The fact remains that Yola's name was on the official list of death sentences, under Dr. Auerswald's signature, "For leaving the ghetto without a pass, sentenced to death. . . ."

This was a terrible blow to all of us, to the whole ghetto. Perhaps Dr. Auerswald was not responsible for the death sentences. Perhaps he merely signed them, while the orders were issued from above. Perhaps his lover took the diamond ring and did nothing. The secret of the truth was known only to a certain few. Are they still alive? What was certain was that Yola Glicenstein was condemned to die despite all our efforts to save her.

But we refused to give up.

The fight for Yola was a challenge for the Jewish intelligentsia, an affair of honor.

In essence, it evoked the struggles against trials for ritual murder, or the Dreyfus case or that of Beilis. But this struggle was not general or public. It was fought within the closed walls of the ghetto.

Anyone with any links to the Germans did what they could for Yola. Those with such influence were the owners and managers of factories working for the Germans, excluding Kohn and Heller, and a few others. The chairman of the Jewish Council, Czerniakow, one of the noblest people in the ghetto, also attempted to use his leverage. The young people even wanted to forge ties with the underground Polish resistance.

Perhaps we did too much. Perhaps if we had made less fuss we might have achieved a pardon. But just at that point, something happened that distracted my attention from Yola's plight.

Every day on my rounds I visited the Glicensteins and tried to comfort them. The apartments on my beat were growing emptier all the time as whole families were wiped out by starvation and typhus. One day, I was walking down Karmelicka Street on my way back to

Leszno Street from Yola's parents'. As always on Karmelicka it was very busy and crowded. The pleading cries of the beggars rang out: "Have pity, Jews!"

Rubinstein, the famous ghetto clown, was there too. Was he a philosopher or a madman? "Everyone must die, except those who do not give up their bread tickets," was his constant line. Rubinstein himself had no tickets. Nevertheless, he lived well, for everyone loved him, and gave him food and drink. He was a hero. . . .

"Only three people will survive the war: Hitler, Pinkiert, and me," he used to say.

Not one of the three survived. He used to tease a certain soldier that in the end he would end up shooting him.

One day, he came up to me and said: "Doctor, whatever you do, don't give up your tickets if you want to live. All men are equal." He looked me in the eye and laughed. That was an extraordinary day. On the corner of Karmelicka and Leszno I was accosted by the wife of one of my patients, who grabbed my sleeve and would not let go.

"Doctor Reicher, tragedy has struck. My husband just died," she lamented, weeping. "Just now, when we have so much work, the typhus had to carry him off. My business is going so well that I can't cope alone. I am earning so much money. When my husband was alive we never had this much work." Tears ran down her cheeks.

"Such a fantastic business, a gold mine, and he didn't live to see it, the poor man. I'm doing a roaring trade now." Intrigued, I asked her what the business was.

"Funerals." The woman was out of her mind. I managed to free myself from her.

Lost in thought, I continued down Leszno Street. Suddenly I heard an engine and turned around. The street was completely empty, but I hadn't noticed. Every day, a truck traveled that way, carrying prisoners from the Gestapo headquarters to Pawiak prison for interrogation. Any Jew caught on the street would be shot at from that truck, so as soon as it came into view on Zelazna Street, which led to Leszno, people fled into houses, gateways or shops. In an instant, traders, beggars, tables, and even whole stalls would disappear. Only corpses remained behind, motionless along the walls. But I had been so wrapped up in my thoughts that I had missed my chance to escape. It was too late. The truck stopped alongside me and three men got out. One punched me in the face and I lost several teeth. It would have been madness to put up a defense. They beat me senseless until I collapsed on the sidewalk in a pool of blood. I was later told they continued to kick me even as I lay there. When the truck drove off, people carried me home. I lay unconscious for the rest of the day. Ever since, I have had poor hearing in my right ear and impaired vision in my right eye. Those ten minutes aged me twenty years. But as soon as I recovered, I turned my attention back to Yola's fate.

Her sentence had not yet been carried out. She was still in jail and we had not lost hope of saving her. She sent letter after letter to her fiancé, begging him to save her. At a secret meeting of our Zionist organization, several possibilities were discussed. Disease did not prevent executions being carried out. But perhaps typhus? We could infect her artificially. But could we accept such a responsibility? What if she died? On the other hand, the unwritten laws of every country in the world state that capital punishment may not be carried out on someone seriously injured or on pregnant women. Yola was neither. Dr. Szwarcenberg, Dr. Konigstein, and I decided we would break her leg. In the meantime, news came that she would be shot the following week. We had to act quickly if our plan was to succeed.

As an accomplice in our task we managed to enlist a senior colleague of mine from Lodz, Dr. Gottlieb, head of the Jewish jail. Despite his position, he was a man with a heart of gold, and full of sympathy. He had a charming wife and a young son. Two days later we had everything we needed to perform our deed. Gottlieb was of great assistance to us.

I will never forget that night. Szwarcenberg, Konigstein, a female nurse, a male nurse, and I went to Gottlieb's apartment, or rather to the little room he occupied with his wife and child. We drank a bottle of wine to strengthen our resolve. Yola was brought to the infirmary by a trusted policeman, a prison guard. Then we ourselves slipped in. We had to be immensely careful, for there were spies everywhere. Yola was waiting nervously. Her fiancé threw his arms around her and they kissed.

"We don't have a lot of time," Szwarcenberg said.

"I know," said Konigstein, moving away.

Szwarcenberg explained to Yola why and how we were going to break her leg.

"My lovely leg," she lamented.

"We're going to take the utmost care. You won't feel any pain, and you'll be just as beautiful as before."

Yola laughed and cried at the same time. "Are you sure the Germans won't shoot me, Doctor?" she asked. She was ravishingly beautiful.

"Out of the question. A death sentence can't be carried out if the prisoner has a broken leg. We're going to make sure the bone doesn't set too soon, so we'll have time to save you."

The operation was performed under general anesthetic. Her right leg was expertly broken below the knee. The broken bones were set and we applied a cast. Young Konigstein broke down and had to be led out, but the operation was a success. We all helped. We looked at each other and I saw hope in my colleagues' eyes. We stayed a while longer in the prison and watched over Yola.

"She's waking up," whispered the nurse.

"Where am I?" asked Yola in a weary voice.

"In the infirmary of the Jewish prison," I answered.

"How did I get here? Am I sick?"

"Yes and no," I replied with a smile, and told her everything. The effect of the anesthesia meant that she remembered nothing.

"Why didn't I fall asleep forever? Why didn't you give me poison?" Yola sobbed. I attempted to console her. I spoke of the future, and told her everything would be all right. By now, it was eleven o'clock, well past the curfew, so we stayed with her and talked all night. We discussed all the themes of the day, including the possibility of an armed uprising.

Dr. Szwarcenberg, a well-known social activist, believed that the Germans were still too strong for an insurrection to succeed. But progressive parties in the ghetto were beginning to speak of that very possibility—not just to speak of it, but to prepare. They were buying weapons and ammunition from Poles who had stashed away considerable stores back in 1939. Jews were even buying guns from German and Ukrainian soldiers. The Jewish underground was growing along-side the Polish one.

The religious Jews, who listened to their rabbis and tzaddiks, were generally opposed to any kind of armed uprising. "The authorities derive their power from God. To oppose them would be an insult to God," they affirmed.

In the wee hours of the morning, Yola was moved from the infir-mary and taken back to her cell. She was in intense pain, and had to be given several shots of morphine. Then she fell asleep. Later that morning we left the prison.

The next morning, Gottlieb, the prison director, our accomplice and friend, reported to the German ghetto board through the Jew-ish Council that prisoner Yola Glicenstein had broken her leg dur-ing an exercise period in the prison courtyard. The explanation was plausible; temperatures were below freezing, and there was ice on the ground. A German doctor and the police physician, Dr. Kantor, came to examine the break the next day. Because of the cast they were unable to arrive at a conclusion, and sent her to the Jewish hos-pital for an x-ray. The German doctor showed a great deal of good will, and followed the Jewish ambulance all the way to the hospital in his own car. There, he confirmeded that both bones in the lower leg were broken. Dr. Kantor, my former assistant from the Jewish hospi-tal in Lodz, later told me that the German physician had been well disposed. He liked Yola. Kantor was confident that he would issue a favorable certificate. We had hope. The German doctor had made a good impression on all of us. He seemed like a good man.

Two days later, however, Gottlieb received a visit from two Polish officers, who showed him an order signed by Auerswald. They were to "execute the sentence of death on Yola Glicenstein by firing squad." Gottlieb gave the Polish police some vodka to stall for time. Then, he phoned Czerniakow, who called Dr. Auerswald. "An order is an order," is all Auerswald would say.

Dr. Kantor was present for the execution. He prepared Yola for the worst. It was a cold winter day, and a strong wind blew the snow from the rooftops. Yola was brought out, deathly pale, on a stretcher. They wanted to blindfold her, but she refused. Her eyes were open wide.

"Do it fast, so that I don't feel anything, I don't want to suffer," she told the Polish policemen. Then, in a strong voice, she said "I go to my death innocent. I did nothing wrong. I committed no crime. All I wanted was to take my parents some scraps of bread and a few potatoes so they wouldn't die of starvation. My murderers aren't here. I curse them! May my death be avenged!" The shots rang out. The bullets flew across the snow and ice. As Dr. Kantor told us, no one breathed a word.

So our Yola, who had united old and young in an immense shared campaign, was no more. Shot by Polish police on German orders, one frigid winter day. The world knew nothing of the tragic fate of that beautiful young girl, which remained within the ghetto walls. Millions of men and women went to work that day around the world without any knowledge of this event. Perhaps there are still people alive who were in the Warsaw ghetto and remember the fight to save Yola Glicenstein.

4

New events eclipsed the old ones. I continued to inspect the buildings on Pawia Street. I continued to see my private patients. Yet despite the strict cleanliness my wife enforced, I succumbed to typhus. Pola and Elzunia were fine, so I had myself admitted to the hospital to avoid infecting them. I saw with my own eyes that the hospital was hell. I have to admit that as a doctor, I was treated better than most: there were only three of us in the room. The hospital was overflowing, and most patients lay two to a bed. Others were on the staircases and on the floors. There were no sheets. The death rate was extremely high.

I developed brain and circulatory complications, but after three weeks I was put on the discharge list. I weighed ninety-four pounds. My body was covered with open sores due to poorly administered injections. My sister-in-law, Alina, had visited me regularly at the hospital to bring me food, fresh linen, and everything else I needed. Although visitors were strictly forbidden, she overcame every obstacle to see me. Pola wanted to help me, but Alina wouldn't hear of it because of Elzunia. With Toni's help, Alina had managed to escape to Warsaw. Toni worked in a German police station, and always found the time and means to visit us in Warsaw. Without Alina's help I would have died there. The soups they gave us were so watery that the few patients still able to joke said that the only way to find a piece of potato in them was to undress and dive in.

A few days after my discharge from the hospital, we were all sitting in our narrow room on Leszno: Alina, Pola, Elzunia, Toni, and myself.

"Alina, let me take you away to my mother's, to the Sudeten Mountains," Toni pleaded. "We can get married, and we'll take Elzunia with us. It's our only chance of escape."

"I can't leave Pola and Edward!"

"But you must," I said. "Things are becoming impossible in the ghetto, and there's no way to know what new trick the Germans will come up with to exterminate us."

"I'm not leaving you," Alina said stubbornly.

Toni's entreaties were in vain. He continued to visit us. He would come to Warsaw and enter the ghetto, appologizing to the Jewish police. Toni was afraid, but love conquers all. His love for Alina drew him to the ghetto walls. He took care of us, and especially because of the child, he made sure we had provisions we could only dream of: exotic fruit, even chocolate. But one day, he didn't show up. He stood outside the barbed wire fence and did not cross over to the ghetto. We never saw him again.

On orders from the Jewish Council, I was called up to work on the construction of the ghetto wall. I was still weak following my attack of typhus, and my wife was terrified.

"Go to the council and tell them you're still too weak, that you'll pay someone to replace you."

I went to the council. Grynbaum, whom I knew, came out of his office. I told him I was recovering from typhus. There was a law requiring all Jews to do physical labor, but one could pay someone else to do the work.

"Believe me," he said. "I wish I could help you, but I'm powerless against the Germans."

He said that the order was in my name, issued by the German authorities, and it expressly stated that "Dr. Reicher himself must work."

There was nothing to be done. At seven o'clock the next morning I reported to the community construction department with my tools—a ladder, a trowel, etc.—set off for the section of wall to which I had been assigned.

The Germans were systematically shrinking the ghetto, which made it easier for them to control the population. Work on the wall was constant, so that the ghetto continually grew smaller. The old wall that had once formed the boundary between the Jewish quarter and the Polish side had to be knocked down, and a new one was being built a hundred yards further in. Apartments "freed" by Jews were handed over to Aryans.

I had to work despite my broken health. I mixed cement, hauled sand, and carried bricks, which I laid one on top of the other. I had to carry heavy loads. I was emaciated and weak, and the work brought on a bilateral hernia which still gives me considerable trouble today. I could not have it operated on, because the typhus had weakened my heart. The work also caused my legs to swell. I had difficulty breathing. Try as I might, I could not find a way out of this duress. We were under constant watch. But I knew that my body could not withstand the backbreaking work; I had to save myself.

It was then that we heard the first rumors that Jews were being sent to the east to work. Many people were relieved, even overjoyed, just as they had rejoiced when they imagined that things would be better in the ghetto. But I was no longer so naive. I knew that deportation meant certain death, and I told my wife so one evening. We decided to become Aryan. But the path between our decision and the final result was long and painful.

5

I finally managed to get a lighter job at the wall, and I put my mind to planning our escape. I thought of converting to Catholicism, but it would be pointless: converted Jews were treated exactly the same by the Nazis. They stayed in the ghetto and prayed in their churches

on Leszno and Nowolipie Streets. Another idea came to me when the
carters who brought the sand for building the wall spoke about the
Tartars. There were a lot of Tartars living in Warsaw, in the Powisle
neighborhood. They were Muslims. I would try to become a Muslim.
It was the only solution.

I asked one of the sand carriers to take me down to the banks of
the Vistula, where they dredged up the sand for building the wall. I
asked him to wait for me for an hour. I removed my armband. On
the streets leading to the river there were lots of horse butchers, with
the emblem of a horse's head in pewter. They were Tartar butchers,
because Tartars are very fond of horsemeat. I asked for the address of
a mullah, and a few minutes later I was standing outside his house. A
woman showed me in to the waiting room.

"I'm here on private business," I said, and handed her my card. I
was dressed respectably; I had brushed all traces of sand from my
clothes, and had even shined my shoes with a cloth.

The mullah received me right away. He sat in a room richly hung
with oriental rugs. He was over seventy, rather short, with a white
beard. He was wearing a long gray coat and had slippers on his feet.
He showed me to a chair, and asked how he could help me. I wasn't
sure if I could trust him, but his smile suggested that I probably could.

"I've come on a very confidential matter. No one must hear a word
of what we say."

"This is my home, you may speak openly here and without fear."

"Master, I am a physician, a well-known specialist. I have a wife
and a small daughter, and I live in the ghetto. . . . I've come to ask for
your help. I've always been interested in the Muslim faith. I would
like to apprentice myself to you and to plumb the mysteries of the
faith. I would like to convert to Islam along with my whole family."

"I've read a lot about Islam," I babbled on, "and the beautiful language of the Koran. The ardor of this faith and its forceful expression have convinced me." The old mullah observed me intently and
looked deep into my eyes.

"I believe you, Doctor. I believe you unreservedly. You are a physician, and I suspect a good one. We value doctors, for they help people. Ours is an ancient culture, and medicine has played a great role

in it. It would be a great joy for me to gain three new followers, but you see, Doctor—" here he paused for a moment, and I could already sense his refusal, "I can no longer do anything. I will tell you why." The old man sighed. "Two weeks ago I received an order from the Gestapo to draw up a list of all the Muslims living in Warsaw. That list has already been sent back. From now on, only people whose names appear on that list are Muslims. Though I deeply regret it, I can do nothing. Even had you not convinced me so entirely, I would have tried to help you."

I was visibly shaken, and could not muster a word. I stood up to leave.

"Please stay and drink a cup of good Turkish coffee with me."

I did. I drank a cup of excellent coffee, black as night. "If I added you now to the list," the mullah said, "the Germans would suspect a trick, and you would be lost, and we as well. Trust in God. He will help you." I made my way back to the sand carrier, who was waiting by the river. I had lost all hope. The whole way home, I didn't say a word.

Back in our room, Pola was waiting for me, looking very distressed. "Two German officers were here. They asked who I was. Then inspected everything. They searched through our wardrobes and trunks, and turned all our pockets inside out, but they didn't find anything. What could they have found apart from me, Elzunia sitting on her potty, and the wash hanging out to dry? When they saw they had been misled, they told me that German security had received an anonymous tip-off that I was an English spy."

That was a strange incident. We knew who must have denounced us: our neighbor's family. We had to cross their room to reach our own, so our relations between us were strained. They usually refused to let us through, and caused problems. At night, they locked themselves in, and we were stuck. After the incident with the German officers, we decided to move out. The raid shook me so much that I stopped thinking about my failed attempt to convert to Islam. One event chased away the one before; there was no time to recover. We were constantly on edge.

6

We quickly found a new apartment. A woman whose family had died of typhus offered to exchange her room for ours; the authorities had wanted to billet a family of five with her.

Moving was a risk because of the "grabbers" and thieves; besides, the German police also entered the ghetto. If they found gold or dollars in someone's luggage, they shot him on the spot. A lawyer named Pinkiert, whom I knew well, had been killed summarily in this fashion, along with his wife and children, without a judgment or trial.

His wife had been the soul of the ghetto's orphanages and a close colleague of the famous pedagogue Dr. Korczak. During a move, gold coins had been found on the Pinkierts, and they were summarily shot.

So I was extremely cautious. I concealed all our gold, jewelry, and gold watches in Elzunia's favorite toy, a brown teddy bear. I packed the dollar bills in a condom that I carried on my person. With everything well hidden, we took a rickshaw to our new apartment on Nowolipki Street. Elzunia carried the precious bear.

When the driver stopped outside the front door of our new building, I began to help him unload our possessions into the house. My daughter started to play on the street with a small boy who was perhaps eight years old. Before I came back downstairs, the boy suddenly wrenched the bear from her and ran away. Pola was standing nearby but failed to notice, for which I was bitterly resentful. That yellow bear contained almost all our possessions—and money often spelled the difference between life and death. I was in despair. I tore off to look for the boy.

On the street I ran into a patient of mine who was a smuggler. I told him what had happened, and he advised me to go to a known underworld hangout, a café on Smocza Street. I ran all the way there, asking passersby as I went where the café was. Many of them mocked my desperate question: "Where is the thieves' café?" People looked at me as if I were out of my mind. Suddenly an elderly man with a broken nose and an unkempt beard appeared before me.

"Follow me," he said. "I'm a go-between." He had a strange way of constantly smacking his lips. We came to a dirty bar, the like of which I had only ever seen in crime movies. Behind the bar stood a fat bartender who must have weighed over two-hundred and fifty pounds. I ordered tea and the middleman went from table to table, chatting up various people. A moment later he returned to my table with a suspicious-looking middle-aged man in a worn suit with a garish scarf around his neck. This turned out to be the father of the eight-year-old boy who had snatched Elzunia's bear.

"What can I do for you?" the thief asked.

"I would like my things back. I will give you cash worth part of the value of the stolen items."

"We shall see." The three of us left the café and headed to Kroch-malna Street. A wooden staircase on the far side of the courtyard led up the outside of the building. There were wooden balconies on every floor, with a door that led to many separate rooms. The stairs swayed as if they might give way at any moment. Everywhere there were clotheslines full of laundry. I was led into a room. The stench was overpowering. I wondered why the inhabitants of the ghetto were so afraid of fresh air; the place was filled with steam and children. A woman was nursing twins. The little thief was there too.

The bear was retrieved from inside the sofa; it had already been professionally gutted. And there were its contents: a dozen twenty-dollar gold coins, two diamond rings, one loose diamond, my 75-gram gold watch (a wedding present from my wife's grandfather), and a woman's watch with a gold chain. Nothing was missing. An appraisal was begun. The middleman's valuations were not very high. The value was established in dollars. We also agreed on the percent-age for the thief—almost half.

"Do you have enough money on you to pay us?" the middleman asked.

"I do."

"Very well. It will cost you nine hundred dollars. And I get fifty dollars as the go-between."

But how was I to produce the money? There was an outhouse down in the courtyard, but I was afraid to leave the men alone with the goods and just as afraid that they might murder me. Then again, they were thieves, not murderers. They watched me intently.

"Well, are you going to pay us or not?"

"I'll pay you, but I don't want your wife and children here."

"Out!" the thief ordered. The children left the room.

"I'm not taking the twins out. Forget it!" the woman said. What was I to do?

"In that case, at least turn around," I said furiously. I was enraged at having to undress before these people, but I removed the condom, wiped it off, and paid the ransom. It was only then that I noticed the woman had been watching everything in a mirror . . .

"We gave you a good price because you're a doctor," the middle-man said, "but you should round it up." I gave them some Polish zlotys. "And we learned something from you," the thief said. "If you don't mind, show us how you did it." I took a fresh condom and showed them how to roll the paper money and tie it with a thread. The men were satisfied with the deal and offered me some brandy to celebrate, but I thanked them and declined. I was glad it was all over. The woman sewed my valuables back into the teddy bear.

"You see, our word is a word of honor. We thieves have our honor, too," they said in farewell. I retrieved my valuables, but I lost almost all my paper money. To this day I have no idea how an eight-year-old thief figured out what was in that bear. It was either instinct or experience. People in the ghetto often hid their wealth in children's toys.

7

I spent whole days trying to think of how to escape the ghetto, but could come up with nothing. It was too risky, and none of my plans had any chance of success.

July 22, 1942, was looming. It was a hot summer. Posters about the first deportation were on the walls, and many people volunteered willingly, lured by the promise of five pounds of bread and two pounds of beet jelly to be distributed at the place of assembly, the Umschlagplatz.

They were convinced they were going east to work, but their true destination was Treblinka, with its gas chambers and crematoria.

I was certain that deportation was tantamount to death, but no one would believe me. They believed the German posters that promised work in the East.

I kept telling people that if they wanted to survive, they would have to hide. In July 1942, they just laughed. They were paying a fortune for permits entitling them to work in German "workshops." These were factories and workshops owned by Germans in the ghetto; all the Jewish businesses and workshops had been officially closed down. People went to great lengths to obtain these permits to be exempt from deportation. They were convinced this was their route to safety.

To my mind, this work permit was just another piece of paper that could be torn up at any moment. There is no limit to human naïveté. Everything in the German ordinances is false: that was my deep conviction. Whatever the Germans ordain, do the opposite: that was my operating rule. I owe my life to those two principles combined.

The siege and progressive shrinking of the ghetto illustrate the methodology used by those in charge of deportation. They applied the same approach to people. They made the ghetto smaller and smaller, like a vanishing object. They reduced the number of people until there was no one left. They exterminated one group and promised the survivors they could stay.

This was a strategy designed to reassure. But they never kept their word and sent to their death people to whom, the day before, they had promised life, just as a butcher calms the beasts he is about to slaughter. Members of certain privileged professions, such as policemen, government employees, physicians, gravediggers, and others were convinced they would be eternally safe from deportation. But they were wrong. I was sure the only safety lay in a good hiding place.

I began to look for one in earnest after the owner of my medical office disappeared. Professor Frankiel's family consisted of his lovely wife, two talented grown daughters, and a son-in-law. They were a charming family. Professor Frankiel gave violin lessons, without being able to make a living at it; his wife cooked for private customers. The whole family looked convincingly Aryan.

They could have crossed over to the Polish side and survived with false papers. But hunger had led them astray. They had gone mad. They wanted to take trains to the East. I begged them not to go, but in vain.

They left of their own free will. They each received their five pounds of dark bread and two pounds of beet jam. That was the price of one Jewish life. And these five intelligent, educated people went willingly to work, in other words to their deaths. I was there when they left their home forever. Alone in a four-room apartment after my assistant left, I fell apart. It was already late. There were no more patients.

Suddenly I heard shouts in German: "All Jews out!" When had they entered the building? What difference did it make—they were already there. Their heavy boots thumped on the stairs. Where could I hide? In one corner of my office there was a cabinet for storing medical instruments, but it was unfortunately on legs. I hid behind it, but my feet were visible. I was afraid. My colleague, Dr. Goldlust, was shot dead in his apartment, where he had gone to hide. I tried not to breathe.

"Open up!" came a shout from outside the door. I didn't move. Rifle butts smashed down the door and soldiers entered my waiting room. "This is the end," I thought to myself. My heart froze. They came right up to the cabinet and started playing with the instruments and cracking jokes. After a minute or so, they left. I was in a terrible state. I lay down on the couch and breathed deeply. I was shaking all over. So they hadn't noticed my feet after all.

Cupboards and wardrobes were to play a major role in my life from then on. With luck, they could save us.

That day, all the Jews in the building where I had my office, at 5 Solna Street, were evacuated. Fifty people were led to their deaths. I alone escaped. On my way home, I ran into the poor woman who cleaned my office. She was beaming. I asked her why she was so happy.

"Doctor, I have good news. I'm going east to work! My child and I will finally be free from hunger and torture. Even if I have to work hard, we'll have enough to eat. We won't be hungry any more."

"Madame, you mustn't go to the train. No one knows what awaits you in the east. It may be that there is no work at all, but something worse . . ."

"What do you mean, my dear Doctor? Such an educated man, and spouting such nonsense. Oh no, my child and I are not going to stay here and starve!" And off she went.

I lost myself in thought. Could I be wrong? Could we really be better off now after all that we had suffered? Had Hitler changed his mind? Were we "parasites in the body of other nations" really being asked to build a new East? No, I was definitely not wrong. The so-called work in the East was just a trick to fool the herd that was being sent to slaughter.

I ran all the way home. I had to find a place to hide. Koprowski, my medical assistant, was looking too, but he found nothing. He was killed on Mila Street, in what they called "the cauldron."

We found a hiding place in the house where we were living, on Nowolipki Street. It was an attic used for drying laundry. About 150 people hid there. The only way in was up a ladder, which was then pulled up. It was a precarious place: a child's tears or cries could give us all away. But I went there anyway, with Pola and Elzunia. Alina hid elsewhere; we planned to join her later.

It was then that the chairman of the Jewish Council, the engineer Czerniakow, committed suicide. The German authorities had ordered him to help with the deportations. His successor complied with the Germans' every demand; he danced to the Germans' fiddle. With Czerniakow, we lost our defender.

Then came the most terrible moment of all: we were discovered. One by one we had to descend the ladder, chased by the SS men's leather whips. Outside the front gate of the house we lined up for the march. . . to the railway siding, to the terrible Umschlagplatz. So our lives were over! There was no chance of escape. Yet I sensed a glimmer of hope. I took Elzunia in my arms, and Pola walked beside me. It was a hot day at the end of July 1942.

We were led to the Umschlagplatz by a cordon of Ukrainians and SS men. Families were allowed to stay together. We were in the midst

of a huge crowd. Thousands of men, women and children were waiting patiently to be loaded onto freight wagons. Anyone who was
there that day knows the meaning of hell. We were being pressed
toward the train. The former Jewish hospital was next to the tracks. I
knew it well; I had been a patient there.

"Let's go upstairs," I told my wife. We climbed up to the top floor of
the hospital. There was no way out now, for the square was cordoned
off and heavily guarded. The hospital was teeming with people waiting to board the trains. We stood by the window.

"Up here we'll be the last to be loaded," I told Pola. "They'll take
the people on the square first, then those from the lower floors. Only
then will they come for us." We had kept a cool head. After the shock
of being discovered on Nowolipki Street, we had managed to stay
calm. We had certainly not given up.

From the window, I could see people being driven into the cattle
wagons. I had been right: they were indeed first loading the people
in the square, and then those from the lower floors of the hospital.
Finally, some Ukrainians chased us downstairs. Shots rang out constantly. Anyone who hung back or put up any resistance to board-
ing the train received a bullet in the back of the neck, like my friend
Pilzer, the lawyer who had drawn up the bill of sale for my house in
Ruda, or nineteen-year-old Marynja Eisenstadt, the immensely talented daughter of the great Jewish synagogue choir conductor. Had
she lived, she would now be a world-famous singer, for she had a
voice of incomparable beauty. She was known as the nightingale of
the ghetto. She was killed because she hesitated for a moment before
getting on the train.

I had done everything possible to avoid reaching the death train.
But how could we resist the mass of people bearing down on us? And
this crowd was being chased by bullets. Suddenly, I caught sight of an
ambulance and a man in a white coat. A doctor! We pressed our way
through. My heart raced as I recognized my colleague, Dr. Rundstein.

"Rundstein!" I shouted. He was dressing a bullet wound. He turned
his head. "Save us!"

He passed me a white coat. "Dress that woman's and child's
wounds," he ordered, pointing to Pola and Elzunia. I understood. I

quickly bandaged Pola's head and put her and Elzunia in the ambulance. I climbed into the front seat with Rundstein. The vehicle pulled away from hell. I gripped Rundstein's hand.

"Thank you, Risyu," I said, using his nickname. "You just saved our lives!"

"I wish I could help all of them," he answered. "But the Germans love order . . . In this factory of death, they first wound people, then they order us to treat them." We were back on Nowolipki Street. Once again, we were safe and sound.

After that, ambulances became redundant. They were used only in the early stages of the deportation. Eventually, the best doctors were fed to the death machine too. Our savior, Dr. Rundstein, was among them.

8

The architect of Operation Reinhard, Hermann Höfle, along with eighteen officers under his command, had established his headquarters at 103 Zelazna Street. Höfle lived there like a king, with his officers as his privy council. The Jewish Council catered to their every wish.

They had been given the finest house in the ghetto, with the most modern apartments. They were assigned workers, chambermaids, and cooks—the most beautiful women in the ghetto. There was even a Jewish orchestra to play soft Viennese waltzes while the murderers enjoyed their meals.

The commander and his officers ate well. It was here that orders were issued every day sending thousands of Jews to their deaths. After a hard day's work, those who carried out the orders needed to rest, which was to be found at 103 Zelazna Street. This was the home of the man in charge of the destruction of the Jews, the *Befehlsstelle*, the headquarters for orders.

Adjacent to that house, at 101 Zelazna, lived the Jews who worked at the *Befehlsstelle*. The janitor of that house, Mohn, had been a patient of mine for years. He wanted to help me find a place to hide. We no longer had a home after that terrible day at the Umschlagplatz. I went to see him. Mohn advised me to build a hiding place at 99 Zelazna. It was a good piece of advice: the building two doors down had been rented by death, who had turned it over to the organizers of this horror show. They ran it from behind a desk, drinking lots of wine.

Mohn and I were standing in the entranceway to 101 Zelazna. "Go upstairs, doctor. This is your only chance." I hesitated. I wasn't sure, because it was so close to the mouth of the lion.

"Perhaps I'll wait. We might find something else," I said.

"No place is as safe as this, right under the Germans' nose. Go up and have a look. Then you can decide for yourself."

99 Zelazna Street was on the corner of Nowolipie. It had been hit by a bomb when the Germans attacked Poland in 1939 and was partly destroyed and burned out. Only a small section of its flat roof remained. The building was higher than everything around it.

But how would we get up there?

"We'll knock a hole through from my roof at Zelazna 101."

"How?"

"You'll see."

And I did. In the attic wall of 101 that faced 99, we carefully made an opening that was just wide enough for a man to crawl through. And there, on that sixty-five square feet of roof, I built a hiding place, the best one imaginable. The idea was ingenius, and I thanked Mohn heartily.

We placed a heavy chest filled with sand in front of the hole in the attic at 101 Zelazna. This chest completely covered up the hole. Then we nailed two brass rings to the chest so that when we were up on the roof we could pull the chest close to the hole. We fastened two hooks into the wall on the roof and tied the rings to the hooks using strong rope. No one in the attic in 101 could possibly suspect the existence of our hiding place across from them.

Once inside, we could only move about lying down and crawling. If we stood up, someone might have seen us from downstairs. As it was, we were invisible to anyone except airplanes. Up there we were relatively happy, although we had only bread to eat. I made sure that we always had ten loaves of bread and two pails of water. If the bread grew stale, we dipped it in water and we ate it. That was our only food.

Ukrainians and SS men came up to the attic several times, but they never found us. We heard their voices and held our breath, and things ended well. Höfle and his employees never worked at night, so after dark we would go down to the Jewish workers' apartments at 101 Zelazna to stretch our legs and replenish our water. We soon struck up new acquaintances and friendships. In times of danger they would bring their children up to our roof. The only people who knew about our hideout were a few of the workers, Mohn, and Edmund Lichtenbaum, the son of Marek Lichtenbaum, the new chairman of the Jewish Council, a relative of mine. We felt more or less safe in our new situation.

In August 1942 I received word from Edmund Lichtenbaum telling me to report to the *Befehlsstelle*. I felt uneasy. I was escorted there by an official from the Jewish Council, who vanished as soon as we arrived. I presented myself to a corpulent blond, Höfle's secretary. While I was waiting, five drunk, shouting SS officers entered the waiting room.

"You a Jew?" one of them asked.

"Yes," I answered.

"Good. You're just what we need." His companions laughed. "Jews are good at Jewish games. How about you?" They were all staring at me. "Come on, Jew!" I took a step toward them.

"Up against the wall!" I obeyed. "Now the game begins. This will be the last game of your life."

I leaned my head against the wall and felt the barrel of a revolver on my neck. Were these people mad? Was this why I had been summoned? How could Lichtenbaum have turned me in like this? I was supposed to be meeting with Höfle! The officer pressed the gun into my head. It hurt.

"So, Jew, how do you like our Jewish game?"

I said nothing. The officer pressed harder.

"The Jew's lost his voice. What a strange dog—it doesn't bark, and it doesn't bite."

"Come on, pull the trigger," someone said to the owner of the gun.

"Patience, my friends," came the answer. "The game isn't over yet. Even Jewish games have rules."

"You know what? When we finish him off, we won't even need to bury him. You hit a Jewish louse with a German bullet—there's nothing left."

"Still got nothing to say for yourself? Lie down on the floor!"

Without a word, I lay down on the rug. Now I could no longer feel the gun.

"Flat on your stomach! So I can take better aim at the back of your neck." I was drenched in sweat. What if this drunkard shot me in pure jest? Today I'm amazed at how calm I was then.

"The doctor is awaited by Sturmbannführer Höfle," came the secretary's voice.

"What? He's a physician?" The officers instantly sobered up.

"Stand up, sir," said my executioner, and helped me to my feet. One might have supposed I had simply been lying on the floor of my own volition. What really took me by surprise was the "sir."

"You're a dermatologist."

"Yes."

"That's good. We need dermatologists." The officers reeked of alcohol.

"Come in, please," said the secretary. I went into Höfle's office. The drunks stared after me with curiosity.

All the rooms were richly decorated, and Höfle's study was no exception: the finest furniture, carpets, upholstery, drapes, and light fixtures. Jewish interior designers had been commissioned to do it all by the Board. Everything there had been confiscated from rich Jews.

I was standing before Hermann Höfle, chief of staff of Operation Reinhard, and one of the most fearsome murderers after Eichmann. (Who would have guessed then that nineteen years later I would testify against him before the presiding judge at Salzburg. . . .) He was a monster in human form, an accountant of death. He lived off those he killed. I had imagined him as brutal and savage. From everything I had heard, my image of him was correct.

I was gripped by fear when I saw him; not because of his terrifying appearance, but by the opposite: here was a man in his early thirties, with a round face, a jovial expression, and bright blue eyes. This was the creature who had already killed thousands of men.

The degree of my astonishment stunned me, but I had no time to consider it.

"I sent for you, sir, because I have a disease of the scalp. The itch is eating me up alive. Please examine me," he said.

He stepped out from behind his desk. I tried to size him up.

As I did so, an obsessive thought told hold of me: "Kill this man, kill this monster, eradicate this beast." My thoughts were feverish. Again, an inner voice said, "Kill him." I could have stabbed him in the neck. I was very nervous. I focused my entire will on staying calm. Supposing I killed him, what then? A new Höfle would sit behind this heavy oak desk. There was no shortage of Höfles. And how many Jews would have to pay for my act? I pulled myself together.

"Well? Have you established what it is?"

"Yes, Herr Sturmbannführer." It was a disease known at the time as seborrheic eczema, and now called seborrheic dermatitis. I prescribed the appropriate treatment.

"It's perfectly harmless," I said, to reassure him.

As I was writing out my prescription, a thin man, about forty-five years old, walked in with a large German shepherd. There was something foxlike about his face. He swept the room with a harsh gaze. I recognized Brandt, head of the Warsaw Gestapo. He saluted Höfle, then strode to the window and opened it. I heard an excruciating scream that stopped my pen. It was a scream racked with desperation. Brandt looked down into the courtyard with a strange expression. Höfle joined him at the window. Neither of them was paying me the least attention. I stood up and saw an extraordinary scene.

The man who was screaming in pain had only pants on. His hands were bound above his head and tied to a hook in the wall. A huge SS man was beating him across the back with a long gridiron. I later learned that it was Scharführer Händke, head of the economic service, whose decisions spelled life and death for the Jews of the ghetto. His victim was moaning and groaning.

I knew this man. He was Meszalem Abramson, son of a chocolate factory owner, who had rented rooms in our house in Lodz for many years. I couldn't bear to witness this scene any longer. Why was he being tortured?

I gave Höfle his prescription, bowed slightly, and left the room. Höfle nodded his head and didn't extend his hand. I was already at the door when I heard Brandt's voice: "The Jews are an abomination. I care more about my dog than all these Jews put together."

I had to pay several more visits to that house, in secret or openly. Some time later I learned that Händke's victims were Jews suspected of having money or valuables. They were tortured until they revealed where they had hidden their treasure.

9

We had not abandoned our plan to cross over to the Polish side. With this in mind, Pola decided to bleach her beautiful brown hair. I went to see Leon Kac, house coiffeur at the *Befehlsstelle*. Kac had his own salon at 103 Zelazna Street, with expensive glass mirrors, porcelain bowls, running water, and all the instruments of his profession. Hairdressers to the rich and powerful are generally thought to have some sway over them, and Kac was the most popular and influential of the Jewish employees at Zelazna. Why? I learned the answer directly from him.

Late one evening, I climbed down from the roof and went to see Leon. He lived on the second floor of 101 Zelazna. He opened the door himself. He was short, just over five feet, with a freckled face, red hair, and a long, white scar down his right cheek. He had sharp, piercing eyes and thin lips, and his head was slightly cocked to one side. There could be no forgetting such a face and physique.

"What can I do for you?" Kac asked, with professional servility.

"I need to speak to you."

"Please go ahead," he said politely. He gave the impression that he didn't want to invite me in. We spoke in the stairwell.

"Mr. Kac, my wife wants to bleach her hair. I've come to ask if you can do this and if so when."

"Do you have your own place?"

"No. Could she come to your house?"

"That would be impossible. She'll have to come to my salon, at 103."

"That's too dangerous. It could cost her her life."

"My dear Doctor, what do you expect me to do? How exactly do you propose this should happen? I would like to help you, but . . ." Leon shook his head.

I begged him to reconsider. Reluctantly, Kac agreed to let me take Pola to his home the next day.

The next evening, Pola and I returned to Leon the master coiffeur. "Come in," he whispered conspiratorially. He led us into the entryway, but did not show us the other rooms. All the doors were closed. We saw no one. We could hear children's voices coming from one of the farthest rooms. Everything was ready for the bleaching. In no time at all, Pola was blond. Leon was clearly in a hurry, eager to be done with such a dangerous job.

We realized afterwards that his work was mediocre, to say the least. He was a men's barber. The color was uneven, and Pola's hair grew dry and brittle. My wife never again recovered her beautiful hair.

"How much do I owe you?" I asked Leon when he was done.

His price made my head spin: twenty times what a doctor would charge for a visit in the ghetto. But those were exceptional times and I paid without blinking. "I did my best," he said with a bow, and showed us out the door.

I had to look again and again at my wife, that night and over the course of the next few days, in order to accustom myself to this new person.

"You look like a real Aryan now," I told her, and indeed, her Semitic origins were undetectable now. So much so that she seemed a foreigner to me.

At the *Befehlsstelle*, rumors spread that a dermatologist lived nearby.

Still, no German knew where I was hiding. One day, Mohn, my adviser, came to see me.

"Two officers have contracted something suspicious," he said, chuckling. "Could you please go see them in their private apartments? Neither Höfle nor anyone else must hear of this."

I took my instrument bag, and Mohn led me to the apartment of one of the officers. He received me courteously.

The patient had gonorrhea, and I was able to help him. In the case of the other officer, Miller, his symptoms did not allow me to make a firm diagnosis. I told him I suspected syphillis.

The big, muscular man was clearly distressed.

"You have to cure me."

"Unfortunately, I can't help you without a microscope and a blood test."

I prescribed him something neutral that would not affect his diagnosis. When I saw him again two days later, the clinical picture was unchanged. Miller was in despair.

"Go see Dr. Nowakowski, my colleague on the Polish side. He'll help you," I advised him.

"I'm not going there. I'm not going to an Aryan. If you won't help me, I'll kill you, and then I'll commit suicide."

He was agitated now, and standing. His illness was very painful; besides, he was afraid of being found out by Höfle, which was why, I imagined, he preferred to be treated by one of the despised "subhumans."

"Be reasonable. We'll send a blood sample to Dr. Nowakowski for analysis, and then we'll see."

The SS man agreed to that. We sent a Ukrainian to Dr. Nowakowski with Miller's blood. I made the arrangements with my colleague by telephone one evening, in secret, using a phone from the *Befehlsstelle*.

When I received a negative result from the blood test—positive news for the patient—I was able to begin treatment. With the help of sulfathiazole tablets, and swabbing the sores with carbolic acid, I managed to cure him. It wasn't syphillis. Miller was very grateful, and earnestly advised me to flee to the Polish side. So these murderers were sometimes capable of human feelings. They were blindly receiving and carrying out orders. They were afraid of their superiors, and feared for their own lives. Moreover, before and after carrying out murders, they got themselves drunk to make it easier.

One day, while I was in the midst of examining Miller, someone knocked on the door. We froze in terror. Miller more than I. I went pale. Luckily, the door to the apartment was locked. He hid me in the bathroom and only then went to open the door.

It was Höfle. I recognized his voice. He said he had come on official business, and began to issue orders as to which streets were to be "cleansed," in other words emptied, of Jews. (Nineteen years later I recounted this incident to the investigating judge in Salzburg. Höfle claimed never to have ordered the deportation or murder of Jews. . . .)

From Miller and others at the *Befehlsstelle*, I gleaned more important information. Höfle was Himmler's special envoy. He had been specifically chosen to liquidate the Jews in the Warsaw ghetto. He received daily orders directly from Berlin.

Every day there were meetings of the Joint Staff of the extermination, where the officers decided which apartment buildings would be liquidated. New targets were marked on a map of the ghetto. Through a gap in the lower barrier of our rooftop hideout, I watched the death detachments march out every day, led by Höfle's officers. Before my eyes, columns of Jews were led to the Umschlagplatz. Germans and Ukrainians made them run. Anyone who walked too slowly or veered too close to a doorway was killed on the spot. Even now, at night, I still hear the telltale crack of a human skull being smashed by a rifle butt.

At the *Befehlsstelle*, I saw with my own eyes several crates of gold that had arrived from Treblinka. They were transported by more than twenty Jewish workers using special supports. Again, Miller urged me to escape.

"Save yourself while you can, doctor. All Jews are going to be exterminated," he told me. "Even those who work at the *Befehlsstelle* will be deported in the end. No one will be left alive. Flee!"

I began to prepare. My wife now had blond hair, but there were other problems to be resolved. We needed a hideout on the Polish side. And we needed to pick the right moment. From the example of Kohn and Heller, I understood that under German "protection," there was no chance of survival. Kohn and Heller were the most powerful people in the ghetto. When they finally realized that they were about to suffer the same fate as everybody else, they asked their powerful Gestapo contacts for protection.

The response was instantaneous: they were killed on a pile of garbage with a shot to the back of the head by one of Höfle's officers. Such was the end of the Jews who had been on better terms with the Germans than anyone else in the ghetto.

I had almost forgotten about Leon the barber, when one day he came up to see me on the roof.

"Doctor, I'm very worried. My son is sick. He has a high fever. Please come see him," he stammered. I followed him back to his house and he led me into the sick child's room. "This is my eldest son; he is twelve years old," he said proudly, gazing at him with fondness. The boy had the grippe. I gave him some aspirin.

"It's just the grippe. Nothing to worry about," I reassured the distressed father.

I was taken aback by the décor of the room. It was filled from floor to ceiling with genuine Persian rugs, rolled up and stacked in piles. This astonished me, but I did not let it show.

"What do I owe you for your consultation, doctor?" the barber asked. He produced a beautiful old-fashioned leather wallet, which looked as if it had not belonged to him for long.

"Nothing," I replied, putting my stethoscope back in my bag. Leon could not contain his surprise. "Nothing? What is that supposed to mean?"

"Just what I said. Put your money away."

"But tell me why."

"Look, you're a Jew and I'm a Jew. Both of us are persecuted, perhaps even condemned to die. We belong to a cursed people. How can I possibly take your money? The most important thing is for your son to get well." I opened the front door. Leon didn't move. I looked at him again and he followed me out with his gaze. My words must have made a deep impression on him. It wasn't long before I learned their extraordinary consequence. When his son's condition improved markedly after two days, Leon invited us to a solemn Friday night dinner.

His wife served us in the kitchen; evidently, he didn't trust us entirely, or he would have received us in one of the living rooms. Considering conditions in the ghetto, Leon had a very large apartment. There were eight of us in the kitchen: the three of us, and Kacs' family of five. His much younger wife, a Jewish beauty, was a head taller than he, educated, charming, and well mannered. Their three sons were there too, aged five, eight, and twelve, sweet, well brought-up, and well dressed. The meal was exquisite—a feast such as we had not had for years: herring, sardines, hard-boiled eggs with mayonnaise, gefilte fish, consommé, chicken, vegetables, and a bottle of genuine Carmel, the wine from Palestine. The Sabbath candles shone in a silver candelabrum, a masterpiece of Venetian art. I could not tear my gaze away from that beautiful silver. Leon smiled to himself, noticing my appreciative gaze.

The food was delicious, and we ate our fill. Imagine, in the ghetto. In that hell. Yes, we feasted and we felt wonderful. We forgot about time and place, about all that awaited us, and abandoned ourselves entirely to the serenity of the moment.

It was a pleasant evening. After dinner came coffee and a cake washed down with a good cognac. For Pola and Elzunia it was all incomprehensible. We barely spoke; we were too absorbed by the food. When it grew late, Pola and Elzunia left the room to sleep. and so did Leon's wife and sons. Leon asked me to stay.

"Doctor, what you see here seems unreal to you. I will tell you how it came to pass, but it's a long, long story. That's why I asked you to stay."

He began to tell me the story of his life. It was one of the most tragic tales I ever heard. I'm grateful to him for telling me. He was unstoppable. And I made no attempt to interrupt him. With a torrent of words, he reconstructed the portrait of his life.

"Doctor," he began, "I wasn't born on easy street like you. I wasn't born into wealth. I never knew my father. My mother was poor. We lived among the poorest Jews of Warsaw. When I was six, my mother died. I was put in an orphanage. But I wasn't so badly off as I was later, when I grew up. When I was ten, they apprenticed me to a tailor. He had a bunch of children, and he took me in to save on paying an assistant.

"I had to get up at six in the morning. If I was slow getting up—because a child needs more sleep—I was beaten. And so cruelly! Then I had to help clean the house, chop wood, fetch water from the well, and scrub the floor. And all this at the age of ten. I was a weak little boy with spindly arms and legs. Several times a day I had to do the shopping or deliver clothes to customers, often up to the top floor and back again. I had to give half the tips I received to the tailor's wife; the other half I could keep for myself. Yet despite everything, my master and mistress beat me for the slightest reason.

"Worst of all, I wasn't being taught my trade. The orphanage had placed me there so that I would learn a trade, but there was no oversight, so the master reneged on his promise. I had no official guardian, so those people could do as they pleased with me—beat me, curse me, starve me. There was no one to stop them. To say I was miserable would be an understatement. I was small, fragile, and powerless to defend myself. The only good thing they did was to send me to a melamed. But my comrades in the heder bullied me and teased me. I was poorly dressed and had no one to stand up for me. No one paid any attention to an abandoned boy.

"In this way, months and years went by. Everybody else had their bar mitzvah, but not me. The parents of other boys held solemn celebrations and balls with fifty or more invited guests. The boys received money and fine gifts. There were prayers and music. But on my thirteenth birthday there was nothing. No ball, no music, no presents, no guests. Nothing!

"That was the day I decided to do something that turned my life around. I went to the barber. I had never been to one before. I had long hair and *peyot* that my mistress trimmed twice a year. With the few pennies I had saved, I went to see Moszek the barber, who was also a physician's assistant. There were cupping glasses and leeches in his shop window; he also dispatched medical advice.

"Moszek's shop was on Niska Street, next door to my master's studio, in the poorest Jewish part of Warsaw. Moszek was very courteous toward me, and that impressed me greatly. Before him, no one had ever said a kind or civil word to me. Moszek was completely different. There were huge mirrors, a basin with running water, hot and cold, the scent of soap and eau de cologne, and a nice man in a clean white apron. It all made an incredible impression on me. I told Moszek that I would gladly become a barber. He asked how old I was.

"'What?' he said, 'Thirteen? I thought you were nine. You're very small. But if you want to be a barber, come work with me.'

"I took him up on his offer and decided to become a barber's apprentice. When I told the tailor, he beat me unconscious, and his wife joined in. Indeed, had the neighbors not stepped in, I think they would have killed me. I went back to Moszek, who dressed my wounds. They took several weeks to heal. The only trace is this scar you see on my face.

"The tailor told the people who tore me from his clutches that he had taken me from the orphanage out of pity, and now I was leaving him like an ingrate.

"I started out with Moszek as an errand boy. I had to sweep up hair and dust, brush the customers' clothes, and open the door to let them out. I could keep my tips, I was given room and board, and I lived an altogether better life. With the money I saved, I bought myself a brand-new suit.

"Moszek had three sons and a daughter named Rachel, who was very pretty. We played together as children, and it became a lifelong love. Rachel became my wife. Moszek warned me not to marry right away, but in the meantime I had become a barber and was making my own money. I thought I would be able to feed Rachel and myself. While Moszek was alive he helped us, but after his death there was no more work for me on Niska Steet. Moszek's sons took over the business.

"I found a new position on Smocza Street, but my wages were not enough. Our life was torture. When the children came along, it became worse still. Not only could we not afford clothes, we were even short of food. Imagine how I felt not to be able to offer my wife beautiful dresses, as every man does gladly. I was ashamed when I saw my children in their poor clothes.

"Rachel and I had dreamt of a life of luxury. We wanted a nice place to live, money, comfort, trips—yet we couldn't even afford tickets to the movies.

"We were determined to give our children a better life. We would buy lottery tickets, and right up to the moment of the drawing we would work ourselves up into a frenzy, imagining everything we'd do with the money if we won. We actually did win, many times, but only the price of the ticket. It was all in vain. Years passed, and nothing changed.

"Then the war came. We were in the ghetto. We had survived everything, even typhus. Then came July 22, 1942, and the transports to Treblinka began. One day, I was shaving a high-ranking Jewish official. Thanks to him I became barber at the *Befehlsstelle*. Of all the barbers, I was the lucky one. Now I cut Höfle's hair, and I shave his officers and soldiers."

Leon fell silent. The clock struck three in the morning.

What life does to a man, I thought to myself. I would have done Leon a disservice had I judged him without knowing the circumstances that had made him who he was.

We were sitting in the kitchen. All around, it was quiet; the candles flickered in the silver candelabrum.

"I want to show you something else." We went into the adjoining room. I was dumbstruck. The room was piled to the ceiling with silver. There was an immense amount of liturgical silver—candlesticks, candelabras, Torah embellishments—but also everyday pieces, such as coffee services and silverware. There was easily a ton. Leon led me into the next room, which was for porcelain: Meissen, Sevres, Old Berlin, and several other houses. There was also glassware, antique bronze clocks, works of Chinese and Japanese lacquer, along with precious and semiprecious stones. But that was not all. The room was also filled with bolts of cloth, but only the very finest: English wools, French silks, brocades, jerseys . . . thousands of silk stockings, and flask upon flask of the most expensive French perfumes. There was a box hidden in the wall for all the jewelry: diamonds, emeralds, rubies, sapphires, topazes, turquoises, as well as rings, earrings, and necklaces of every description.

My head was spinning. Was this a scene from *The Count of Monte Cristo*? I was looking at a priceless treasure vault.

Next door, huge quantities of more prosaic things: razors, scissors, shaving brushes.

Leon shot me a strange look.

"My children won't go hungry anymore. They won't suffer. They won't have to look on while others enjoy life," he said vehemently. I said nothing. While I sympathized with him, I could not approve. How could he have come by all this? I wondered. It was as though Leon had read my thoughts.

"It's late now," he said. "But come see me again. I'll show you something even more important. I'll tell you how I came into possession of all this, and how I'm going to get even more." He led me to the door. Day was breaking when I got outside. I was unable to fall asleep. Everything I had seen and heard appeared before me again and again, as in a dream.

Before Leon revealed the origin of his riches, he asked me to treat a Ukrainian soldier, a man with a venereal disease. I managed to cure him in just a few days, and Leon was very grateful.

But I could not stop wondering how he could have acquired all his treasure. From his story it was clear these were recent acquisitions. Every day I would see Leon go out into the city with the Ukrainian I had treated and one other. The two Ukrainians were armed with rifles. Where they were headed was a mystery, but I could already guess what Leon was going to tell me.

Meanwhile, something happened that strengthened my resolve to fight. One night we were asleep on the roof when we were awakened by the hum of bombers. It was as bright as day. Suddenly, shapes like candelabras lit both earth and sky. Bombs were falling onto Warsaw. It was the Russians. For the first time, standing on the roof, I was beside myself with joy at every bomb dropped from the Russian planes. I asked God to have mercy on us and cause a bomb to fall on the *Befehlsstelle*. I prayed the whole time. I wouldn't have cared if we were killed in the process.

Germans cowering in fear crowded to the cellars in their nightgowns. It was strange to see how quickly those heroes in the fight against the Jews turned into cowards. They feared for their lives—the same men who thought nothing of murdering innocent people.

Alas, the *Befehlsstelle* and the adjacent houses survived that air raid unscathed.

The German antiaircraft defenses tried to fight back. Their searchlights combed the sky, but they didn't down a single Russian plane.

With arms raised to the sky, I stood on the roof amid the drone of the engines and begged the heavens for deliverance. The planes receded, but from that moment on I firmly believed that our survival would only come from the Russians. Unfortunately, there were no more air raids.

And life continued.

The next day I returned to see Leon and listened to his tale.

"Doctor, you're wondering how a poor barber came by such riches. This time, my story about this will be much shorter. I was appointed Höfle's 'court' barber. I was then given soldiers and a truck and told to find a proper salon. I amassed everything I needed from the most exclusive salons on Leszno Street: furniture, mirrors, instruments, and everything else. Then I set up my salon in number 103 Zelasna.

"You know yourself, as a physician, what happens when one works with people or takes care of them. At such times one speaks of many things. I always chatted with my customers: about the weather, about hair loss, about illnesses, and many other things. The officers wanted me to give them the addresses of rich Jews. I gave them those addresses, and will continue to do so. The Jews are doomed in any case; they will all be deported. The fact that I betray their financial status means only that their apartments are searched more thoroughly. Since they're going to be deported, I'm doing nothing wrong.

"Where they're going, no wealth or jewelry can help them. The officers only search the apartments once the owners are deported. They take the best things, and leave the rest for the Office of Estimates. But I can do exactly what the officers do. They do it for their own personal gain. And the officers have so much work that I do it not only for myself but also for them.

"Every day, I go out with the two Ukrainians assigned to me and load valuable things onto a rickshaw. The officers get wristwatches, gold cigarette cases, cuff links, and tie pins studded with precious stones. Those are things they can easily hide and sell. They trust Leon the Jew. The rest I keep. I'm sure you were astonished to see me with the Ukrainians.

"But I haven't shown you the most important things yet, Doctor. Read this."

He handed me two letters. One was a safe conduct pass in the name of Leon Kac. It read as follows:

"Mr. Kac may enter any Jewish apartment. He may take therefrom whatever he sees fit. The authorities are bound to assist him. Kac has two Ukrainian aides for this purpose." The sheet bore a stamp with a swastika and the name of an SS detachment. I read it over word by word. To think that they had issued something like that to a Jew! I returned the letter, and took the second. It read, in typed capital letters: "The Jew Leon Kac and his wife and children are entirely exempt from deportation." Below was Höfle's signature and a stamp with the Nazi raven.

It all seemed incredible. Dumbfounded, I stared at Leon, who smiled proudly.

"As you can see, they put everything in writing, in black and white."

"Is it true?" I was skeptical.

"Naturally. You know the Germans. They have blind faith in anything written on paper. They would sooner be torn to shreds themselves than ignore anything contained in a real document. Bureaucracy has its good side, too, Doctor."

"So you believe this letter from Höfle can save you at a critical moment?"

"But of course! It's an absolute certainty. But I have other passes and certificates. Every time I shave an officer's neck and tickle him with my razor, I can have any piece of paper I want," Leon laughed.

This man is mad, I thought to myself. Does he really believe what he's saying? His gold fever has evidently robbed him of his sense and his foresight . . . He interrupted my thoughts.

"Come, Doctor, I'm going to show you something else."

He opened a door to the left. I had thought it was a bathroom, but we stepped into an art gallery, or better still, a museum warehouse.

"And this too is yours?" I exclaimed. I was a passionate collector of paintings, and considered myself a connoisseur.

"Yes, this all belongs to me," Leon said proudly. I was looking at his art treasures. There were hundreds of paintings, almost all oils on canvas, with just a few sketches. A number of paintings were together on a single roll, all good or very good. There was nothing bad or even mediocre. There were Renoirs, Matisses, Degas, and works by the old masters, including one small canvas, *Young Girl,* which portrayed a thirteen-year-old girl in gray-green tones. A masterpiece. What eyes that child had. All the nostalgia of the Jews in the ghetto was in her gaze. The portrait was from the beginning of the twentieth century. What a genius, that painter. I found it hard to turn away.

"Well, Doctor?"

"Leon, you amaze me. You've taken the cream of the crop from the best Jewish collections," I said, touched by the artistic treasures before my eyes. Warsaw's Jewish community had once been the biggest in Europe, but I had not suspected that it harbored so many outstanding works of art.

"But tell me, how did you know which paintings were the best?" I asked him.

"I'm going to tell you that secret too. My wife was once an auditor in the art history department of Warsaw University. So we would pry the paintings from their frames and bring them here so she could to choose the best ones. We delivered the rest to the Office of Estimates. I don't know a thing about painting, but these are worth a fortune," Leon said with great assurance.

"You have a marvelous collection; I'd even call it priceless. But the only thing that interests you is what it's worth. I appreciate your honesty."

"You can see how careful I've been. Now my children won't have to be barbers when they grow up."

"We can talk about that another time. In any case, I thank you for trusting me enough to show me your treasures."

I took my leave of Leon. In fact, I was to see him only one more time.

One evening there was a great party at the *Befehlsstelle.* Many Germans came from the city with their ladies. They were served by

Jewish waitresses. Although the officers entertained themselves every evening after their "onerous" work, there had never been such a grand ball. That evening and the next we were unable to sleep because of the loud music and the boisterous guests.

After the ball, in the early hours of dawn, the chairman of the Jewish Council and two councillors, Wielicowski and Sztolcman, were summoned to headquarters. Sturmbannführer Hermann Höfle informed them that all Jews were to report to the place known ever after as the "cauldron," on Mila Street, where a selection would be held. It was an unconditional order. Anyone who resisted—either by staying in their apartment or attempting to hide—would be shot.

The news reached us on the roof via the servants from the *Befehlsstelle*. We decided not to go to Mila Street, so we survived. Most of those who went did not return. Even work permits were of no avail. People believed in documents, and they paid for it with their lives. Höfle was just like Hitler: he promised things he had no intention of honoring. Even his privileged Jews went to Treblinka.

Händke, the sadist who had tortured Abramson in the courtyard, was the antithesis of Höfle the bureaucrat: he attacked and killed with his own hands. On the eve of the great ball he had spent hours torturing a pig until it died. Its shrieks were heart-rending.

Höfle had a beautiful Jewish servant, Klara, the widow of a Polish Jewish officer who had been murdered in Katyn. She had a small daughter. Klara was blond, with nothing Jewish about her. Was she Höfle's mistress? Eventually, after the war, I received information that suggested such a possibility. Höfle's former secretary, the blond who had received me on my first visit to the *Befehlsstelle*, was jealous of Klara, and was waiting for an opportunity to take revenge. That moment had arrived.

Höfle and a few assistants had gone to Otwock and a few other small towns outside Warsaw to finish off the Jews there. Händke had stayed behind in Warsaw. The secretary convinced Händke to send Klara to the Umschlagplatz. Klara was cleaning Höfle's apartment when Händke arrived with two Ukrainians to take her and her child to the Umschlagplatz.

This came as a horrifying shock to Klara, and she resisted. The

Ukrainians dragged her and the child out. She was playing for time. She must have hoped that perhaps Höfle would return soon and set her free. When they reached the entrance to the house, she threw herself to the ground and hugged one of the thick iron guardrails that stand to either side of Polish entryways to prevent entering cars from damaging the walls. Klara grasped the rail with one hand while holding her little Stefcia tight with the other. The child was crying and shouting. The Ukrainians stood by uncertainly, but then Händke showed up. He grabbed Klara's magnificent long hair and pulled with all his might. Klara screamed in pain. But she did not give up, still waiting for help that didn't come.

One of the Ukrainians stepped in to help Händke by tearing Klara's hand from the post while Händke pulled her hair. Klara was still lying on the ground. But when the Ukrainian fired a warning shot into the air, Klara gave in and went with the child to the Umschlagplatz.

I saw it all from the roof. Apparently, when Höfle came back, he screamed like a wounded beast when he heard what Händke had done to Klara.

I saw Klara again in 1943, on the Polish side. She had managed to leap from the window of the cattle car en route to Treblinka. She was free, but her child perished at Treblinka. Klara lived for vengeance. She would not die until she had attained it. And her revenge would come.

I will never forget the sight of Dr. Korczak marching to the Umschlagplatz with his orphans. From up on my roof, I could do nothing to help him. A well-known teacher, he had several opportunities to flee to the Polish side, but he refused. He wanted to stay with his children. He walked at the head of the line of children, carrying one small child in his arms. All the children were well dressed and carried identical knapsacks and bread bags. . . . This great man (for his greatness was acknowledged) accompanied his children to their death. Two men: Korczk and Höfle. Where is humanity? Where is justice? Where? Does it exist?

"We don't always understand the ways of the Lord. His ways are different from our own," my father used to say, my father who let himself starve to death as an old man in the Lodz ghetto and who had built a synagogue to the glory of his God.

Justice exists if God exists. But we don't understand justice, just as we don't understand God.

This same Hermann Höfle, who nineteen years later claimed not to have given the orders for the liquidation of the Warsaw ghetto and to have "seen nothing, heard nothing, and said nothing," sent three hundred fifty thousand people to be exterminated—men, women, children, old people, newborns, pregnant women, and invalids. He, the accountant of death, with his calculating, perverse, and ice-cold intellect, was in the process of winning the war against the Jews without losing a single soldier. Good strategy. He, the head of a band of murderers, was afraid of the dark. He worked only in daylight.

What did he do to his underlings, who swallowed their victims whole and choked on their blood? He bought them alcohol, assigned Jewish women to wait on them hand and foot, wined and dined them, offered them elegant balls and music. Hermann Höfle knew how to buy souls. He knew the exact price of every single one. It cost him nothing. As a backup, he could always lie. He never kept his word; lies were his best weapons. Just as dictators have known for centuries, lies still work and always will.

How strange these past few days and hours had been. I asked myself to what extremes naive humanity could be pushed. When they arrive in hell, do people still believe that they've been saved? And saved by a scrap of paper with a few words scribbled on it? People actually believed that they possessed a guarantee as solid as iron or concrete. Leon Kac more than anyone.

Once again I went to see my new friend. We sat and talked in his kitchen.

"Leon, have you really considered what you need to do?"

"There is nothing to consider, Doctor. I plan to keep cutting hair and shaving beards," Leon laughed.

"Leon, do you really believe that the *Befehlsstelle* has finished its work and that those who survived the cauldron on Mila Street will be left to live in peace?"

"Naturally. Why would I not believe it?"

"But Leon, do you seriously think that when the *Befehlsstelle* has finished its work, they will pack their bags and go?"

"What's it to me?"

"You yourself and all the Jewish workers at 103 Zelazna Street know too much about the Nazis. Believe me, Höfle will tidy up after himself before he leaves."

"Perhaps, but that's no concern of mine. My safety is guaranteed by a letter from Höfle and his officers. Our safe conduct passes confirm that I and my family are exempt from any and all orders of deportation."

"And you really trust the Germans?"

"Yes, and I've already told you why. Höfle has promised to take me and my family to his home in Salzburg. There, I'll live out the war in peace and quiet."

"You believe that?" I was profoundy disturbed.

"It goes without saying. I'll take my treasures with me and begin a new life. Höfle will make sure I can take my whole fortune with me."

He was quiet for a moment. Then, radiant and self-asssured, he continued speaking.

"One day, I'm going to build myself a beautiful villa on the Riviera. And my children will do whatever they want. They'll become doctors, engineers—whatever they choose. I'm so rich now that I can spend the rest of my life without working. In fact, I plan to buy a yacht and sail around the Mediterranean with my wife."

"And what does your wife think of your plans?"

"She tells me I should leave it all behind and escape with the jewels to the Polish side," said Leon. He shook his head. "She says we should save the children. . . . As if anything could harm us here.

"On the Polish side we'd be at the mercy of informers. They'd strip us of everything we have. And then when we had nothing left to give they'd report us to the Gestapo and we'd be killed."

"But what awaits you here is annihilation and death," I said, cutting him off sharply.

"I have more faith in the word of the German officers than in Polish informers, or of the Poles in general," he said. "I'm *their* Jew. It's a whole different thing. I'm irreplaceable for them. They need me."

I understood at that moment that there was no point in replying, and I left. Leon would remain imprisoned in his blindness.

I continued to hide up on the roof, eating bread dipped in water. Every day I watched Leon and his two Ukrainians haul all sorts of precious objects into his house.

Yom Kippur 1942 was approaching. The pace of deportation picked up. Some fifty thousand people remained in the ghetto, many of them, like me, in hiding. The others were officially employed in the ghetto workshops. Pola, Elzunia, and I were still sleeping on the roof. The whole time we lived there, it rained only once.

Suddenly, one beautiful autumn day, we heard wild, terrifying shouts: "All Jews into the street! *Alle Juden raus!*" What was happening?

I looked down through an opening in the outer wall of the roof. The Jews from the houses at 101 and 103 Zelazna Street were being driven out. They had nowhere to hide. SS men and Ukrainians were everywhere. By now whole families were standing in the street, because the Jewish workers were allowed to have their wives and children with them. Leon Kac was there too, furiously waving his papers in the air. He showed them to Miller and the other officers, but none of the Germans paid him the slightest heed. My heart was pounding and began to ache. In despair, Leon ran over to Händke and handed him the papers, but he had picked the cruelest criminal of all. Händke roared with laughter and ripped the papers into tiny pieces.

"All this is . . . shit!" he said.

"But it was written by your superior, *Sturmbannführer* Höfle!" Leon shouted. His whole body was shaking.

"It's shit! I know what I'm doing. Now beat it, you filthy Jew!" The Ukrainians fired into the air. An order rang out: "To the Umschlagplatz!" The Jewish workers, together with Leon and his family, were marched away. I watched as the group grew smaller and smaller, like the end of a movie. I never saw any of those people again. And not one of them betrayed our hiding place.

Poor Leon! Your treasures sealed at once, that very day, along with your whole apartment. How could you have trusted your assassins? Can a man already strapped to the electric chair trust the man about to flick the switch?

Lipinski, one of the handful of people to come out of Treblinka alive, told me later, in the hospital in Piastow, about the murder of Leon and his family. Leon's wife and children went directly to the gas chamber when they arrived at Treblinka. Leon saw their bodies, because he was assigned to the group that removed gold teeth from the mouths of the dead and searched for other objects of value. Leon himself was shot two days later while "working," atop a heap of corpses in the forest. He was suspected of pocketing gold. Such was the end of Leon Kac, who wanted to asure his children a better life, different from his own . . . His time and place doomed all his dreams to failure.

10

The *Befehlsstelle's* work was done. Those who were still alive and living in the ghetto began to feel relatively safe. But the Germans were lying again. They announced that things had been definitively stabilized. . . . They carved the ghetto up into several smaller ghettos, each of which held several thousand people. I was convinced this was the beginning of the end. I had understood the methods of our destroyers.

It was all but impossible to cross from one ghetto to another; it could easily mean death. SS men patrolled the areas between the ghettos and used the slightest pretext to kill a man on the deserted streets. With people crammed into small neighborhoods, it was much easier for them to maintain control.

The largest ghetto included Muranowska Street, Zamenhof Street, and Gesia Street. The other ones were centered around German shops and were inhabited by Jewish workers. Jews were killed every day. The Germans were constantly sending people to the Umschlagplatz. If this could be called calm, it was the calm before the storm.

Since the *Befehlsstelle* had been disbanded, there was no longer any reason for us to stay on the roof. Different Germans were now in charge of the ghetto. We moved to 42 Muranowska Street. On the festival of Shemini Atzeret, the residents of our building gathered in one room to pray. There were nine men; all the others were at work. In the Jewish religion, certain prayers require at least ten men (a minyan). They were one man short. Two men came to see me and asked me to join them as the tenth. I agreed to go.

We prayed with all our hearts and asked God for help. The men wept and pulled out their beards. They believed in God's help and trusted in him. Their deeply rooted faith gave them hope.

In the midst of the prayers I was called away to attend to a woman in the next building over who was having a kidney stone attack. She was in terrible pain. I gave her a shot of morphine. When I returned half an hour later, the room in which we had been praying was empty. The Germans had taken the men who were begging God to help them to the Umschlagplatz. That day I lost my faith.

The youth of the ghetto created the Jewish Combat Organization. They took up arms against our oppressors. They did not want to go to their deaths like cattle. They made contact with Polish underground organizations, from which they purchased all kinds of weapons. They also began to attack lone Germans in the ghetto and stole their arms and ammunition. The Germans began moving around in groups. The young fighters knew that despite their struggle they would not survive, but they preferred to die fighting rather than let themselves be slaughtered. Rich inhabitants of the ghetto were forced to donate money for arms. Food was stockpiled and hand grenades began to be produced. Life in the ghetto changed. Now it was officially led by the young.

The Jewish Council was indeed the puppet of the German authority. The lethargy of the older generation gave way to the energy of the young. They understood that the attitude of the previous generation had been a failure. If they didn't take things into their own hands, no one would do anything.

Despite the tension, detailed plans were made for an uprising. Anyone who collaborated with the Germans, like the chief of the Jewish police, was sentenced to death by an underground tribunal.

The young were following their own path now. What moved me most were the children's games: selections, uprisings, battles between Jews and Germans. Their minds could not encompass the evil that surrounded them, yet through their games, they took part in everything. Elsewhere, people's morale was giving way because of the terrible trials they had been through. Everyone had lost parents and friends. With their nearest and dearest among those who had perished, the brakes loosened and moral rigor no longer held sway. The young fighters considered the old ways obsolete. Religion no longer meant anything to them. A God who would tolerate such injustice was no longer God. Free love flowered in the dying ghetto. But there were also many weddings.

I was living with my wife and child at 42 Muranowska Street. I no longer had a private practice. I worked in the Jewish hospital, which was now on Gesia Street. I would work there until midday, after which I would go to the *Werterfassung* (the Bureau of Estimates), the German institution in charge of picking up Jewish possessions, which was short of manpower. The apartments and possessions of people sent to be exterminated were therefore unguarded. I had been charged by the Jewish Combat Organization with chopping the more valuable pieces of furniture into pieces to prevent them from falling into German hands. This was my new hobby, and gave me great pleasure. Older ghetto residents were set to work by the Jewish Combat Organization building shelters and hideouts.

We, too, began to build a hideout at 42 Muranowska. We found a suitable cellar, and we bricked up the little window so that it was entirely invisible from outside—or so we thought. From the floor directly above, we cut out a square of the parquet; this was our entrance. Our hideout could be locked from inside, and was hard to detect. It was 150 square feet of floor space with a ceiling height of six and a half feet. The space was intended for thirty people. When we were done, I felt much better and much safer.

11

On January 17, 1943, we were celebrating the marriage of my wife's cousin, Ewa Grunfeld, a lovely, charming girl of seventeen with blond hair and green eyes who had fallen in love with a twenty-year-old boy. The wedding was held in Szulc's workshop, where Ewa worked.

It was a Sunday. We arrived by ambulance, for reasons of security. The meal was excellent, with duck and good wine. Almost all the wedding guests were young, since their families had almost all been killed. A well-known rabbi, the author of many religious and philosophical works, but whose name I have unfortunately forgotten, married the couple. The atmosphere was provided by a piano and drinks.

We listened to *"El Maleh Rachamim"* (God full of mercy), the prayer of mourning sung when a bride and groom have no parents. Everyone wept and embraced, including the newlyweds.

The young couple received many presents, which were not hard to come by in the empty ghetto. Almost all the guests were members of the Jewish Combat Organization. They laughed, sang, and danced. There were songs in Yiddish, Polish, and Russian. We also danced the hora. Everyone was joyful and in high spirits. For a short while we managed to block the war out of our thoughts. The ghetto did not exist. This was life in all its fullness—youth and happiness. And here, thanks to the young people's enthusiasm, we felt the flicker of hope in the future.

Even a member of the *Werkschutz* (industrial defense), a German from the Szulc factory, took part. He tolerated our revelry and even joined in, perhaps because he had had a lot to drink.

That was the last wedding I attended in the ghetto. The atmosphere peaked at around midnight. At that very moment everything came to a halt. A liaison from the Jewish Combat Organization arrived and told us to return to our homes at once. They had received word that a major anti-Jewish action would begin at dawn.

The young people went straight to their combat units, and the older people to their hideouts. That was the Jewish Combat Organization's strategy. As to us, our situation was complex. We could not go home; it would have spelled certain death. One of the Jewish commanders had been at the wedding, and he sent a liaison officer to help us. Half an hour later, an undertaker's hearse was waiting for us at the door. It was a horse-drawn wagon with an appropriately dressed coachman. Two coffins lay inside; I climbed into one and Pola into the other. We rode like this, each in our dark box, seeing nothing.

All we could hear was the bump of the wheels against the street. The Germans didn't stop us for inspection. They gave us the green light or "free passage" for dead Jews. Maybe the dead are finally happy, I thought to myself from inside the coffin.

12

We did not get back to Muranowska Street until 2:00 A.M. We woke everybody in the house and quickly told them what we had just heard. Yet even then there were people who refused to believe us and would not go into hiding. The next day they were at the Umschlagplatz.

We slipped back beneath the floorboards into our rabbit hole. More and more people began to arrive. In the end, instead of thirty, there were seventy of us, counting friends and relatives of residents along with residents of the adjoining buildings, including the elderly, the sick, and many children. How could we say no? It would have meant certain death. Seventy people in a space of 150 square feet, and only six and half feet high.

Standing one pressed against next, we could barely move. There wasn't enough air, and after a few hours we were running out of oxygen. There was no electricity. Our candles flickered and began to die. The sick and elderly were suffering from the lack of air, but we were helpless to do anything for them. Upstairs, the Germans were combing the building floor by floor, looking for Jews.

By now, the Germans had sensed the existence of the Jewish Combat Organization. That next morning, on January 18, the resistance began, a kind of trial by fire ahead of the uprising that was to break out three months later: a heroic struggle, hopeless as it was.

While we waited, fighting raged between Jews and Germans on the streets nearby.

Down in the cellar, we could hear isolated shots, the roar of submachine guns, and the explosions of bombs and hand grenades. From the apartment above our heads came the heavy footsteps of German soldiers in search of victims. We were no longer able to stand. How much longer? Many people sat down, which made things even more cramped. Some lay down on the ground; others, their strength and will ebbing, fell on top of them. The older people could no longer get up. And the children had to urinate, but where? On those lying down.

Then the worst came to pass. The first victim was an elderly man who died of a heart attack brought on by the lack of air. Under normal conditions, he could have survived. He died because he was there. I could do nothing to help him. I was the only physician present, but I did not have the right medication. After that incident, however, with the help of four strong men, I managed to impose a certain order in the cellar.

We succeeded in setting off an area of about forty square feet, no small accomplishment under such conditions, where we placed all the weak and the sick. By this point, the air was so thin that even matches went out. Then, just as we heard a soldier's heavy steps above us, a baby began to cry. Panic filled the room. The child's cries could have given us away.

The desperate mother tried everything she could, to no avail. People began throwing items of clothing on the child to muffle its cries. They even pressed a pillow to its face, at risk of suffocating it. A fight broke out between the mother and a woman who had become hysterical. Up above, we could still hear the Germans' heavy steps while the two women tore each other's hair in a silence broken only by the baby's cries. Every moment could have doomed us all. The mother was fighting like a lioness for the life of her baby. It was then that I felt something give way inside me; invoking the memory of my parents, I promised myself that if I survived this night in the cellar, I would cross over to the Polish side.

That first day in our underground hideout, January 18, 1943, felt like a year.

The women eventually calmed down but the child was dying. Despite the danger, as soon as the soldiers' footsteps began to fade, I led the mother and child from the cellar.

We carefully closed the trap door, and right there, in a ground floor apartment, I did everything I could to save the child. I used mouth-to-mouth resuscitation, pressing the baby's lips to mine. The mother knelt beside me, deathly pale. At last the child began to move. It gave a cry like a newborn and began to breathe normally.

The child was alive and breathing, and was turning pink. It was a beautiful year-old girl.

I stood up and peered cautiously through the curtain onto the street. Before my eyes, I saw armed Germans and Ukrainians driving Jews toward the Umschlagplatz. With haggard faces, people were allowing themselves to be herded along, offering no resistance. They knew what awaited them. Many, perhaps, even wanted their torment to be over and to find peace at last. Silent and stunned, they passed before my windows just as others had passed months before during the *Grosse Aktion*, the big deportation.

Where was God? Didn't he see what was happening here? I felt empty and unconsolable. Even if I managed to survive, how would I ever be able to feel joy after living through all this? I was jolted out of my reverie by the sound of approaching footsteps. Germans! We couldn't return to the cellar; the door was bolted from the inside. Besides, how could we put the sixty-seven people there at risk? The woman sat on the floor cradling her child. The footsteps came closer, but I was calm, resigned to anything. Could the same be true for Pola, down below?

But it was not a German! It was Gottlieb, a Jewish policeman, brother of the Jewish prison commandant who had helped us try to save Yola Glicenstein. He was a good man, and I had nothing to fear from him. He looked distraught. Several other Jewish policemen followed him in.

"What's wrong?" I asked. "A few days ago they killed my brother and his family," he said. "He was having dinner with his wife and four-year-old son. The Germans burst in all of a sudden. 'What's this? Jews, still eating bread and sausage?' Enraged, they killed the whole family."

Gottlieb also told me that the Germans had herded several thousand Jews to the Umschlagplatz that day, with no regard for work permits. They had simply rounded up everyone they came upon. But there had been an enormous change. The Jews had begun to fight, and fierce battles had broken out between the Germans and members of the Jewish Combat Organization.

Thanks to the fighting, many people had managed to escape from a column that was being marched to the Umschlagplatz, and had returned to hiding. This was unprecedented. The Jewish policeman advised me to remain in hiding, and he left.

I knocked on the entrance to the cellar. They let the three of us back in. That night we all left the hideout. Some people returned to their homes; we and many others slept in the ground floor apartment. We knew that the Germans were too lazy to conduct their operations at night; still, we posted sentries in the courtyard and at the entrance to the street.

13

The night was calm. At eight the next morning another day of fighting began. In the cellar it was just as cramped as before. People leaned against another, and it was unbearably close. I had to provide medical care without a break. There was another heart attack, and another elderly man suffered a pulmonary edema. This time, however, I was prepared; in the early hours of the morning I had brought down syringes, instruments, medicines, and dressings.

That day a woman lost the baby she was carrying. With everyone watching, I tried to help her. . . . I even carried out a minor operation. The battery-operated flashlights people had apparently obtained during the night from abandoned apartments were of great use to us. Once again we repeatedly heard German footsteps overhead. Once again, in the silence, a baby began to cry. And once again, as on the day before, it was pressed against a pillow, but this time the child was weak, and it suffocated. There was nothing I could do. That evening, the distraught mother hung herself in her apartment. We found her body four days later. On balance, then, that second day was more tragic than the first. The battles in the ghetto continued; the shooting did not cease. And that day too came and went.

The following day was January 20, 1943, a Wednesday. Strangely enough, we had become accustomed to our hideout. We had stopped seeing everything as such a tragedy. It was also less cramped, for a few people had found other places to hide.

That night, the news spread through the ghetto like lightning: the

Germans had been defeated at Stalingrad, with heavy casualties. The news came from the Combat Organization's clandestine radio. The optimists among us rejoiced that we would soon be free, but the pessimists moaned that Stalingrad was about one thousand eight hundred miles from the Warsaw ghetto. By the time the Russians came, not a single Jew would be left alive.

Beginning at dawn, still in our basement hideout, we were already dreaming up strategies.

At eleven o'clock, disaster struck.

Suddenly, we heard something dangerous just outside the bricked-in window on the far side of the cellar facing the street. It sounded as if the sand were being swept away or plaster scraped off. Even worse, a few minutes later a few bricks were knocked in with rifle butts, and daylight streamed into the cellar. We had obviously not done a good enough job of bricking up the window. We sat frozen with fear in our mouse hole when we heard German voices. We understood two words: "hand grenades." Before we had a chance to think, a grenade exploded in the middle of our cellar. There was chaos, confusion, screams. Our throats rasped and we began to choke. Our eyes stung. Beside me, Pola shrieked with pain. Two people were killed and twelve were wounded. Two of the most badly injured died the next day in the hospital, where we took them that evening.

Pola was wounded in the neck. Even today, long after the war, she still suffers from the fragment of that grenade that can never be removed, because of its proximity to her vagus nerve. How many painkillers has she swallowed since that day in January 1943?

I suffered a slight wound to my head, which took a long time to heal. Down in the basement, the wounded moaned with pain, while those in mourning wailed in grief. We were back in the grip of our fate as persecuted Jews.

But the Germans had moved on, not even waiting to see the result of tossing a grenade into a crowded basement. Were they afraid that the explosions would come back to haunt them? The German High Command must have realized that Jews were hiding in the basements and given the order to oust them with grenades.

Despite the danger, we had to open the trap door and remove the dead and seriously injured. We ran out of dressings and fashioned bandages from sheets. That third day in the cellar was especially cruel, and even the optimists among us were reduced to silence.

We remained in hiding a fourth day. Finally, the German operation eased up and very few Jews were caught. Things gradually calmed down. By Saturday, life had returned to the way it was before January 18, as if nothing had happened. . . .

Everyone returned to their apartments. When we returned to our one room, I was astonished to find it completely empty: no furniture, no kitchen utensils, no linens. While we were in hiding, the *Werterfassung* had taken everything away, as if we had been deported. The same thing happened to our neighbors.

Fortunately, we had taken a few warm clothes with us into the cellar. I also had our money and a few objects of value.

We spent the night in another apartment that had not yet been emptied, although its inhabitants had been deported to Treblinka. We borrowed their furniture, sheets, and linens and took them to our room. By now it was Saturday. Once again, I told myself we had to cross over to the Polish side.

For the previous few weeks I had been in frequent contact with a friend from Lodz, the lawyer Olek Rozenholc, who had changed his name on the Polish side to Olek Budzynski. Olek left the ghetto every day to work at a train station on the Polish side, the Ostbahn.

He was part of a large number of Jews who went out in groups to work in various German industrial plants, workshops, and construction businesses on the Polish side. He had come to know a number of Polish railwaymen and wanted to help me escape.

He found us a place for seventy *zlotys* a day at the home of his friend Kaczynski, another railwayman, who lived on Bema Street.

The whole undertaking was fraught with danger. Everywhere, informers lay in wait hoping to strip the Jews of everything we had.

For a Jew, things on the Aryan side were terribly expensive; worst of all was the rent, which was dozens of times higher than normal, supposedly to guarantee our safety. For every Jew turned over to the Germans—a guarantee of certain death—the Germans promised special rewards. Naturally, there was no shortage of candidataes. For starters, informers were given the clothing of those they turned in, along with cash; peasants in the countryside were paid in kind, receiving coal, salt, sugar, rationed food, and other goods.

Poles were not allowed to harbor Jews on pain of death. No wonder, then, that our rent was set so high. Despite the immense danger, we wanted to cross over to the Polish side. Here in the ghetto we faced certain death. On the Polish side we had a real, however slight, chance of survival.

Alina, Pola's sister, crossed over to the Polish side every day with a group of Jewish laborers who were constructing a building at 6 Narbutta Street. I discussed my plan with their foreman, a Jew and someone I could trust, and he agreed to lead me to the other side with Pola and Elzunia by blending us into his group. We settled on Tuesday, January 26, as the day of our escape.

"Tuesday is a lucky day," my wife said. I wanted to keep the promise I had made to myself: we would cross over to the Polish side, and we would become Aryans.

PART III

THE OTHER SIDE
PASSING AS ARYAN

1

We stayed up late the night before that fateful day, preparing our escape. It was still dark when we woke at five o'clock. We ate our breakfast and at six o'clock we set off for the day laborers' assembly point. Pola was wearing a short peasant-style shearling jacket, boots, and a woolen kerchief from which her golden curls—poor Leon's handiwork—escaped. She was holding Elzunia. I was dressed in more elegant fashion, in a new navy suit and a green Tyrolean hat with a feather, which made me stand out from the other laborers in their work clothes. Our attire was supposed to give us an Aryan look. Later we noticed that all Jews wore just such hats with just such feathers, making them an easy mark for the informers.

All the workers had knapsacks in which they smuggled "rags" for sale on the black market, but ours held only a few items for our personal use. Our valuables were safely hidden elsewhere.

We joined the group of workers on Kurza Street, as had been arranged with the foreman. Alina had taken care of all the formalities. It was understood that she would bring us all the rest of the things we had left behind in the ghetto. The plan was for her to come live with us shortly on the other side.

On Kurza Street we lined up in twelve rows of four and set off. We stopped at the ghetto gate. The German officers counted us. There was no list of names; the foreman had announced that there were forty-eight of us, and forty-eight there had to be.

I was exhausted after the stressful events of the preceding days. The trials we had lived through in the basement of Muranowska Street had sapped my energy. All I could think of was the present; I had no strength left to think of the future. Escaping the ghetto to the Polish side was the most difficult moment of all. The wound on my head hurt badly and I felt empty. As we went through the gate we were carefully scrutinized by the German officers and Polish police. My turn came.

"My, my. We're looking elegant today. What kind of work does such a chic Jew do on Narbutta Street?" asked the fat, ruddy officer.

"I am an engineer and architect," I answered.

"Well, go build then. Let's hope the house you're working on doesn't collapse."

I made it through. The man behind me was not so lucky.

"What's this?" shouted the same German who had just interrogated me. There was no answer.

"Well, what is it, you filthy cur?" More silence.

I heard the impact of a rifle butt and a man moaning. The beating continued after he was lying on the ground. He must have been trying to smuggle something out. We continued on, not looking back; now we were only forty-seven.

We walked at a military clip down the streets of the Aryan neighborhood. There was hardly anyone in sight at such an early hour. It was still dark out. Suddenly, someone at the front of the line began to sing. Everyone chimed in. I picked up the tune, and it was like drinking a glass of fine cognac. My head still hurt, but my lethargy was lifting.

We marched and sang light-hearted songs: "Kurza, Narbutta, to paradise we go, lads and lasses, Ho-ho, ho-ho!"

I looked around me as I walked; I was surrounded by young couples. They sang, marched, and cast happy glances at each other as they walked. That was how one went to work on the Polish side: marching along with a song and a smile.

The first Polish traders materialized, and deals were struck as we marched along: clothes for bread, sheets and pillowcases for potatoes and vegetables. The Poles vanished as soon as a policeman appeared in the distance. You could live for a week from a single knapsack stuffed with clothes.

On Pulawska Street there was a streetcar stop where lots of people were waiting. As we passed them, Pola and Elzunia dropped from our group and disappeared into the crowd. No one noticed her slip off her Jewish armband. She had the address of Kaczynski the railwayman, the landlord of our hideout. We manged to exchange a final glance, and then she was swallowed by the crowd.

2
—

We were putting up a building on Narbutta Street, and we were each assigned a specific task. Down in the basement, the foreman ordered me to shovel coal into the boiler for the central heating system.

An SS man of about twenty came downstairs and watched me as I worked. It was hot, so I had removed my vest and hat. I was now wearing only my navy blue pants with white stripes, which were known as "tennis." The young SS man laughed.

"I can see you're not a worker," he said. "That's not the way to shovel coal into a boiler."

He took my shovel, and full of strength and youthful energy he thrust the coal into the boiler. "Now you do it," he said. I grew nervous. I was not accustomed to physical labor. I tried to copy him and throw the coal as he did, but I couldn't get it right. More than half the coal fell on the floor.

"Take it easy. Something isn't right. What's your profession?"

"Physician, dermatologist."

"A physician, sir?" The SS man raised his eyebrows. "I would never have guessed." He addressed me as sir, and that calmed my nerves. "If you're really a dermatologist, please examine me. That will prove you're telling the truth."

He led me into his room on the first floor, where the apartments were already finished. I examined him. He had acne on his face and back. I prescribed alcohol swabs for his face, and a special diet.

"Now I see that you really are a physician," he said, and left the room.

I was terrified. What was he planning to do? Where had he gone? Maybe a physician had no right to work here, and that might hurt my chances. But a few moments later my fears were set to rest. My patient returned with another SS. He, too, had come for treatment. When I examined him, it turned out he had a fungal infection.

"We've netted a Jewish dermatologist, and the Jews are good

doctors," said the first man to the second. They both laughed. They called in one of the Jewish workers and sent him to the pharmacy with the prescriptions. The SS with the fungal infection left, and the other one stayed with me. We began to chat. He asked about my background and my family. The young SS was amazed to hear that I still had a wife and child. He was convinced that almost all the Jews had been exterminated, especially the women and children. He himself had spent some time on assignment to a death camp.

"Nobody survived there," he said. "It's astonishing that you and your family were still alive, and living in the ghetto."

This surpassed his understanding. For him, there were no living Jews now, only walking corpses who bore within them the stigma of inevitable death. Of course I didn't tell him that Pola and Elzunia were in a safe place, on the Polish side. We sat together and conversed.

He told me about himself and his life. He seemed quite sincere. He came from Strasbourg, from a mixed family: his father was German and his mother French. His father was suspect now for having held French citizenship between 1919 and 1940. In order to make amends, the father had decided to be extremely cooperative. The son had joined the SS, even though with his dark hair he did not fit the ideal image of a German. Despite his SS training, he didn't strike me as a killer. He even made a rather good impression, if one can say such a thing about an SS. But perhaps that was just because he was alone. Two Nazis and you have a merciless gang.

"We're in the middle of a war, and I have to obey orders. If not, things will go badly for my family and me," he said. "I know why you came. You want to take some food back to your family in the ghetto. You can buy as much as you wish—even ten bags of potatoes. By all means, take advantage of the situation, because tonight our truck will take the Jews back to the ghetto. I'll even go with you, to make sure you don't have any problems at the entrance to the ghetto."

I gulped. I was supposed to slip away onto the Polish side and join Pola and Elzunia. Now I had an SS man offering to help me! I had to play for time.

"You guessed it. I need to buy some food so we don't die of starvation."

"Go ahead, then," the young man said amiably. "Nothing will happen to you."

But it was too light out to escape, too early. I managed to consult Alina in secret. She advised me to buy two bags of potatoes, which weighed over a hundred pounds. If I didn't return to the ghetto, she would take them herself. I carried them down into the cellar. The young Strasburger was very pleased.

It grew dark around half past four. The truck that was to take us back to the ghetto had arrived.

I loaded the potatoes. The Jews climbed into the truck, but I held back; if I returned to the ghetto now, I might not find it so easy to get out again.

I made my mind up quickly. Very calmly, at an even pace, I walked away down Narbutta Street toward Pulawska Street, before the very eyes of the young SS man and his colleague. I took off my armband and threw it under a tree. He surely saw that. It would now have been clear to him that I was trying to escape. Would he kill a fleeing Jew? When I had gone a few dozen paces, I heard a sharp "Halt!"

Now I had to make a split-second decision. I could still tell him I wanted to buy cigarettes, or some candy for my daughter. Returning might save me. . . . Then again, out of fear of his comrade, he might shoot me on the spot. A simple shot to the back of the neck, as was the custom by then. If I kept going, he might kill me too. Once again, I heard the shout: *"Halt!"*

But I kept running. Doing the opposite of what they ordered had become the motto that never failed me. By this point I was only about thirty feet from Pulawska Street; a few more steps and I would be safe. On Narbutta Street there were just a few passersby, but Pulawska was full of people. I managed to disappear into the crowd and continue running. I could feel his sight trained on me, his eye taking aim at my dark silhouette. Don't be afraid, keep going, stay calm. Once more I heard, *"Halt!"* but faint now, and unclear. Then suddenly a few shots from a sub-machine gun.

I threw myself to the ground, but immediately jumped to my feet. Terrified people ran for cover into gateways. I reached the corner of Pulawska Street: I was saved. Slowly and calmly I entered a small grocery store on the corner of Pulawska and Narbutta. The shop was jammed. I pressed my way through the crowd, into a corner of the shop where I was invisible from the outside. Everyone was talking about the shooting on the street.

"They're at it again, rounding people up to deport them for forced labor to Germany." The door opened and a man came in.

"A Jewish day laborer escaped from Narbutta." My face flushed burning red.

"Some nerve! The bullets could have hit us too . . . us Poles."

"Hitler keeps killing Jews, but they're still everywhere!"

"The Jews bring nothing but misfortune!"

"We should be grateful to the Germans for destroying those Jewish lice!"

The fearful voice of a woman pierced the onrush of words:

"First it's the Jews, and then it will be our turn. And in the meantime they are turning us against each other. . . ." But that timid voice was shouted down in the general mêlée.

The street was calm again. Some brave soul stepped out to assess the situation.

"They're gone," he announced.

The shop emptied out, and I left too. I was free, at least freer than in the ghetto. I was supposed to make my way to our hideout, to Pola. I thought of the SS man from Strasbourg. I was sure he had fired only because there was another German watching my escape. He had deliberately fired late, when I was already on Pulawska. And he must have aimed high, or else he would have hit someone from the crowd. All of which suggested that he hadn't wanted to harm me, and had only fired from a sense of duty.

Be that as it may, I had managed to escape. . . . How many times would I have to escape again?

3

It was an ink-black night. Only a narrow band of blue light fell from the streetlamps, which were dimmed with paper. Bema Street was far away. I had to hurry if I was to make it before curfew. What if I got lost? I groped for my identity card. I relaxed when I felt its shape in my vest pocket. The name on the card was Wladyslaw Jankowski. It was counterfeit, of course; Mannowna, a famous ballerina before the war, who had won a competition in Brussels, had obtained forged cards for all of us.

She had a special permanent safe conduct pass that allowed her to cross unaccompanied to the Polish side. She knew people who created forged Polish IDs. She was among the most privileged people in the ghetto and was enormously helpful even without being asked. People said she was a Gestapo agent and mistress of the infamous General Stroop, who crushed the Jewish uprising in April 1943 and razed the ghetto to the ground. She was shot to death under mysterious circumstances on the Polish side of Warsaw.

"You're a Pole now, Wladyslaw Jankowski, so see to it that you act like one."

I decided to take the tram. I boarded the car and paid, but was not given a ticket. That's the way things were done then. The money went into the conductor's pocket, and the Germans received only the small change. It was a tiny act of sabotage. The tram rattled along dark streets. The journey seemed endless. On the steamed-up window, someone had written: "Your underpants may be lined with fur, but you'll never win the war!"

It was clear the Poles lacked neither humor nor courage. A Jew would never have dared to use such words.

I wasn't exactly sure where to stop, and I was afraid to ask. In the end, I just got off.

I tried to find my street. I wandered round for quite a while. An old lady had pointed me in a certain direction, but it proved wrong. I asked a railwayman where Bema Street was.

"Walk along the tracks," he advised me. "Who are you looking for?" I didn't want to give away our hideout.

"To Nowicki's, at number 30."

"There's no one by that name there."

"He just moved there, and he's subletting," I assured him.

The railwayman gave me a suspicious look.

I stumbled across the tracks, shivering with cold. The houses on the other side looked like black monsters. I felt uneasy, and the whole neighborhood gave me the creeps.

"*Halt!*"

I stopped. A man in uniform approached me and shone his flashlight in my face. I closed my eyes. When I opened them, I saw a German sentry guarding the tracks.

"What are you doing here?" he asked in German. I pretended not to understand.

"You don't understand German? Your papers!"

That I had to understand. I handed him my identity card. Using his flashlight, he examined the photo and then me. Then he handed back the card and, without a word, went on his way. I wiped the sweat from my brow. With my last ounce of strength I finally arrived at 20 Bema Street.

It was a separate building, slightly larger than the low connected houses that shared communal gardens. I knocked. The door opened.

In the evening light I could make out a large man with a soot-covered face, in greasy, ragged clothes, dirty from working on locomotives.

"Mr. Kaczynski?"

"Good evening, Doctor."

The front door led straight into the room, with no vestibule. My eyes searched for Pola and Elzunia, but they were nowhere to be seen. What had happened? Had they been apprehended on their way here? Had they fallen into the hands of the Germans or the informers?

Kaczynski understood my fear, and pointed to a partition. There was my family. Pola laughed and cried with emotion and joy. Elzunia clasped my hand in both of hers and would not let go.

4

The train conductor Antoni Kaczynski lived with his wife Veronika and fifteen-year-old daughter, Irka, in a small house in a working-class neighborhood. There was a larger house across the street, but otherwise we had no neighbors, which was very lucky. The house consisted of a single room divided by a curtain into two unequal parts. The front part was the kitchen, where we ate and spent the day, and where the Kaczynskis slept. Pola and I slept behind the partition, and Elzunia slept with Irka. Mr. and Mrs. Kaczynski slept in a double bed, and Elzunia shared a single bed with Irka. For the Kaczynskis' family, friends and neighbors, it was understood that Pola and Elzunia were refugees from the area around Lublin, from where, in fact, large numbers of people had indeed been pushed toward Warsaw.

Pola was introduced as the wife of a Polish officer imprisoned in a German camp. I, on the other hand, did not exist officially at all. If anyone came in, I would hide behind the curtain or slip under the bed. For greater security, Kaczynski and I constructed a hideout, because I preferred them. Behind the curtain we cut out a few floorboards to make a hole about two feet square. The house had no cellar, so we dug away the earth beneath the floor and carried it out in a pail during the night into the nearby fields. We nailed together the boards we had cut out to make a lid for the hideout, just as we had done on Muranowska Street, and covered it with an old rug. It was an ideal hiding place, but after a while it became wearisome.

As it turned out, the Kaczynskis had a lot of visitors: Antoni's co-workers, friends, neighbors. It was wartime, and people dropped in on one another and exchanged all kinds of news. Besides, Irka had numerous admirers. She was a fresh young thing; a real little morsel. I was forbidden to appear, for the Kaczynskis claimed there was something Semitic about my features. In any case, it was a time when every stranger was suspected of being a Jew. It was easy to find something Semitic in a face—a turn of the nose, protruding ears, or a slightly thicker lower lip. Sometimes I would have to dive under the floorboards twenty or thirty times a day. I would come out filthy and matted with lumps of clay. I had to brush myself clean and wash many times a day, and there was no running water in the house.

Veronika, Kaczynski's wife, wasn't happy to have us, and took every opportunity to show it. There was no toilet in the house; instead there was a shed out back, country style. I was not allowed to use that stinking outhouse. Despite these unusual conditions, we were relatively safe there. Our rent was seventy zlotys a day, the amount the lawyer Olek Rozenholc had arranged for us to pay. It wasn't expensive, but neither was it cheap.

For Kaczynski, it was a considerable amount, because he earned very little as an engineer, and food and clothing had grown very expensive. Still, his monthly rent was less than what we paid him by the day. But Kaczynski was a decent man and behaved respectably toward us. With Veronika, however, it was a different story. She argued constantly with Pola and made her life miserable.

Pola used to go shopping every day on Narbutta Street, as an Aryan, of course. Alina would bring old clothing from the ghetto, and Pola sold it at a far higher profit than the Jewish building workers could get. Since they could not take unsold clothes back into the ghetto, they had no choice but to accept the prices that the Polish traders offered.

Since the *Werterfassung* in the ghetto worked so slowly, the clothing trade was a brisk business. The virtually limitless amount of clothing from the four hundred thousand Jews who had been sent to Treblinka awaited customers.

Pola learned from Alina that on the day of our escape everything had proceeded calmly when the workers returned to the ghetto. There had been no investigation into my escape, and none of the Germans knew that Alina was my sister-in-law. Out of prudence, however, Alina had left the one-hundred-pound bag of potatoes in the truck; she thought one of the Jewish workers must have picked it up.

We had a lot of linens and clothes to sell, since Alina supplied us daily. Veronika wanted to act as our agent. She knew she had us in her clutches. She wanted to buy our clothing at a price even lower than what the Polish traders paid the Jewish workers. She had us over a barrel. Moreover, she was vulgar toward us, aggressive and rapacious, unlike her honest husband, who was under her harsh rule. Veronika did whatever she could to keep us from making any money on those clothes. Since Pola refused to be exploited, there were constant arguments, which always ended with our giving in. That little hell was the detonator of something far worse, all because of some secondhand clothes.

5

One day, Pola was about to set out for Narbutta Street when we heard that a raid was underway: young Poles on the Polish side of Warsaw were being chased and caught like dogs. They were being thrown onto a convoy of trucks and driven to Germany to work as forced labor, without even the chance to say good-bye to their families. Since Pola was young—still under thirty—she was advised to stay at home.

The used clothing business between the Jewish day laborers and Polish traders took place in the apartment of the concierge at 6 Narbutta Street. The concierge received a commission, and she also bought food for the Jews. When Pola did not show up at Narbutta that day because of the raids, Alina left the day's allotment of clothes with the concierge and asked her to take them to the Jankowskis, who were staying with the Kaczynskis. But the concierge went to a neighbor's house instead, telling them that she had Jewish clothes from the ghetto, and that the Jankowskis were probably Jews themselves. Naïveté, or malice?

The least suspicion was enough to put our lives in danger. The result? Our stay with the Kaczynskis was over. Everyone on Bema Street knew that the Kaczynskis were harboring Jews. Kaczynski did not want to keep us a moment longer. Alina had acted very irresponsibly in giving our address to the concierge.

Now we could expect to be betrayed at any moment. Where were we to go? Where would we hide next? All kinds of people kept dropping in to see the Kaczynskis and I was constantly having to slip beneath the floorboards. We didn't have a moment's peace.

We could not go to a hotel like normal people, for they were searched every day. Neither could we rent an apartment, because just then, in February 1943, the number of Jews escaping from the ghetto was at its peak, and anyone looking for a place to rent was suspect. We could see no way out of our terrible situation. But if we stayed with the Kaczynskis we faced death and so did they.

We decided to trust our luck. Pola was an optimist by nature. For the moment we were completely dependent on Veronika, whom we plied with valuable gifts. We begged her to give us two more days on Bema Street. But Antoni Kaczynski did not want to keep us even one more hour. "Just two more days," we begged him. Finally, even Veronika put in a word for us. . . .

"Word hasn't gotten out yet. Nothing will happen to you, Antoni," we said.

"Maybe no one will tell the Gestapo. Just give us two more days. You'll be saving three human lives."

Antoni Kaczynski was a devout Catholic, and that last argument convinced him. He wanted to do a good deed; we were allowed too stay. I also cut a deal with him. I gave him my English overcoat and my navy-blue suit, and he gave me his oil-stained overalls and an old rail worker's cap.

Now I looked like a true Aryan worker on the Ostbahn—the Eastern line. I also found some old-fashioned oval nickel-framed spectacles. I broke the left ear piece and tied it back together with a piece of string. I now looked like a disheveled worker down on his luck, and I looked much older than my age. Kaczynski studied me carefully.

"Well, Edward, you really could work on the railway now. You look like a real Polish railway man." He promised to find me a job at the Szczesliwice station.

But for the moment I had more important business on my mind: I needed to find a place to live. I knew that my oldest brother's mother-in-law, Bronislava Tobias, was in hiding on the Polish side, but I didn't have her address. Her niece, Marynia Landau, had married a Karaïm* and was now called Krall. I figured that the Krolls' address should be registered with the address bureau on Teatralny Square, so I left my rabbit hole and headed there.

On Bema Street not far from the Kaczynskis', an old, miserably dressed woman cast me a quizzical look. Evidently, she knew or suspected that I was a Jew. I quickened my step. For as long as I remained on the Polish side I would experience sheer panic when

---

* A Turkish-Jewish group from the Crimea, the Karaïms were not persecuted: they were considered Aryans, even though their religious practice was almost fully Jewish.

I felt such looks. Even now, such looks make me shudder. They tell me I'm a despicable Jew.

By the time I reached Teatralny Square, I felt perfectly disguised, and that lifted my spirits. When I stepped inside the Warsaw city hall, I could not believe my eyes. I knew the porter. It was my professional rival from back in Lodz, Dr. Krynski, a famous dermatologist.

Now he was a porter in the town hall, hidden beneath an official hat with a broad visor. He had grown a thick mustache. He looked at me but did not recognize me. I resolved to grow a similar mustache myself. Dr. Krynski and his family also survived the war, and he is now a renowned specialist in New York.

In the address office, which adjoined the census bureau, I did not remove my railwayman's head cover, which I called my magic cap. I found the Kralls' address.

The Kralls lived in a big house on Poznanska Street. It was a large apartment, but they were subtenants there. Their landlady opened the door and once again I felt that strange stare that recognizes a Jew.

Marynia burst into tears when she saw me.

"They deported my mother to Treblinka," she sobbed. "I don't want to live without her."

I attempted to calm her down, pointing toward the door through which her landlady might overhear us. It was then that Marynia told me her husband wasn't a true Karaïm; he had false papers. The Gestapo already suspected that he was a Jew, and the landlady was sure. In any case, she already knew that Marynia was Jewish, and I now understood why she had stared at me the way she had when I walked in.

Krall dealt in gold and foreign currencies, a business that had made him many enemies, competitors who were jealous of his success. Although Marynia did not love him, she was a good wife. He was twenty-five years older, and his sole ambition was to accumulate more money. His gold fever snuffed out all the fears and concern his wife expressed. Marynia felt certain that death was closing in on them. There was a long silence when she finished her story. How could I help her? What could I advise her? My own situation was worse than hers.

Marynia gave me the address and telephone number of her aunt Bronia, who was in hiding under the name Lozinska, and begged me to come back and visit her with my wife and child.

On my way home I called Bronia, who was delighted to hear my voice. She had thought I was dead. She was living legally with a professor from the Warsaw Technical Academy, Zawadzki. I arranged to meet her the next morning in the coffeehouse opposite his school. Buoyant with hope, I returned to Bema Street, to the Kaczynskis'.

At four that afternoon I took Pola and Elzunia to see the Kralls. Marynia's husband was a thick-set man of sixty-five, with crafty, darting eyes. I explained our situation.

"You cannot become a Karaïm, because the Gestapo has a list of all the Karaïms." He thought for a moment. "I know," he said. "There's an old Polish woman named Malinowska, a Pole, who has two rooms. Maybe she would rent you one of them." He gave me two addresses, one on Emilia Plater Street, the other on Nowiniarska Street. After that he began to tell me of his success in business. He was very proud of his collaboration in the diamond and currency black markets. He drew a leather pouch from his pocket. It was brimming with jewels and gold coins. His eyes sparkled as he showed me each and every piece.

"I'm rich. Money is all-powerful. Nothing can happen to me."

Once again, the pale, freckled face of Leon Kac appeared before me. Gold must be more blinding than the sun. Its victims no longer see what is going on around them; all they see is that blinding light, just when they should keep their eyes on everything else.

We were offered afternoon tea with pastry. There was also wine, and the landlady had been invited to join us. The atmosphere improved. In the ghetto, Elzunia had taken dance lessons for children, and now she wanted to show off her accomplishments. She danced gracefully, leaping with passion. Her little face was red, warm, and happy. She was so carried away by the dance that she forgot everything around us; by now, she too was aware of our situation. Suddenly, she was forced to stop.

The landlady had an attack of nerves. She sobbed and writhed spasmodically. "Jewish children are dancing on top of a volcano, while their heads are smashed against a wall. . . ." She laughed and cried at once, spitting out words we could barely make out. Our cheerful mood was gone for good, and we took our leave as soon as propriety allowed. We made our way home weighed down by somber thoughts.

Just like the SS from Strasbourg, the Kralls' landlady was treating us as if we were already dead. In their eyes we Jews were living corpses.

The landlady's panic attack worried me greatly. There must have been a reason for it.

The Kralls were taken away by the Gestapo the following night. Krall raged that he was a Karaïm, but to no avail. He and Marynia were killed in Pawiak prison. So Marynia's premonition was correct. No one knows what became of Krall's fortune. I learned of the affair from their landlady, whom I had not trusted from the moment I first saw her. I don't rule out the possibility that she betrayed the Kralls herself, to gain possession of their wealth, but neither can I affirm such a possibility.

6

Kaczynski received us badly when we got home. He asked us to decamp immediately, saying that the Gestapo might arrive at any minute. With presents for Veronika and Irka, we bought ourselves a night's reprieve. The next day we went to meet Bronia Tobias in the coffeehouse as we had agreed to. She arrived with a pleasant, cheerful man called Tomek.

Bronia was a good woman—elderly, but jovial and gay. She had lost weight and looked sick, complaining of stomach pains. Despite her advanced age and feeble appearance, it was clear that she had once been very beautiful; her smile was still charming. Her husband, Maksymilian Tobias, had been a high-ranking official with a Swedish-Polish bank before the war. Influential Swedes had asked Nazi dignitaries to free Tobias so he could join his wife, who was described as an Aryan, although in fact she was a Jew. But attempts to reunite this "mixed" couple failed, and Bronia's husband perished in the Lodz ghetto.

Bronia was a mensch in the true sense of the word. She went out of her way to help people. She knew the Szenwald family; Szenwald senior had been the director general of a Warsaw company, Natanson, before the war. Now they were in hiding on the Polish side under the name Ziembinski. Their former porter, Gniewkowski, who was devoted to them, was protecting of them, and it was Gniewkowski with whom Bronia wanted to put me in touch. She hoped he would know somewhere we could stay. I also had the address of Malinowska, an old wet nurse, from Krall. We stayed a long time in the café, and Bronia tried to reassure us. She told us of the enormous losses the Germans had sustained at Stalingrad.

"Did you know that Stalingrad is now called Hitlergrab?"* she whispered.

All kinds of people came and went as we sat there. I could tell from their features that many were Jews. Tomek, the pleasant young man who was sitting with us, was trading glances with a pretty blond sitting at another table. I thought they were flirting, but Bronia whispered to me that they were brother and sister. Bronia and I talked about my brothers, who had gone to live in Palestine, and who sent her letters through Portugal, a neutral country. I complained about Pola, who continued to reproach me for not leaving with them. In the end, I hadn't managed to save my father, even though I had stayed behind for his sake.

An exaggerated wink from the owner of the café interrupted our conversation. What could he want? Was he trying to blackmail us? Had he recognized us? I stood up calmly, so as not to draw attention to myself, and went out into the hallway as if I were going to the bathroom.

"Watch out. There are two Gestapo agents here who've been observing you since you arrived," he whispered. I thanked him, returned to our table and told the others what he had said.

We settled our check and left the coffeehouse. As we were leaving,

---

* A pun: *grad* means city in Russian, while *grab* means grave in German: thus Stalingrad, where the Russians dealt the Nazis their first crushing defeat, would now mean "Hitler's grave."

Tomek made a sign to his sister and she left at the same time as we did. We parted ways with her out on the street. She was going in the opposite direction, to have her hair done.

From a distance, we noticed that two young people were following her, but we paid no particular attention to them. We assumed they found her attractive and wanted to speak to her. Two days later, Tomek told me, with tears in his eyes, that his sister was dead. The young people following her were secret agents. They had followed her to the beauty parlor. As she was having her hair washed, they walked in.

"You don't need to dry your hair. You can go to the Gestapo with wet hair."

The men took her away, the hairdresser told Tomek. She was shot in Pawiak prison the next day.

We went to see Mr. Gniewkowski, who looked after the Szenwalds (now the Ziembinskis). He was an elderly, white-haired gentleman, slender and tall, bent slightly forward. Bronia explained our plight.

Without a moment's hesitation, he took us to see his his sister-in-law, his brother's widow, who lived at 47 or 49 Hoza Street, in a single basement room with a kitchen. The walls were bare and damp. It was a poor refuge, unfortunately, because it had no hiding places, but it was better than nothing. I thanked Bronia and Mr. Gniewkowski sincerely and we went back to the Kaczynskis to pack up our affairs.

I wanted to part with them on good terms. We told them all our troubles. They were above all pleased that we were leaving.

That was our first move on the Polish side. There would be many others.

7

Since I was supposed to be a Polish railway worker, I couldn't stay in the house all day. It would look suspicious to the people who came to see Gniewkowski. I needed to find a job. Luckily, Antoni Kaczynski had talked to the stationmaster on my behalf, and a few days later I was hired as a coupler.

The work was straightforward, but dangerous. The stationmaster interviewed me before taking me on. I said I had prior experience at a small station in the Lublin region. I was very nervous about this interview, but Kaczynski assured me I had nothing to fear from his boss.

It was only some time later that I learned that the stationmaster had not believed a word of what I said. He was a Polish patriot and assumed that I belonged to the Polish underground.

Everyone at work was Polish. I rarely saw any German railway men. I received a German railway document with the Nazi raven— a precious asset, no doubt.

I got along well with my coworkers. I offered them brandy from a bottle that I refilled every day. I even learned to drink myself. I spoke little and contented myself with listening.

The railway men often talked about the Germans and the Jews. Many of them were pleased at what was happening to the Jews, but there was a small minority who defended them. Nevertheless, I heard a lot of bad things about the Jews, and I could do nothing to defend my people without arousing suspicion. I kept my mouth shut, even though that too could have seemed suspicious in those days. Surprise, surprise, no one showed the slightest doubt. I was a Pole, Wladyslaw Jankowski, a railway worker. If anyone had suspected I was a Jew, I would no longer have been there, because there were informers among the workers, and I would certainly have been denounced. The worst of them, one with a German name I no longer remember, used to boast about his successes whenever he got drunk. He would force Jewish girls hiding on the Polish side to give themselves to him. When he tired of them, he turned them over to the Gestapo, to their deaths.

I had to listen to all this. The Poles hated the Germans, and their favorite topic was the dream of their defeat. The workers took turns declaring whom they would wipe out first after the war: the Reichsdeutschers or the Volksdeutschers. The choice was always the Reichsdeutschers, of course, for business must come before pleasure. . . . They hated the Volksdeutscher most of all. There was a joke circulating around this time: "Why is there no pork to be had with ration cards? Because the last pig signed up as a Volksdeutscher."

I worked on the Ostbahn from six in the morning until four in the afternoon. I liked the work. I could forget about everything else, and the brandy did the rest. After work I went home, and from the window of our basement room I watched the legs of the people passing by.

Mrs. Gniewkowska had a boarder in her kitchen, a thirty-year-old woman with a fiancé. He was a decent guy who had one fault: he drank too much. There was good reason to be afraid, because he could have talked, and it was clear that he suspected us.

There was also a new complication: we were subletting, and we had to register with the authorities. Our identity cards were false.

To minimize the risks, I went alone to see the building administrator. I filled out the registration form, but didn't know that I was also supposed to bring proof of having left our previous address. The address I had given as my prior residence was also false. It was an abandoned building that had been bombed in 1939. I told the administrator that I would bring my proof of prior address at a later date, and left my registration form with him for the time being.

I then began a feverish search for a counterfeiter who could get me out of this tight spot. Meanwhile, however, the administrator summoned Mrs. Gniewkowska and told her he suspected me of being a Jew. Evidently either I or my papers had not been to his liking. Mrs. Gniewkowska reported all this back to us. She said that the administrator had an excellent relationship with the Germans and might even be in cahoots with them. We had been living there less than two weeks and already our hideout was compromised. How much longer would this torment last?

I walked the streets of Warsaw. Of course I was depressed. Before each window, I thought of the people inside, who had cares of their own, their own misery and luck. At least they had a place they could call home. There were so many houses in this city, a sea of houses one after the other lining both sides of the street, but there was nowhere for me and my family.

It was the end of March. A beautiful, sweet spring in premature bloom brought nostalgia and brilliance to the air. Dozens of young couples walked the streets arm in arm, or embraced on the park benches. My heart was heavy. I thought of Bronia Tobias, but did I dare worry that poor ailing woman again?

Bronia had a very nice room free of charge at the home of Professor Zawadzki, the rector of the Technical Academy, who knew she was a Jew and risked his life for her. I believed that good deeds lead to noble actions, and that people who do good always find others willing to help them with devotion.

So I phoned Bronia. Just hearing her voice was enough to reassure me. She said she would come over right away. What energy that good woman had when it came to helping others! Bronia and I took a droshky to the Ziembinskis, who lived far away, in the Grochow district. Bronia went up first alone, but after a few minutes she took me up to meet her friends.

The Ziembinskis were a charming couple, gentle and polite. They had a two-room apartment with a kitchen. He was about fifty-five, a tall, handsome man with a square, honest face. She was ten years younger, on the obese side, very pale and soft. Mrs. Ziembinski's sister, who was even more obese, shared the apartment along with her little son, who was not allowed out of the house because he was too Semitic in appearance, especially because of his nose. Big noses were persecuted. Before the war the Ziembinskis had been wealthy, and even now they still had a considerable fortune. Their former porter, Mr. Gniewkowski, had obtained false identity cards for them using a borrowed name.

Gniewkowski had also found them a summer house outside Warsawa, in Falenica, which he rented from a peasant named Mucha.

The Jews of Warsaw had often summered in that region, which was prized for its fresh country air and its ease of communication with the city. The guest houses and dance halls of Międzylesie, Falenica, Otwock, and Srodborow were full of life during the summer. Poles were nowhere to be found. Everyone was Jewish.

Although Mucha was well acquainted with the Jews' appearance and demeanor, he did not for a moment suspect the Ziembinskis. All he knew was that before the war his tenant had been a high-ranking civil servant and well-known dignitary.

Gniewkowski had taken the summer villa for the Ziembinskis

just in case. If their Warsaw hideout was ever compromised, Falenica would be their backup. Since it was a beautiful spring, the Ziembin-skis were eager to go out there, and therefore agreed to let us stay in their Warsaw apartment while they were away. This in response to Bronia's fervent imprecations, as she described the dire situation of her brother's brother-in-law.

And so we obtained our third hideout. I was at a loss for words in expressing my gratitude. On a lovely spring day, we moved into the apartment of Ziembinski, the ministerial adviser. The other residents of the building looked askance at the grimy railway man who was now living in the home of a dignitary in these mixed-up times.

8

I had left the details of my false identity card with the Hoza Street house administrator, on the registration form. Since he was clearly suspicious, that document was now completely worthless, even dangerous. I therefore had to obtain a new one. Warsaw had a thriving counterfeit industry, serving Jews and members of the Polish resistance. Gniewkowski gave me the address of a certain Zygmunt, who lived at Jagiellonska Street. I went there one afternoon. It was a big, old house, and the apartment was on the sixth or seventh floor.

The door was opened by a man who was completely drunk.

"Are you Zygmunt?"

"Yes, my dear railway man. Come in."

Swaying and smiling, he led me into his apartment.

"Come sit down and have something to drink," he said hospitably, not asking the purpose of my visit. After the first glass came a second, then a third. Zygmunt began to tell me various jokes, most of them connected with his trade.

"A man comes to get an identity card. 'Your name?' 'Schultz.' 'First name?' 'Siegfried.' 'Place of birth?' 'Berlin.' 'Are you German?' 'No, Polish.' 'Where was your father born?' 'In Strasbourg.' 'And your mother?' 'In Frankfurt.' 'Then you're one hundred percent German!' 'Sir, if a chicken lays an egg in a pigsty, will that egg produce a pig?'"

This joke emboldened me, and I brought up the subject of an

identity card, adding that I would prefer to return to the matter when he was sober.

"I'm never in another state. So go ahead and tell me exactly what you need."

"I need an identity card."

"That's all? A mere bagatelle! Come back tomorrow with a photograph."

The next day I went back to see Zygmunt with a bottle of brandy and one thousand zlotys. Once again there was a great consumption of alcohol before we got down to business. Zygmunt could drink vast quantities of alcohol. After this well-watered preamble, he led me into his other room, which was entirely occupied by a printing press.

His wife, a petite blond with a dainty face, worked tirelessly. Zygmunt showed me examples of his work: identity cards, German passes, counterfeit stamps of various Polish and German ministries and offices, including the Ostbahn, blank birth and baptism certificates, and a variety of other documents.

I showed him my German railway card, and he promised to make me another one exactly like it, but in the name of Jan Kalinowski, the name my new documents were to bear. Wladyslaw Jankowski had ceased to exist. I was afraid there might be complications at the station, but I had no choice. In case I was stopped on the street, I could not have Kalinowski on my identity card and Jankowski on my railway pass. I also bought my daughter a blank birth and baptismal certificate, issued by a Catholic parish in Lublin. I filled it out myself, in the name of Elzbieta Zofia Jankowska. I suspect Elzunia would not have survived the occupation without it.

I picked up the false papers from Zygmunt the next day. He was dead drunk. He wanted a thousand zlotys for the railway pass and five hundred zlotys for the birth and baptism certificate, but with a bottle of brandy he agreed to twelve hundred zlotys for both. He had already pocketed a thousand the day before for my identity card.

"My dear railway man, I know you're a Jew, but you have nothing to fear from me," he said. I was not so sure, however; decent as he may have been at heart, he could easily have sold us down the river if he got too drunk. Alas, my fears were to prove justified.

On my return home, I found Pola almost unconscious, her eyes brimming with tears. She was unable to say a word. Only after several minutes did I learn what had happened. Almost every day, Pola went to Narbutta Street, where she would meet up with Alina at the home of a Polish trader who lived nearby and could be trusted.

Since losing our hideout on Bema Street, we had avoided the concierge at Narbutta Street. The trader didn't know that Pola was Alina's sister, since she was passing for an Aryan. When she went to Narbutta Street that morning, the Pole told her that all the Jewish workers from the construction site at number 6 had been shot the previous day.

This was such a shock to Pola that she fainted. With this, the trader and the other Poles present in the apartment now found her suspect. Fortunately, they did nothing to blackmail her, and let her go in peace. Devastated, she went to Narbutta Street, and, throwing caution to the wind, asked the concierge there what had happened.

That day the building at number 6 had been finished, and the workers from the ghetto were told they were going to build another house in Otwock. A truck drove them to the forest near Otwock, where they were ordered out of the vehicle and told to undress. Five by five, men and women, they were lined up in the woods and shot in the back of the neck. Those in the back rows had to watch the others fall while they awaited their turn. The corpses were taken to the Jewish cemetery on Gesia Street in Warsaw and buried. The concierge had learned all this from the SS men living in her house. Pola dragged herself home to Grochow. She saw and heard nothing of what went on around her. She couldn't cry, for that could have given her away. It was the Jews who were sad, the Jews who wept, and the *szmalcowniki*, the informers, were on the lookout for people with sad eyes. Only when she got back to the house in Grochow, where nobody could see her, could Pola dare to cry.

So our beloved Alina had been murdered. Now I was filled with regret that I had resented her for giving us away, compromising our hideout at Bema Street. How often we had begged her to come live with us, to escape from the work site on Narbutta Street. But she said she felt safe as a worker, and she felt useful.

It may be too that she was afraid to be a burden to us, especially financially. That is probably closer to the truth: Alina sacrificed herself for us.

9

Alina was dead, lost to us forever. Her enormous kindness, the smile that we loved so much, were only a memory. And life went on, with its endless troubles.

We could no longer stay at the Ziembinskis'. We were highly suspect to the neighbors; after all, what was a low-class railway worker doing in the home of a government minister? We were afraid of being denounced. I felt those strange stares and feared the informers, who were everywhere. There was no hiding place in the apartment. If anything happened, we were defenseless. Our only comfort was Hitler's defeat. The Battle of Stalingrad had lifted our spirits.

I was on my way to see Mrs. Malinowska, at Emilia Plater Street. The streetcar was packed, and a large peasant woman was standing right in the middle with her milk cans. "What are you doing standing there like Hitler at the gates of Stalingrad?" one wise guy cracked. . . .

I had been given Malinowska's address in Otwock by the late Krall. Malinowska was an old woman, about seventy, with white hair, and illiterate. Her room was filled with holy images. She was constantly crossing herself and praying, but her religiosity was just skin-deep. In fact, she was a greedy, crafty woman.

She had two rooms available, one on Nowiniarksa Street and one on Emilia Plater, which had once been part of the ghetto, although it was now outside the wall. Despite her size, Malinowska, I sensed, was not a strong character. I felt uneasy renting a room from her on Nowiniarska Street. For some time now a certain instinct in me had been growing sharper, and I had learned to rely on it and on my intuition. This may sound strange, but a few minutes or hours before impending danger I would feel a painful pressure in my chest. I called it the "evil spirit." This "evil spirit" became so well honed over time that I felt it long before the actual danger threatened us.

Before we moved to our new apartment I paid a visit to Professor

Zera. I had a small leather valise and several other items of value that I wanted to leave in a safe place.

"Who could be more trustworthty than Zera?" I thought. After finishing medical school in Warsaw, we had pursued our specializations side by side in Paris, he in cardiology and I in dermatology. We had been inseparable in that charming city, and had spent hours together strolling along the banks of the Seine. I have fine memories of the magnificent trips we took around Paris. We also made a longer voyage to Normandy, stopping in Rouen, Deauville, Trouville, and Le Havre . . . In Rouen we saw the square where Joan of Arc was burned at the stake. In Le Havre, we climbed the tower of the cathedral and enjoyed a splendid meal in a top-notch restaurant where we paid next to nothing because it was their first day in business. Marvelous days. We were young and our lives stretched before us like a wonderful lunch in the middle of a beautiful, long excursion.

I wrapped up my little case and went to see Professor Zera. I hadn't seen him in fourteen years. He had a private practice, and there were many patients in the waiting room. The white-aproned cleaning lady refused to let me in.

"You must register a week before your visit," she said.

"I'm not a patient; I've come on a private matter."

She went to speak to the professor, and a moment later emerged to lead me through another door into his office, whose furnishings bespoke success. There were oriental rugs and paintings. Zera stood up. He was clearly not pleased to see me. I asked him to keep my valise until I could come back for it, and he agreed. He didn't ask me how I was faring, but he certainly knew the situation I was in. He made no offer of help. Perhaps he was too busy. . . . Still, I was relieved to know that my beloved valise was safe.

That same day, when I returned from seeing the professor, we moved into Malinowska's apartment at Nowiniarska Street. I expressed my sincere gratitude to the Ziembinskis, who happened to be in Warsaw that day, and who invited us to dinner the next Sunday at their summer house in Falenica. Mrs. Fuks, a well-known lawyer from Lodz and an old friend of mine, would be there, too. I promised we would go.

10

Malinowska had a second-floor apartment that faced the street. There were three rooms: we lived in one, a Polish student in another, and the third was occupied by an aging hack violinist who played on the street and in courtyards. The building faced the ghetto walls, which we could see from our windows, along the buildings that housed the Jewish brushmakers' workshop. We could see Jewish children playing beyond the wall. The people in the apartment on Nowiniarska Street, and in the whole house, were convinced that we were Aryan. Only old Malinowska knew the truth. We had been living there for several days, and we felt calm. I went to work every day and my life took on a certain rhythm.

On Sunday we were supposed to go out to Falenica. It was a glorious spring day, and everything was in full bloom. But Pola had a sore throat and cough, so she and Elzunia stayed home while I took the little shuttle train to Falenica alone. So much had happened there! Many Warsaw Jews had summer houses there before the war, a number of them in a fin de siècle style, with terraces and balconies. Others belonged to local peasants who rented them out to city dwellers for the summer.

Gniewkowski had rented one of these smaller houses for the Ziembinskis from a farmer named Mucha. Mucha was proud to have a dignitary living in his house, and Ziembinski had a good relationship with Mucha, from whom he purchased milk, butter, eggs, cheese and vegetables at very reasonable prices.

Officially, Ziembinski was living there with his wife, but his sister and her young son were in hiding with them. The sister had rather Semitic looks, and the little boy was clearly Jewish, but Mucha had never seen either one of them. Mrs. Fuks, the lawyer, and her own son also came from time to time to visit the Ziembinskis, but she was a natural blond, and both she and her son looked Aryan.

The two boys, the Ziembinskis' nephew and Mrs. Fuks's son, had become friends, and longed to play outside, but because one looked so Semitic, they had to stay indoors.

Yet who could force such active children to stay within four walls in such beautiful weather? The Ziembinskis' nephew kissed his mother, his aunt, and his uncle, begging them to let them out in the yard. "We'll be very careful," he promised.

Alas, the Szenwalds, alias Ziembinskis, let them go. It was a Saturday afternoon. Mucha was an old man and rarely went outdoors, but his sons were always out and about, so it was little wonder they noticed children playing in the garden. They were quickly drawn to the Ziembinskis' nephew.

"That boy's a Jew!"

"Who are you and what are you doing here?" young Mucha asked.

"I'm here with my uncle, Mr. Ziembinski," the boy answered timidly. "I'm very good. We're only playing ball."

Mucha's sons went back to their father. They said they wanted to report the boys to the Gestapo, and old Mucha agreed. He was very greedy, and believed the Jews had duped and wronged him. He wanted their clothes and other belongings as well as a reward in money and in kind. With all of that he could even buy another cow.

So without further ado, one of Mucha's sons rode on horseback to the Gestapo headquarters in Otwock. The result was instantaneous. At six o'clock on Sunday morning, a car with five armed Germans pulled up outside the house where the Ziembinskis were living. They roused the sleeping Ziembinskis, who had prepared no hiding place. They herded them all into one room. One of Mucha's sons was a witness.

Ziembinski was calm and collected.

"Would you kindly tell me what this is about?" he asked.

"You're a Jew!"

"No, sir, you're mistaken. I am a Pole."

"So how come you speak German so well?"

This itself was suspicious. Almost all Jews could speak German.

"I used to be a teacher of German language and literature."

"If you are a Pole, recite a prayer."

"Our Father, which art in Heaven, hallowed be Thy name. Thy kingdom come . . ."

"That's enough. Anyone can learn a prayer. Drop your pants."

"But why?"

"We know what we're doing."

"Forgive me, but I would rather not to do this in front of the women and children. Surely you understand."

They slapped Ziembinski in the face, and the women and children started crying. The old man had to do as he was ordered.

"You have no foreskin. You're a Jew."

"No—that's because of an operation I had to undergo as a young man."

"We'll see about that as soon as the boys drop their pants."

"But we were good!" the children wailed.

One of the Germans spoke Polish and translated. The boys were made to lie down on the table one by one.

"They're Jews," said the German examining them. He turned to Ziembinski: "The boy said you were his uncle, so you're a Jew and so are the boys' mothers."

"I'm not Jewish. My husband was a Jew," Mrs. Fuks answered. This could be, for she looked like a Nordic beauty from the legend of the Nibelungen.

"Very well. We'll look into that further, but for now all five of them are coming with us." Ziembinski, his wife, her sister, and the two boys were led outside. Mrs. Fuks followed. The Germans ordered the young Muchas to dig a grave, and all the residents of Falenica were summoned to witness the execution.

I had no idea of all of this as I crossed the fields between the station and the Ziembiskis', lost in thought.

I came to my senses suddenly when I saw a horde of people running in a single direction alongside Mucha's house.

"What's going on? Why are you running?" I asked a passing peasant woman.

"They're about to shoot some Jews, and I don't want to miss it," came the answer.

It would have looked suspicious if I had turned on my heels, so I joined in. I soon found myself on a hillock in the midst of a dense crowd of peasants. Next to a large hole that had just been dug, a brown-black mound of earth grew higher as we watched. The work seemed to take forever, although two other peasants were assisting the young Muchas. To one side stood the victims: one man, two women, and two children, all in their underwear. The women and children were crying. The man was grim and silent. A few yards away stood Mrs. Fuks, the only one fully clothed.

A tall Gestapo officer lined the victims up overlooking the grave, and killed all five with shots to the back of the neck. At that moment, Mrs. Fuks threw herself at the murderer.

"What have you done?" she screamed. "In God's name, what have you done?" grabbing his hands.

"She's a damned Jew too," came a voice in Polish. The executioner shoved Mrs. Fuks away from him. She fell to the ground and he fired three shots at her. She wasn't dead yet, so he finished her off with two bullets to the head. Then she joined the others in the tomb. Shovels dumped earth onto the corpses. A young woman next to me threw up.

"Well done. We have to get rid of the Jews," shouted someone in the crowd. Others nodded their agreement. But the spectacle had etched its horror on the sunburned, wrinkled faces of a number of old peasant women. They looked with revulsion at the murderers.

"It's an insult against God," they whispered.

I myself was incapable of thinking. I turned back toward the station. All I wanted was to return to Warsaw.

When I told Pola, she broke down.

"I can't take it any longer! This life is unbearable. We can't go on like this!" she sobbed. But in fact, we had to go on living.

When Mrs. Fuks failed to return home on Sunday evening, her husband became anxious. He sent his oldest son, a boy of twelve, to Falenica, to find out what had happened. The Muchas took the boy and handed him over to the Polish police, who held him at the station. When the boy too, did not return, Fuks turned to Gniewkowski, who went out to Falenica himself and learned everything. Only through great effort, and with a ransom, was Gniewkowski able to free Fuks's only surviving son, who in a single stroke had become an only child and a half-orphan.

11

A few days after the events in Falenica, I woke up at five o'clock in the morning with a strong sense of foreboding. The pressure in my chest warned of impending danger. At six o'clock there was a knock on the door.

"Who's there?"

"Police! Open up!" Two men came in: a Polish policeman and a streetcar driver. Pola was sleeping with Elzunia. The two men surveyed the room. The streetcar driver had made sure to close the door behind him.

"You're Jews!" the policeman shouted in a menacing voice.

I was in such shock that I didn't know what to say. I was speechless with fear.

"Get up! Get dressed! We're taking you to headquarters. We have proof you're Jewish."

"But we've done nothing wrong. Leave us alone."

"What you've done or not done is no concern of ours. You're Jewish, and that's enough for the Gestapo."

Meanwhile, they were ransacking the room in search of valuables. They found nothing of interest.

My wife begged for mercy, and five-year-old Elzunia fell to her knees before a holy image lit by a small red lamp and was praying aloud. Kaczynski, who had taken her to church a few times, had taught her some Catholic prayers, and she firmly believed she had been baptized. Now she knew that she and her parents were in grave danger. With tear-filled eyes uplifted to the image of the Virgin Mary, and hands folded, she was pleading for salvation. The policeman looked at the child and ordered a halt to the search. The child's fervent prayers had moved him, and he let Pola speak.

It turned out they were informers and wanted a ransom of ten thousand zlotys. Pola bargained them down to four thousand. We handed over all the money we had in the apartment, and gave our word of honor that we would pay them the rest within the week.

"I will sell a few things and give you what I get for them," I assured them.

The policeman looked tenderly at Elzunia.

"I swear on that sacred picture and on the Holy Cross, and on the head of my son, who is the same age as your daughter, whose prayer went straight to my heart, that you may continue to live here in peace. No one shall find out about you."

I took the informers to a nearby bar. When they were suitably drunk, they told me who had given them our address: Zygmunt, the forger. He had probably not done it intentionally; because he was an alcoholic, cheap booze had probably loosened his tongue.

When I returned home, we discussed our situation.

We had no other hideout, and we had no choice but to stay there and take the informers at their word. That was an unforgivable mistake. We should never have stayed in a compromised hideout. But Gniewkowski could no longer help us; after the tragedy of the Ziembinskis he was suffering from anxiety. We should have gone back to Bronia's, but we didn't.

We knew how vulnerable we were, though, so we resolved to place Elzunia in safety. If we were to die, then at least the child would live. But first I had to come up with the rest of the ransom.

I went to see Professor Zera. The same cleaning lady opened the door, but this time I did not have to wait. Zera received me coldly. He said that many things had changed in his life, because he had married. I congratulated him and asked for my valise. He said he wasn't sure where it was, because he had a number of different properties, and told me to return two days later.

On the appointed date, a different cleaning lady opened the door. Zera announced that he had not found the case, and that perhaps the previous maid had taken it. I looked him straight in the eye. He smiled and lowered his gaze.

The valise I had left with him was very valuable; in those days it would have been worth at least ten thousand zlotys. Perhaps his wife had taken a liking to it. In any case, whatever was in Zera's mind, a Jew was powerless. When I was almost at the door, Zera called me back. "Good luck, dear colleague—and be careful. And if you have any jewelry or diamonds, I'll be glad to buy them from you."

So spoke a professor, a physician, and the good friend of my youth. . . . Now I knew what to think of him.

But I went out onto the street with a light heart. Things could have been worse—he could have reported me. I had lost my suitcase, but I still had my life. Through Bronia, who knew all kinds of people, I managed to sell some dollars. I used the money to pay off the informers, who had lost no time in coming back for it. Now our number one priority was to find a safe haven for our child.

12

Elzunia looked completely Aryan. She was blond, and she had a combined birth and baptismal certificate. Although it was very hard for us, we made up our minds to part with her, so she would be spared in case we eventually perished.

For this I needed to get in touch with my cousin Basia, a Catholic who had been baptized as a young child. Deeply religious. Eleonora Reicher, born Barbara Reicher, was a rheumatologist as well as a scholar, and was known as much for her many scientific papers as for her writings on Christianity, thanks to which she had extensive contacts in the upper ranks of the Polish clergy.

Bronia arranged for us to meet at the home of Princess Aniela Woroniecka.

It was an elegant building, with a marble staircase. I rang the bell, and an elderly woman in clothes resembling a nun's habit opened the door and led me into a large salon filled with antique French furniture and a beautiful piano.

I sat down gingerly on the edge of a gilded chair, so as not to dirty the seat with my greasy clothes. In came a pale, frail woman of perhaps forty-five, with a kind, profoundly spiritual face. This was Princess Woroniecka, modest and shy like a country girl on her first visit to the city. A riveting, fascinating woman, she spoke in a warm voice, choosing her words with utmost care.

The princess told me about herself and her family, speaking with a strange, objective precision. Her father, one of the Czartoryski princes, was deceased. Her mother's brother, Prince Lubomirski, had been the Polish regent during World War I. Princess Aniela Woroniecka's ancestors had played major roles in Polish history.

One of the Czartoryskis, Prince Adam, had been at the center of a circle of émigrés in Paris after the Polish uprising against Russia in 1831. The Czartoryskis were related to and intermarried with many of Europe's royal houses, including the Bourbons and the Hapsburgs. Now Princess Woroniecka shared this seven-room apartment with her mother, née Lubomirska, and her sister, Maria Czartoryska. They owned the building, which stood on the corner of Nowogrodzka and Krucza Streets; it had long been their city residence. Their permanent residence was in the region of Poznan, where they had a large landed estate that had been confiscated by the Nazis and annexed to the Reich. They had thus fled to Warsaw.

In time, I learned that Aniela Woroniecka was a deeply pious woman. It was said that she had once planned to be a nun, but never took her vows. After the death of her husband, she resolved to become a doctor so she could treat the sick as an act of charity.

She had begun her studies in Warsaw before the war. She was the oldest student in the medical school, which is where she met my cousin Basia, who was a member of the faculty.

These two devout women shared a rare quality: the calling to do good. The war had changed nothing in that respect.

"We are living in difficult times, and it is the duty of every man to help his neighbor. This does not take much by way of courage," Aniela Woroniecka said to me one day. "You just need to do your part and have faith in God." Everything she did, she did with modesty and spontaneity.

I hadn't seen my cousin Basia in many years. She could not pass for an Aryan, and I was sure she had taken a great risk in leaving her hiding place to help my child. Before the war she had treated all of Warsaw's clergy, so she could now count on their help. She herself was in hiding in an institution for blind children.

Basia and the princess deliberated, and it was decided that Elzunia should be placed in a convent. The princess's housekeeper, Jadwiga Turek, the woman who had opened the door to me, would take her there and the nuns would know nothing of Elzunia's background. The governess would say that the girl's Catholic parents, originally from Lublin, were dead. She was also to allude to the child's presumed aristocratic origin. In fact, Elzunia's birth and baptismal certificate were from Lublin.

I thanked these three women from the bottom of my heart. Despite their different backgrounds, they came together through their strong faith and the actions that flowed from it.

It was hard for us to part with our child, but we painted her forthcoming stay in the convent in glowing colors. She listened to us attentively, with big eyes.

"But where are *you* going to stay?"

"We'll find a safe place to live. And on Sundays, Mama will come out to visit you and you'll take lovely walks together to the woods."

When the appointed day came, we went to meet Jadwiga Turek at Princess Woroniecka's. From there, we went together to Międzylesie, outside Warsaw, to the convent of the Sisters of the Family of Mary. When Madame Turek took her by the hand, Elzunia asked: "Will you really come on Sunday?"

When they disappeared behind the convent gate, Pola broke into sobs. But Elzunia was safe. Now, we thought, it would be easier for us to hide.

13

After the visit from the informers, we no longer wanted to keep our room, but we took the policeman at his word and stayed there. In any case, for the time being we had no prospects of finding something else.

To be on the safe side, we fashioned a hideout in the hallway. It was a cubbyhole concealed between the bathroom and the corner where the electricity and gas meters stood.

It was so cleverly hidden that from the exterior it was practically invisible. We hid our valuables under the floorboards, creating several niches so that if one were plundered, the others would remain.

Then the fateful day of the uprising in the Warsaw ghetto arrived:

April 19, 1943. From our windows we could see how fiercely the Jewish youth fought the Germans, who outnumbered them in men and weapons. Before my eyes, on Nowiniarska Street, I saw German soldiers fall under Jewish bullets. . . . I also saw Jewish fighters tumble from the windows of the brushmakers' warehouse. The Germans returned single rifle shots with artillery fire, canons, and aerial bombardment. The uneven fight dragged on. Marszalkowska Street, teeming with armed Germans, Ukrainians, and Lithuanians, had become a battlefield. I saw bleeding Germans fall in the dust and filth of the streets. There was a moment when it seemed that our whole building would be evacuated, but then the fighting moved onto Bonifraterska Street, and we were left where we were.

I stood by the window. The Germans had set up canons in front of our building and were firing them along with machine guns. Hand grenades were exploding everywhere. My body was inside, in the house at Nowiniarska Street, but my heart was in the battle that was being waged beyond the wall, and my thoughts were with the heroic young defenders of our people.

Houses, doused in gasoline and set alight, exploded one after the other. One after the other, I saw mothers jumping with their children from the balconies and shattered windows of burning buildings. Tears poured down my face.

That night, a sea of fire illuminated the heroic ghetto. The wind bore the suffocating, piercing smoke, and there was no let-up to the bombs and the deafening roar of exploding bricks, metal, and wood.

Suddenly, somewhere close by, I heard the sound of music. Our neighbor, the elderly violinist who rented the room adjoining ours, was playing Paganini on the balcony. I peered at him more closely. His eyes were bright, and he was playing feverishly. The glare of the flames distorted the sharp features of his aged face.

"Why are you playing?"

No answer.

"Why?"

"Why do you ask?" he answered with another question, and continued playing.

A moment later, with astonishing calm, he said, "This is the most beautiful moment of my entire life. I feel like Nero watching Rome burn. He recited his poetry, and I'm playing my violin. My heart is bursting with happiness. I'm playing to show the world my joy, because I've lived to see the Jews burning up like lice!"

Horrified, I pulled back to stop myself from hitting the old man. That madman's music accompanied the cruel fall of my people's brightest sons.

Pola and I went down onto the street. On Nowiniarska Street and Krasinski Square we passed fairground stalls, carousels, and swings. People were out having a good time. Loud music was blaring and couples were dancing. It looked as though they were celebrating the fall of the Warsaw ghetto. A drunk man threw his arms around me. "The Jews are burning!" he laughed.

I said nothing.

In the next few days, part of the ghetto was reduced to dust and ashes. But on the Polish side, just across the wall, life was merry and gay.

14

My own scream woke me from a dream. Drenched in sweat, I looked around. It was still dark, and Pola was fast asleep. What was happening to me? I felt the crushing pain in my chest that was a sure sign of impending danger. Just as a seismograph records the least tremor half a world away, this dull pain was a warning. I woke Pola.

"We have to get out of here!"

"But why?"

"I have that ominous feeling."

Pola felt my anxiety; she trusted my premonitions.

"Where can we go so early in the morning?"

"It doesn't matter. We just have to leave."

"But it's still curfew. We'll be stopped, and we have false papers. At least here we have a place to hide. "

I said nothing, and Pola fell back to sleep. I tried to fall asleep myself, but my anxiety only increased.

At five o'clock in the morning, there was a knock at the front door. We leapt out of bed, for we knew such early visits boded ill.

"Make the bed," I whispered to Pola, but there was no time. Half-dressed, we slipped into our hiding place. Crammed in as we were, we had to hold in our breath.

Mrs. Malinowska, who happened to be spending the night at Nowiniarska Street, came out of the kitchen and shuffled across the corridor. Muttering to herself, she opened the front door. We heard the whole conversation from our hiding place.

"Where is the railwayman?" asked an urgent voice.

"He and his wife left for work," answered Malinowska, who had heard us scuffling into our hiding place.

"Where does he work?"

"At the train station, of course."

"Which station?"

"That I don't know."

Several men were ransacking our room.

"You lied. This bed hasn't been made, and it's still warm. Quick—check the windows! Maybe they went down the side of the house."

The men went back into the foyer.

"You're the landlady here. You're hiding Jews. But you won't be lying anymore: we're from the Gestapo."

We heard each word perfectly, and our hearts were pounding so hard that we were sure they could be heard out in the hall.

"Madame Malinowska, the penalty for hiding Jews is death. You can feel my revolver on your forehead. Do you feel how cold it is? Just tell me where the Jews are, and you shall be free."

Malinowska remained silent, but she must have pointed to our hiding place, for the door was smashed in and we were dragged out, bathed in cold sweat.

Three revolvers were trained on us, in the hands of three men: a Polish policeman, an elegantly dressed Ukrainian, and a small, thin, evil-looking man, who turned out to be a Volksdeutscher.

First of all, they searched us for weapons—in vain, of course. The money we had on us went straight into the pockets of the three blackmailers.

Threatening to turn us over to the Gestapo, the small Volksdeutscher demanded that we hand over all our valuables: gold, currency, and jewelry.

"I have no gold, diamonds, or jewelry here," I said. "I left it all with friends. As soon as I sell something, I'll give you some."

The thick-set Polish policeman began to punch me in the head. My nose started to bleed, but he didn't stop. I tried to speak to him, but he kept beating me. My head was killing me, and bumps appeared, but I would rather have dropped dead in my tracks than reveal where our valuables were. Nothing could stop the policeman; he just kept hitting me. But the Volksdeutscher realized that beating me was not going to work. They called him Schultz.

"You're stupid, Jew. You're going to the Gestapo, and once you get there you'll give up everything. Not only that—they'll make mincemeat of you."

I washed the blood off my face and got dressed. Schultz was already pushing me out the door. I turned around and saw Pola looking at me with wide eyes.

15

Schultz took me by the arm. We went downstairs and he led me toward the ghetto walls. My brain was working feverishly. I needed to get rid of Schultz, but it was too risky this close to the ghetto. Besides, he was armed. There was no way to escape. By now it was daylight, and laborers were already on their way to work. Arm in arm like two drunks, we drew closer and closer to the wall, on Swietojanska Street. Beyond the walls, there was the sound of gunfire. The hunt was on for Jews still hiding in bunkers and ruins. The battle was in its death throes.

Schultz dragged me toward an armed German soldier. "Arrest him," he said, pointing at me. "He's a Jew from the ghetto." The German looked at me in disbelief. I smiled at him and pretended to be drunk.

"I'm a Jew, oh yes siree, murder me, tee-hee, tee-hee," I babbled in Polish.

"Don't believe him, he's just playing drunk," Schultz urged, in German. "He needs to be arrested. He's a Jew." I cackled like a madman. The German stared wide-eyed at my railway uniform; the Germans respect uniforms. And Schultz was in civilian clothes. I tapped my hand to my neck conspiratorially to show the German how drunk Schultz was.

"Watch out and keep moving," the German said benignly, giving us a gentle shove. He had taken us for a couple of drunken chums and set off in the opposite direction. Schultz lost none of his bravado. He pulled me on toward downtown Warsaw. The whole way there, I attempted to convince him. "Just let me go. I'll get the diamonds, sell them, and bring you the money."

But he refused, and we walked on. A few minutes later, I started up again. I talked him into going to Professor Zera's. My plan was to borrow some money and pay the ransom. Schultz finally gave in. When we got to Zera's house, he wasn't home.

Schultz thought I had tricked him, but I had bought myself a little time, even though he was still pulling me toward the Gestapo headquarters on Szucha Avenue. On the way, on Ujazdowskie Avenue, he stopped me in front of the SS *Polizeiführer*. A tall German with a machine gun was standing by the guard post. He looked at my railway uniform and I repeated my role as a drunk, just as I had by the ghetto wall. Once again I escaped with my life.

Schultz was furious, and pushed on toward Szucha Avenue, which was no longer far away. From Szucha Avenue no Jew returned alive. The Gestapo was looming ever closer. . . . I made a last attempt to change the informer's mind. I told him about the cache under the floor at Nowiniarska, and promised to give him all I owned. We were standing across the street from the Gestapo. The officer at the guard post watched us with interest.

"If you're lying, I'll kill you in your apartment!" Schultz roared. We walked the whole way back to Nowiniarska Street, because he refused to take the tram. I could barely drag myself along, for I had had nothing to eat or drink that day, and his attempts at blackmail had sapped all my strength.

Schultz was running, so I had to run too. He said he had been given our address by the Polish policeman, the one who had sworn on the cross and on his son's head. . . .

At last we reached Nowiniarska. Malinowska opened the door and was struck dumb at the sight of us.

"Where's my wife?" I asked.

"She left with the Ukrainian."

This came as a shock, for although the Ukrainian had made a better impression on me than the policeman and Schultz, he was clearly an agent of the Gestapo.

Before entering our room, I asked Schultz to leave me alone for five minutes. Amazingly, he agreed to wait out in the hall. I went into the room, which unfortunately had neither key nor bolt. With a penknife, I pried open the cover to one of the caches in the floor, where we had hidden a diamond ring, my gold watch, and a few dollar coins. I removed only the ring, but just as I was about to close the cache, the door opened and Schultz burst in. He bent down and grabbed the entire contents of the cache. Then he started to test the floor of the whole room, which happened to be composed of a large number of small slats. He lifted one of the loosened floorboards; luckily, there was nothing underneath it.

"You won't find anything. You already have all there is."

He shot me a glacial look, and said that if I gave him more, he'd free me.

"I don't know if this diamond is worth anything. The watch is old. It won't fetch much, and these dollars don't add up to much."

"That's all there is. You have everything."

"It's not enough."

"Have mercy, sir," I said. "Even bandits don't behave like this. I'm telling you, you have everything."

"In that case, we'll go to the Gestapo. If things change, you're a useless witness." Schultz was clearly mocking me. He wanted to rob me of everything and then hand me over anyway to die. He took out his revolver. "Let's go!" he said.

16

We took a horse-drawn droshky.

"Szucha Avenue," Schultz instructed the driver. My head began to spin. Szucha Avenue, the Gestapo, the house from which no one comes out alive. Undress, lie down on the ground, a shot to the back of the neck, the end, eternal sleep. People with vivid imaginations are at a disadvantage in such situations.

I knew now that I would not escape Schultz's clutches, but I did not want to die on Szucha Avenue—anywhere but there. Every step of the horse took me closer to the end, my death. I saw people strolling along, the blue sky, Warsaw beautiful in the sun's rays. All for the last time. We turned onto Zbawiciel Square, the Square of the Savior, where all the streetcar lines intersect, which was thronged with people. I prepared to jump. Tensing all my muscles, I threw myself under an approaching tram. As I jumped, various scenes from my life flashed before me, like a film in fast forward, in which the starring roles were played by my father, Pola, and Elzunia.

I heard the screech of brakes, then loud shouts from the crowd. All I could feel was the pressure of the hard cobblestones. I was a little dazed, but there was no pain. I was alive. The streetcar driver had managed to brake at the last moment.

Could he have dreamt that his rapid reflexes, which had just saved a human life, would mean the continuation of my torture?

I stood up, moaning, dusted myself off, and smoothed my clothes. Two policemen were approaching, but Schultz grabbed me by the arms and pulled me back to the droshky, opening a path through the excited crowd.

Now that I had miraculously evaded death, I realized that suicide was not the way out. Clearly, I was meant to die a different death. Or perhaps all this was merely chance, and there was no such thing as destiny? As I was musing, the droshky drew up outside the large Gestapo building on Szucha Avenue. Schultz whispered something to the guard standing outside.

This time, playing drunk would do no good. I was immediately handed over to a civilian employee inside the building. I spoke only

Polish, pretending not to understand a word of German. They sent in an interpreter.

"Are you Jewish?"

"No, Polish. Catholic."

"Your papers!"

"Here you are. Just call Szczesliwice; they'll confirm all the information." The Polish stationmaster at Szczesliwice who had hired me was aware of my change of name from Jankowski to Kalinowski; on that score I was confident.

It was astonishing that the Gestapo did not detect that my papers were forged. Evidently the counterfeiter had done an excellent job, or else they checked my documents in a very cursory way.

Be that as it may, the main interest here was circumcision. I was shown to a specialist in the matter, who pronounced that I was circumcised.

Recalling the tragic events of Falenica, I told him the story Ziembinski had invented: that I had been circumcised in my youth, due to an illness.

"We shall have to wait for a physician to rule on the matter," the foreskin specialist decided. I was led down to the basement. Hours passed, and I could hear shouts, cries, curses. All the time I sat there in my tiny wooden cell, trying to come up with a way to defend myself.

At last the door opened and I was led back up to the second floor. A moment later a tall man with a neatly trimmed dark mustache, Hitler style, came in. His face looked familiar but, try as I might, I could not remember where I had seen him before. He ordered me to undress.

Suddenly, as I was standing there naked before him, I realized who he was. His identity was clear beyond the shadow of a doubt.

"Doctor," I began cautiously. "May I ask you a question?"

"Certainly."

I was whispering now.

"Are you from Vienna?"

"Yes, but how do you know?"

"You're Dr. Sonnenwald."

"That's correct, but how do you know me?"

The Gestapo physician studied me carefully, but he didn't recognize me.

"Dr. Sonnenwald, do you remember when you worked in Dr. Kezel's clinic? Do you remember the lecturer, Dr. Konrad, and Sister Eva? I was working there at the same time."

"Then you are Dr. Reicher?"

"Yes, in this disguise."

The doctor looked at me for a long time. Then he gazed in front of him, lost in thought.

"Yes, those were happy times, in Vienna, in 1928," he murmured. "But what exactly have you done and said up to this point? I need to know, so I can save you."

I told him everything that had happened to me in my few hours in the Gestapo building. He heard me out attentively and left the room. Fifteen minutes later he was back.

"You may go, my friend, you're a free man," he said softly. "I wish you luck and endurance in these difficult times. Remember me from time to time, and think good thoughts for me."

He escorted me back downstairs right to the entrance. Then, in a loud voice, he shouted to the guard, "Let the railwayman out."

And so another miracle had taken place: I had left Szucha Avenue alive. My torment had lasted from five o'clock in the morning until six o'clock in the evening: thirteen hours. That was the hardest and most trying day of my whole life.

17

So I was free. I inhaled deeply and filled my lungs with the precious air of freedom. I was very hungry. I felt like going into the closest café for a cup of tea and some rolls, but then I realized that I didn't have a penny to my name. It was a beautiful, mild evening. Laughing and joking, people strolled lazily down Ujazdowskie Avenue, cars rolled along, and droshkies moved slowly past.

I was walking toward Nowiniarska Street, looking for Pola. I had no idea where the Ukrainian had taken her. I broke into a run, staring at every woman with blond hair whose silhouette resembled hers. At last—miracle of miracles!—I spotted Pola, my darling Pola, on Krasinski Square. I ran to her, and tears streamed down our faces.

The elegant Ukrainian had done her no harm. He had invited her to a café to chat. I had to tell her again and again the events of that extraordinary day. Pola still had a little money that she had hidden away, so we ate dinner in a restaurant.

We could not return to the apartment on Nowiniarska. We had nowhere to go at all, so we decided to split up. Pola went to Princess Woroniecka's, and I planned to spend the night with one of my coworkers. With a flask of brandy in my pocket, I headed for his home. He was astonished that I hadn't been to work, and that I had come to see him so late. I apologized, using the curfew as my excuse. I mumbled something about politics and an apartment in a distant part of town, to make him think I must have some connection with the underground movement. When I put the bottle on the table, all was forgiven. The atmosphere grew cozy, and my colleague brought out something for us to nibble on.

The sky was still red from the fires in the ghetto, and although we were far away, we could hear the roar of collapsing walls.

The alcohol loosened the tongue of my solitary host, who was thought of at work as a Communist or Socialist, or at the very least, a man of the left.

"We Polish workers are opposed to Hitler, because he is a dictator and a murderer. But for one accomplishment alone he deserves a monument," he said, pointing toward the glow above the ghetto. I was forced to hold my tongue and listen to his thoughts, revealed in their true colors, as so often happens, by alcohol.

He spoke for a long time. At last we lay down to sleep.

A huge trunk served me as a bed. It was so hard that it was like lying on a stone—but that was not the worst of it. Before long, I felt a terrible itching all over my skin. Hundreds of lice had claimed their victim. I spent an awful night, and left that hospitable house with immense relief at five the next morning.

It was very early, and I met no one on my way to Szczesliwice station. When I arrived, the first thing I did was to take a much appreciated cold shower. I washed my shirt out too, and hung it out to dry in the yard.

"Why didn't you show up for work yesterday?" the supervisor asked me.

"My wife was sick and . . ."

"Very well."

No one here had any suspicions. He may have thought I belonged to an underground organization, since that was the image people somehow had of me.

That afternoon, Pola and I returned to Nowiniarska Street for the last time and removed our valuables from beneath the floor. From there, we went to Princess Woroniecka's. She had taken Pola in the night before and had agreed to store our things.

Aniela Woroniecka had found Pola a job. There was a vacant domestic position with the countess Karczo-Siedlecka. The princess vouched for Pola, and even told the countess that Pola had worked for her as a chamber maid for several years. So my wife set off for the countess's beautiful palace at Piekna Street, near Ujazdowska Avenue. The countess took a liking to her. Before the war, Count Karczo-Siedlecki had been a well-known Polish diplomat who had supposedly left the country. The countess, of Irish descent, was a friend of the Germans, and always had a full house during the occupation.

In the countess's house, Pola was known as Pelagia Jankowska, the name that appeared on her identity card. This position made her relatively safe and accorded her a degree of stability. I, on the other hand, had nowhere to sleep.

Princess Woroniecka, who was goodness itself, invited me to stay with her. But just as we were speaking, her mother, Princess Czartoryska, entered the room.

"I have no objection to your wife spending the night at our house, because she doesn't look the least bit Jewish. But you—under no circumstances may you stay here. If you were caught in this house, our whole family would be held responsible. I'm not afraid of death; I'm an old woman and shall soon be dead in any case, but they would shoot my daughters or put them in a concentration camp. We're not going to throw you out onto the street. You may spend the night in the cellar, but if you're found there, you must say that you crept in there yourself."

With the greatest precaution, Jadwiga Turek led me down to the cellar, which was filled with coal. A small window, its pane smashed, looked out onto the courtyard. I was exhausted from the events of the previous day.

I thought I would be unable to fall asleep on the coal, but my weary body needed rest, and I was soon out like a light. I was awakened by a conversation in the courtyard.

"There's someone in the basement. . . ."

"You're hearing things. It's probably a cat."

"There's a man in there."

"You're seeing ghosts."

"It must be a thief."

I sat upright on the coal, motionless. The slightest shift of a lump of coal seemed to me to make a racket.

"That's the princess's cellar."

"We can't wake her this late."

Footsteps on the stairs drew closer to my hiding place.

"What are you doing here?" someone called out.

In the faint light of a candle I saw four burly men armed with big sticks. One of them even had an iron bar.

"I had a bit to drink and fell asleep. . . ." I shook my head drowsily, once more playing the drunk. The men saw an inebriated railwayman and calmed down.

"Come on out. That's no place to sleep."

"Why don't you all come on in and join me?" I slurred. They chuckled. They probably felt foolish now, with those sticks.

"Out you come now. It's time to go home."

"I don't have a night pass. . . ."

"You can come to my place," one of them said. So, staggering and swaying, I followed him up the stairs, but his wife wouldn't let me in.

It was a mild night, so I collapsed on a bench in the courtyard and fell asleep at last.

18

Well rested, I got up and went to work. Later that day I began my search for a place to live. I spoke to the superintendents of large apartment houses, and on Wolska Street I found a room to let with an elderly couple. It was ideal for me. The rent was a hundred zlotys a month, whereas a hideout could cost up to a hundred zlotys a day—thirty times more.

"Thank God you're not a Jew!" The old woman laughed at her own joke.

Now my life began to settle down. I had somewhere to live, Pola was a maid for the countess, which gave her a certain degree of security, and my little girl was safely hidden in a convent.

In those days, there was an altar in almost every courtyard in Warsaw, where the residents of each building would join together in prayer. I was glad that I had learned a few Catholic prayers and songs by heart. It was a necessity. Every evening, I prayed in the courtyard with all the other tenants.

On Sunday afternoons, Pola was free, and she and Jadwiga Turek, Princess Czartoryska's housekeeper, would go out to Miedzylesie to visit Elzunia. Jadwiga Turek knew the nuns well, and was allowed to take Elzunia for walks in the woods. The nuns turned my daughter into a devout Catholic; in fact, she was confirmed by none other than the bishop. She chose the name Aniela for that occasion, since she had heard so much about Aniela Woroniecka.

Elzunia told Pola that she spent every minute of her free time praying to God for our survival. Little as she was, she was well aware of the continuing danger that threatened us. My little six-year-old didn't have an easy life in the convent. She had to pretend to be an orphan and a Pole.

The children had to scrub the floors themselves, and food was scarce, for the convent had no assets. Pola did what she could to keep the child supplied, but this was a delicate matter vis à vis the other girls, who had neither parents nor visitors. Elzunia was dazzled by the fruit and sweets Pola brought. She ate them as soon as they were in the woods.

When they parted, Elzunia threw herself into her mother's arms. She wanted to go with her. She said she would rather die than remain in the convent. The sisters took care of the children and taught them, but they were powerless against the Germans. Once the convent had had several cows, but the Nazis had confiscated all the animals and all their stocks of food. The Germans also carried out periodic searches, looking for Jewish children. One evening, they had surrounded the convent and examined all the children, looking them over one by one. Girls with dark hair or black eyes were suspect. Once they were about to deport several of them, but the mother superior gave her word of honor that they weren't Jewish.

Pola was always upset when she returned from Miedzylesie. She told me everything Elzunia had told her, and I did my best to calm her down.

In the evenings the countess Karczo-Siedlecka often threw parties, and the house would be full of guests, mostly high-ranking German officers. My wife was young and pretty, and she caught the officers' eye. She worried that they might suspect her of being a Jew, but her fears were groundless; they all believed her to be an Aryan, and the countess was very pleased with her.

Pola received a good salary, along with generous tips from guests. She had her own room and was well fed. But this relative happiness was not to last. Elzunia came down with scarlet fever and was hospitalized in the ward for infectious diseases at Wolska Street. The only visiting hours were on Sunday afternoons. Pola went, of course, but no one was allowed into the ward, so she could only see the child through a little window.

One Sunday afternoon at four o'clock, at the end of visiting hours, I was waiting for her outside the hospital. Luckily, our daughter was slowly geting better.

It was June, the sky was blue, and the sun was pleasantly warm. We wanted to make the most of the beautiful day, so we took the tram to Bernerowo. We spent a few hours strolling along peaceful woodland paths and reminiscing about the beautiful days of our former life, so long ago and so hard to imagine. When we came to a green glade full of birches, we sat down and turned our faces to the sky.

We drank in the happiness of the moment. When we're aware of it, happiness doubles. We also thought of our brothers in misery, holed up in hiding places and hovels, subjected to blackmail and denunciation. In the prison at Pawiak, according to the underground press, thirty prisoners were shot each day, which meant ten thousand people a year. And the Jews perishing in the ghettos and the camps . . . would anyone manage to save *them*?

How much longer could this go on?

19

We were on our way back from Bernerowo, rested and feeling optimistic. Pola went inside the tram, while I rode outside on the front platform. Suddenly, a few stops further on, when we were already back in Warsaw, a young man jumped onto the running board and took his place beside me. He reeked of alcohol.

"Give me a nip!" he shouted.

"Beat it, you scoundrel," I said with a vigorous peasant tone, hoping to throw him off course, since he was beginning to stare at me.

His eyes sparkled. "You're a Jew," he said. "You're that factory owner, Reicher, who had a silk ribbon factory at Leszno and Mlynarska Street. Now it's payback time!"

"What nonsense is that? I've never heard of that Jewish factory owner. I'm a Pole, and a worker just like you."

In fact, my cousin, Stasiek Reicher, had been the owner of a large factory that employed about four hundred workers. We looked so alike we could have been taken for twins, which had led before the war to some amusing mistakes; now, though, it could have cost me my life. Stasiek was a great lady-killer, and his sweethearts often used to accost me on the street or in cafés, offended that I hadn't recognized them.

In the Warsaw ghetto, Stasiek had paid a large sum of money for a certificate proving that he worked in a German workshop, where he did indeed have a foreman's position. He was an expert on textiles. Nevertheless, he was taken from his apartment to the Umschlagplatz and perished in Treblinka.

How was I to persuade this one-time employee of my cousin that I was not his former boss? Telling him I was his cousin would have solved nothing!

"Get off the tram with me right now, or I'll call a policeman."

Pola joined us from inside the tram and asked what was going on, which was a mistake, for now she was embroiled in it too. The three of us got off the streetcar.

"We're not Jewish. Look at my wife. Here's my identity card."

"Bullshit!" said the young worker. "Follow me."

"Why?"

He pushed me into the nearest doorway.

"Pull down your pants!" he ordered.

"Are you mad?" I had to get rid of him at all cost, which was virtually impossible. I sized him up. He was no taller than I, but more solidly built. I pulled together all my strength and punched him in the chest. He fell, but managed to kick me in the groin. I thought I would die from the pain.

Now I had no way to escape. All this took place on Wolska Street, the main thoroughfare of Wola, the workers' district of Warsaw, just a short distance from my room. That Sunday evening, the street was thronged with people out for a stroll, so we were soon at the center of a crowd of curious on-lookers.

"It's Reicher, the Jewish factory owner!" the informer screamed. People jostled closer to catch the unusual sight.

"But he's a railwayman. . . ."

"That's just a disguise."

"To the Gestapo with the bloodsucking Jewish capitalist!" came voices from the crowd, which was growing bigger and bigger. Fortunately for me, there were neither Germans nor blue-clad Polish police officers in sight. A few men, among them the first worker, dragged me from the crowd and pushed me into a nearby doorway. They emptied my pockets. All my money, documents and other papers vanished. Pola managed to slip away unnoticed.

My assailants suddenly disappeared, and I was left alone in the doorway. I was afraid to go back out on the street in case any of the residents from my new building had been in the crowd. The curfew was fast approaching, but I was afraid to return to my apartment, because the informers might be watching to see which way I headed. I waited until it grew completely dark, and then I slipped onto one of the side streets off Wolska.

"Hand over your money, Jew!"

It was a young boy of about thirteen or fourteen in his schoolboy's blazer and cap.

"Your money, Jew!" he insisted in his little boy's voice that was beginning to change.

"So your idea of making money is to steal it?"

"It's not a crime to take money from a Jew. They extorted us before," the boy replied.

"I have nothing to give you. The only thing you can take from me is my life," I said with resignation. The boy pushed me toward the latrines, where he pried open my mouth, yanked out my gold crown, along with two healthy teeth, and ran away. I was almost paralyzed from the pain in my mouth and groin; if not for that, I would have kicked him. That would have been my only form of self-defense, for he had also taken my penknife.

The streets were deserted. I slipped through a hole in a fence and found myself in a large scrapyard. It was unguarded, so I lay down on the ground amid the rusting pieces of scrap metal. I didn't sleep a wink the whole night, pondering my strange situation. Everyone on Wolska Street now knew I was a Jew; my railwayman's uniform and my magical "invisibility cap" were now incriminating evidence. I couldn't show myself again on Wolska. Too many people knew who I was.

I thought again of suicide, but rejected the idea, recalling the tram that had screeched to a halt on Savior's Square and how I had been saved by Dr. Sonnenwald. At dawn I lifted the board in the fence and found myself back on Wolska Street. There was no one around. I wandered aimlessly, but eventually returned to where I had spent the night, and noticed that there was a wooden hut. The door was open. As I approached, I could see a man sitting inside. I recognized him at once—it was Stanislaw Reich, a friend from my youth in Lodz, an Aryan and a Pole. His wife, a teacher by profession, was Jewish. He was a red-faced man bursting with energy and verve.

When we were both eighteen I had been infatuated with a girl whom Reich and I had met together, but he managed to steal her from me that same evening. My old friend Reich! A journalist before the war, he was now a scrap-iron merchant. I judged that I could trust him, so I went closer to the hut. He recognized me right away. He looked at my railwayman's uniform and broke into a hearty laugh. "I am Reich and you are Reicher . . ."* He invited me in and we hugged each other. I told him about my Aryan life and about the incident with the informers on Wolska Street. Reich offered me some sandwiches and hot tea. He couldn't take me in, because he had to take care of his Jewish wife, but he gave me a wool sweater and lent me two thousand zlotys. I put on the sweater and took my leave.

20

I managed to reach Countess Karczo-Siedlecka's palace without mishap, and knocked at the kitchen door, which was opened by Pola.

"You look like death," she whispered, and let me into the kitchen. I sat down on a stool and Pola made me a cup of coffee. I told her of my escape and all my wanderings, and how everything had been stolen from me, even my shirt. She had not had such a tragic time of it. A boy had snatched her purse, which had money in it, but she had managed to escape.

I took the streetcar to Wolska Street, packed up some of my things, and took them to Pola. I thought of renting a room in another part of town, far away from Wolska, but that would have been impossible because I had no papers.

It was a hot summer, so I decided to sleep in the abandoned brickyards on the outskirts of Warsaw. I was a little late to work, and my coworkers could tell from the way I looked that something wasn't right. "You're sick, you need to see a doctor. Get yourself checked out and ask him to put you on medical leave," they advised me.

"But don't forget to bring us back some lard, butter, and meat.

---

* A pun in German, meaning "I am rich and you are richer."

We'll drink some brandy with it." What could these people know of my misery? I was glad that none of them had seen me on Wolska the previous day.

After work I went once more to see Zygmunt, the forger who had once betrayed my address to the informers. He had surely been drunk when he denounced me; he could not be held accountable for his actions. I had only myself to blame for having told a drunken counterfeiter about my living arrangements. Now I was going back to him; I had no other option.

This time, as before, Zygmunt reeked of alcohol. He was really lit up, and I had to sit down and drink with him, or I would have gotten nowhere. He gave me a new identity card, in the name of Jan Szewczak. Kalinowski was dead. Szewczak was born.

I plucked up the courage to go back to the apartment on Wolska one last time. I found my landlords at home. I told them I had to move as I was being relocated to Lublin, but they did not believe me. They were convinced that I was a member of the resistance movement, and even offered me their assistance. And if they had found out I was a Jew? It was out of the question for me to let them know.

I put all my remaining affairs in a cardboard box and bade them farewell.

As soon as I got out the door, I was ambushed by three youths. They snatched the box from my hands and took off with it. I ran after them, for I wanted to recover the last of my belongings.

"Beat it, Jew, because if you don't, we'll hand you over to the Germans and they'll turn you into soap." I begged and pleaded with them, but in vain. All this was being played out as we ran. I was out of breath. The thieves disappeared into the neighboring fields.

Devastated, I returned to Pola. She gave me some hot borscht, which tasted so delicious that my troubles melted away. But I couldn't stay for long. At any moment the countess or her daughter might peek into the kitchen.

From that day on I never showed my face again on Wolska Street or the surrounding area.

21

I spent the night in the cellar of one of the old brickyards beyond the city limits. Wrapped in my railwayman's trenchcoat, I slept on the floor and awoke the next morning numb with cold. It took me a long time to brush the dirt and dust from my wretched clothes; then my shaving brush, soap, and razor sprang into action. Those were the things I always had with me. Through all the years of war and occupation I never skipped my daily shave. Closely shaved and with a bracing splash of cloudy water to my face, I headed off to work, where I was met by suspicious glances from my coworkers. I tried to work as hard as I could, even at the risk of being crushed between the cars, but my dark thoughts did not subside. The searching, penetrating gaze of one man in particular, who examined my face long and hard, filled me with unease.

I willed the day to pass as fast as possible. I decided not to return to Szczesliwice, and even to forgo the wages I was owed. My colleagues' stares spelled impending danger. They were clearly suspicious, but said nothing in the open, for they weren't sure. Still, my hooked nose and mournful eyes were reason enough for them to suspect that I was Jewish.

A single word, a turn of phrase, a brief remark, an opinion typical of the Jews, and you were on your way to Szucha Avenue or Pawiak prison. If you answered a question with a question, you were a Jew. There were certain expressions only Jews used, and throughout whole conversations, even while drinking, you had to keep your guard up. Until now I had always managed to deceive my colleagues. I spoke perfect Polish and, to improve the camouflage, I even knew some peasant slang.

At last the clock struck four in the afternoon. I slowly gathered my things and walked away. From time to time I turned around, but no one was following me. Done! Good-bye! Hunched over, with gloomy thoughts, I walked toward the ghetto wall. Something incomprehensible was pushing me in that direction.

The ghetto uprising had been suppressed, and the place was now a ghost town. The few people on the street resembled ghosts. There was sporadic gunfire.

Apparently, they were executing prisoners of war and members of underground organizations. When people heard the shots they made the sign of the cross, as if to ward off evil. I stared at the ruined walls of burned-out houses and found myself unable to turn away.

I recognized the skeleton of the house where my friend Olek Rozenholc had lain in bed gravely ill with lung disease. When I was still in the ghetto, I used to visit him, but it was hard to get there across attics and rooftops, the only way of reaching him alive. It was diabolically slippery in the rain. The brushmakers' quarter, where Rozenholc lived, was surrounded by empty houses which were patrolled by gendarmes with machine guns slung over their shoulders.

What is Olek Rozenholc doing now? Is he alive? Where is he? Buried somewhere underneath the ruins, below the rubble?

In this way I wandered along the ghetto walls, bent over as if I bore the weight of the dead on my back. Everything was devastated, burned, plundered, black from the flames. Here and there the remains of a wall still stood, like a finger pointing to the sky; the empty windows looked like the hollow eyes of skulls. There my friends, patients, and colleagues had lived; and here, on the other side of the wall, Jan Szewczak walked. Doctor Edward Reicher had perished in the ghetto. On this side of the wall stood a mock railway worker with false papers, a false name and a false trade.

As I stood there, lost in thought, I noticed two silhouettes. I would have liked to avoid them, but it was too late; they had already spoken. One was a tall blond Pole, a farmer from the countryside, judging by his clothes. Beside him stood a boy of thirteen, as blond as his father, with a sweet face and mild manner such as are rarely seen in a child.

The three of us stood together by the wall.

"I came in from Grojec to the Tax Bureau," the farmer said. "And I brought my son to Warsaw, so I could show him the capital and the ghetto. He's my first-born." He was proud of his handsome son.

It was a glorious, hot July day and the leaves on the hundred-year old trees on Krasinski Square were completely still.

"And what did you tell your son about all this?" I asked, breaking the silence. The man's eyes lit up.

"I told him about the Jews, who were rightfully destroyed here. Like parasites, like leeches, they sucked the blood of the noble Polish people. The Jews owned all the buildings and streets, and all we had were the paving stones, even though it was our country!" He glared at the rubble all around us.

"Hitler was right to exterminate them. We should be grateful to him for freeing us from the Jewish plague." He placed his hand on his son's shoulder.

"Take a good look over that wall, boy. That's where they burned the Jewish vermin to death," he said, almost gently.

My blood was boiling and my temples were pounding like a hammer.

Quiet. Not a word, I told myself, but this time I couldn't hold my tongue as I had done so many times before.

"But aren't there both good and bad people in every nation?" I asked. The farmer listened intently.

"Don't you think that among us Poles there are also good and bad? It's not possible to generalize. Christ was a Jew, too. Can we really burn and destroy everyone?"

I had evidently said too much, for the man turned livid.

"You don't know what you're saying. Jesus lived two thousand years ago. I don't know what the Jews were like back then, but the ones who died here in the ghetto were forgers and thieves. I'm sure the old ones—the ones who crucified our lord—were no better."

The farmer looked at me malevolently and took his son by the hand. "Come along. Don't believe that railwayman; he's probably a Communist."

They went on their way. I was lucky that no one else had heard our conversation. I could have been denounced.

I left that part of town and headed toward the center of the city.

22

Marszalkowska Street—the main artery of Warsaw—was pulsing with life. I passed Germans in uniform, young people, and numerous couples locked in embrace. Street traders openly sold smuggled goods: butter, lard, meat, cigarettes, chickens, and soap, which many families knew how to make at home.

Whenever a German patrol showed up, the traders scattered and hid in doorways. The stores were full of customers and goods: business was booming. There were no more Jewish merchants, but the Poles had taken over and were zealously pursuing their new profession with success.

Observing the crowd more carefully, I realized there were many Jews. There were said to be some fifty thousand Jews on the Polish side, although that figure strikes me as inflated. Their eyes gave them away: they were full of grief and pain. They had lost everyone and everything; all they had left was life itself. But for how much longer?

At every corner, on Marszalkowska, on Nowy Swiat, and on every other busy street, informers lay in wait like spiders in their webs. Once they snared a victim, there was no escape. A ransom had to be paid, in money or jewels, or else they would go straight to the Gestapo, where they received a reward for denouncing a Jew. Many Jews perished in this way.

The largest number of informers was always on Marszalkowska. They stood on the street corners like prostitutes. But what they had for sale, at a high price, was the opportunity to keep on vegetating.

Suddenly, I saw a good friend of mine from school, the engineer Dobrzynski, a Jew like me, and an architect. We had known each other since childhood.

He and his wife were walking right beside me. He was a very handsome man, who didn't look the least bit Jewish. He didn't recognize me at first, but when I introduced myself he laughed heartily at my appearance.

In order not to draw attention to ourselves, we took refuge in a church, where we confided in each other. Dobrzynski was doing well for himself. He was working in a German architectural firm, and had never had a problem. Unfortunately, he couldn't offer me a place to spend the night.

As we sat there on the hard church pews and chatted, we lost track of time. It grew late, and the curfew was approaching. Dobrzynski had to leave. He didn't give me his address. That was the unwritten law on the Polish side: Jews did not give out information on their hideouts, which meant safety and life.

Dobrzynski was apologetic for not being able to put me up, so he offered me a loan, but I refused. I never saw him again. A Volksdeutscher from Lodz recognized him on the street and refused to let him and his wife go. He turned them over to the Gestapo. I only learned about it much later.

Meanwhile, after I parted with Dobrzynski and left the church, I stood on the corner of Marszalkowska and Koszykowa Streets. I had no idea what to do. I had nowhere to spend the night, and the curfew was approaching. In fifteen minutes, the street would be completely empty and all the doorways would be shut. Then the night patrols would come through and round up all the laggards. If they checked my papers thoroughly, I would be lost.

Where was I to go? The nearest brickyard was an hour away, and it was too late to get there by tram. The streetcars ran only until nine. It was too dangerous to go up to a concierge at random and ask for shelter for the night. I would instantly be suspected of being a Jew.

The hands of the clock on the street corner crept inexorably forward. There were only five minutes left. Was there really no way out? I began to dream of a hotel, although that might have looked strange: a grimy railway worker spending the night in a hotel.

In any case, the police made frequent checks on hotels, looking for Jews. With my forged identity card, I knew that if I fell into the hands of the Gestapo again I would not escape alive; miracles like Dr. Sonnenwald happen only once.

The street was almost deserted. There were only three minutes left. The hand on the clock seemed to have no pity on me as it continued its course. Suddenly, someone tugged my sleeve. Terrified, I turned around.

"Come with me, sugar. I'll cheer you up," a woman's voice

murmured. Standing before me was an old, careworn prostitute. I was able to get a good look at her, because it was still daylight.

She must have been well past fifty. She had a puffy face, sallow, wrinkled skin, black eyes without a trace of kindness but a deeply intelligent gaze, a full lower lip, and a double chin. She was curiously dressed for such a warm evening, in a thick brown coat, a long, winter skirt, and scruffy, heavy boots.

As I stood there observing her, I began to feel faint. Never, even in my youth, had I had anything to do with women like this. The look of this prostitute and even her smell repulsed me, but I had no other option.

It was better to go with her than remain alone out on the street. But what would happen when she realized that I was a Jew? Would she call the police right away? After all, these women had no morals, and in all likelihood no conscience either. . . . But I left with her, although I couldn't bring myself to touch her arm. That was how I met Roza Chmielewska.

23

She lived at 15 Koszykowa Street, in a building that had been partially destroyed by a bomb in 1939. On the second floor of the left wing, a small kitchen had remained unscathed, along with a maid's room, and a nice bathroom with white tiles and a toilet. The whole part of the apartment that faced the street had been destroyed. The door closed behind me and I was alone with the prostitute.

"Have a seat, Mr. Railwayman."

I sat down on a chair in the kitchen, which functioned as a living room. It was sparsely furnished, but unexpectedly clean.

"Do you want to stay just for a while, or for the whole night?" Roza asked. She was surprised that I did not reply at once. After a moment, I decided to put my cards on the table.

"I'm not a railwayman," I said. "Forgive me for having deceived you. I'm actually a doctor. I worked in the station until recently, but now this uniform is nothing but a camouflage. I'm a specialist in skin and venereal diseases. I'm sure you've met some of my colleagues."

I paused for a moment and observed her face. She was listening attentively, which reassured me, so I continued.

"I'm a Jew. The curfew was approaching, and I had nowhere to go. Please allow me to spend the night here. I will pay you. But if you prefer, simply throw me out onto the street. That will be tantamount to calling the police. . . . I have a wife and daughter. . . ."

"No," she responded calmly. "I know decent people when I see them; I have an eye for that. You may spend the night here with me, and I hope that nothing will happen to you."

Roza gave me bread and cold cuts, and some tea. I felt I could trust her so much that I told her all about my life under the occupation, especially my trials and tribulations on the Polish side.

"Under no circumstances must you go back to work at the station. It would be too dangerous. You'd better stay here with me for a few days, and then we'll see."

I warned Roza Chmielewska that I did not have enough money to pay her what I should, but she ignored my comment.

Just then, I noticed on her dressing table a greeting card with roses on one side. I turned it over; the other side was blank.

"If after the war you come to visit Doctor Edward Reicher in Lodz at 28 Poludniowa Street, you will receive a diamond ring or a gold wristwatch," I wrote carefully on the card. Roza tucked away this "voucher" with a smile, and we talked late into the night.

Roza was a rather primitive woman, but well versed in life thanks to the many years she had spent working as a prostitute. She scorned and hated men, but she had to make a living. This old rather unattractive woman still managed to find lovers.

Roza understood my situation, for she too was persecuted, an outcast from society. She knew exactly what it meant to live as an outlaw, which is why she decided to help me. She had a heart of gold. Roza slept on a bed in the kitchen, and gave me the narrow couch in the maid's room.

If she had customers during the day, she told me I should hide in the bathroom. For now, she put fresh linen on the bed and I lay down to sleep.

Early in the morning I was awakened by a loud knocking at the door. I jumped out of bed and began to dress. Roza got up too.

"Who's there?" she shouted.

"Open up! It's the police!"

Roza closed the door to the maid's room and put her finger to her lips, warning me to remain silent. I heard the heavy steps of two men, and tried not to move.

"What you want from me, gentlemen?" Roza asked energetically. "How dare you interrupt my sleep! Did I steal something from someone?"

"You practice fornication. You're a prostitute, and for that you owe a tax!"

"Shame on you. You won't get a *grosz* from me, you rogues!"

"In that case we'll report you and you'll end up paying twice as much."

"Beat it, you good-for-nothing lowdowns. All you want is your palms greased, you filthy pigs! You can forget all about your report. I'm the one who's going to do the denouncing here. Now beat it, or I'll throw a chair in your ugly mugs!" Roza thundered like a storm. My whole body was trembling. The cops walked toward the door behind which I was hiding.

"What kind of birdie are you keeping in there? We'd like to have a look at it. . . ."

Roza leant against the door. "That 'birdie' happens to be a German lieutenant, and you're lucky he doesn't understand a word of Polish, or else he'd show you where your money is!" Roza threatened them.

That worked. Swearing under their breaths, the policemen retreated. Roza bolted the door behind them, and when she saw they had left the courtyard, she came in to see me.

"Now you know how to deal with people like that," she said, breathing heavily, but with a triumphant smile. "The best system of defense is to attack. If I'd acted vulnerable or been polite, we'd both be done for by now."

24

Roza took good care of me. Every day she brought me the lunch supplied by the community welfare organization. In the afternoons and evenings I hid in the bathroom, because that was when she had customers, mostly young German soldiers.

She didn't speak a word of German, but love is a universal language. Roza's many years in the trade had given her great savoir faire, and soldiers who could have been her sons or even grandsons came to see her eagerly. They appreciated her, and perhaps even desired her.

One day, a German soldier, middle-aged, entered the bathroom without warning. He looked straight at me but saw only a railwayman. To smoothe things over, Roza brought out a bottle of brandy and the three of us polished it off. In order not to arouse his suspicion, I did not utter a word in German.

From that day on, if there was anybody in the house, I had to lie in Roza's bathtub and she would cover me with sawdust. I was almost drowning in it, with just my mouth and nose above the surface. I have no idea where she managed to obtain such quantities of sawdust, but when I came out I had to spend a long time cleaning myself off.

I often thought of Balzac's *Splendors and Miseries of a Courtesan* while I was hidden at Roza's. I felt sorry for her when sadistic customers beat her, which happened all too often. And so the days passed. I managed to let Pola know my circumstances; there was a telephone in a nearby café.

Pola decided to visit me, and good, warm-hearted Roza prepared a spread to welcome her. We dined well, and as we parted, Roza pressed some money into my wife's hand. Pola didn't want to take it.

"It's a pair of shoes for your little girl," Roza said gently. Pola was moved and took the money, asking Roza to help me find another hiding place.

Two weeks had elapsed from the memorable evening when I had first taken shelter at her house. One morning, she woke me up at five o'clock.

"I had a strange dream, Doctor," she said dolefully. "It was a dream of my whole life," she said. "It was terrible; I was laughing and crying. It didn't start with my life now. I saw the whole thing in reverse, from today back to my early years. I relived everything. First I saw my life as it is now, my life as an old whore. Then I was younger, and just like in the movies, I saw myself in a brothel from before the war, where we were completely dependent on the proprietress, a closed house where she kept practically everything we earned. Then the dream rewound some more and I saw myself as a bar girl in a charming area of Warsaw. There was a kind of balcony with little private booths where I would get a percentage of the check, especially on drinks. Then farther back, I was even younger and working as an entertainer at the Adria, the most elegant nightclub in Warsaw, as you know. Everything was going well with me; I lacked for nothing—I had rich suitors, money, and fancy clothes."

Roza fell silent for a moment, lost in her memories; she seemed suddenly sad, but then she continued. "Later, I was the mistress of a wealthy man, then of another and another, until I saw myself as a pretty, young provincial woman, arm in arm with my fiancé, who took me to Warsaw and then robbed me of everything before abandoning me here. I was ashamed to return to my family in our little village. I was too weak-willed to throw myself into an honest job, so I just kept falling lower and lower."

"And then?" Roza stopped, and a look of anguish crossed her face. "And then," she stammered, "I saw my mother, a good, kind, modest woman. In the dream we went into a church, and there were thousands of skulls, all swaying as if in a strange dance. My mother took me by the hand and warned me that I was in danger."

Roza looked at me, and I was sure she had really had this dream, because she was so shaken. "It's a warning, Doctor. Something terrible is going to happen. You need to leave right away. This is a true prophecy."

I washed, shaved, got dressed, and thanked her sincerely for her hospitality. Before going out the door, I reminded her of the promise I had written on her visiting card. That day nothing happened. But three days later, the Gestapo burst through Roza's door in the middle of the night, looking for a Jew.

25

It was too early to go to Countess Karczo-Siedlecka's, so I headed over to Lazienki Park. It was a beautiful morning. The trees and flowers gave off a delicious, fresh scent, and I recalled the magnificent Warsaw park of my student years. I sat down under an ancient tree and tried to think things through.

I could not return to work at Szczesliwice. It was too dangerous. Nor could I walk freely in the city; too many people from Wolska Street would recognize the Jewish railwayman.

I had thought about trying to procure the robes of a Catholic priest, which would have been the perfect camouflage. Pola had even asked Princess Woroniecka to find me a cassock, but that devout woman refused, considering it a sacrilege and an insult to religion.

So my thoughts turned to another angle. There were many Cossacks in Warsaw. They had sided with the Germans, and when their country had been occupied by Soviet troops, they had fled to the Polish capital. I downed a quarter liter of brandy with a Cossack I met on the street, and took the opportunity to try on his uniform: a short, leather coat called a *bekiesza* and a fur-lined hat. This get-up suited me. It was an excellent disguise, and made me unrecognizable. I asked the Cossack to find me such an outfit. I even gave him an advance, but I never saw either the money or the Cossack again.

At seven o'clock that morning I went to see Pola. She was afraid when she saw me and wondered what had happened. I told her Roza's dream. Pola got dressed, and after breakfast we went to see Princess Woroniecka. We were received by Jadwiga Turek, who smiled graciously and led us into the salon. Princess Aniela appeared soon after, her pale, delicate face filled with benevolence.

"You're in luck. My mother has left for a time to see my sick brother, Prince Lubomirski, so I can hide you. My mother would never have agreed to this, but you're welcome to stay until she returns.

"You will sleep in this salon, on the sofa. But you must never leave this room. We have visitors all day long: friends, relatives, tenants, and employees. They all expect to be received in the salon. For now I will see them in another room, but to be on the safe side, you will hide behind the armoire until curfew." The princess pointed to a beautiful Gdansk oak wardrobe standing in the corner of the room.

"I will never forget your kindness as long as I live, gracious Princess."

She brushed my thanks aside with a wave of her hands.

This woman who was risking everything for us considered her behavior absolutely ordinary.

Now a new chapter of my life began. All day I sat on my stool behind the Gdansk wardrobe, with a bucket for all my vital needs. In the evening the princess would bring a basin of hot water sufficient for me to wash and shave with. She herself emptied the bucket each morning and night. Aniela Woroniecka was an angel in human form. She was a woman who required nothing. Her whole life was devoted to helping others. She was the finest human being I've known in my entire life. Jadwiga Turek, the princess's housekeeper, kept me supplied with varied meals.

In the end, I found my own solution to the problem of my excrement. Of course there was a toilet, but I was not allowed to use it, for the housing office had recently billeted a subtenant in the Czartoryskis' apartment. She, too, was an aristocrat, but unfortunately a violently anti-Semitic one. Had she learned there was a Jew hiding in the house, there was no telling what might happen.

What was I to do then? Pola supplied me with vast quantities of newspaper, and I made up neat packages tied carefully with string. Pola collected them and threw them in the garbage. If for some reason she couldn't come, I would toss them out onto the sidewalk across the street in a wide arc—at night, of course. It was amusing to peek through the curtains at the passersby who thought they had come upon something valuable, and whose hopes were dashed when they opened up my packets.

I spent two months behind that wardrobe. I had only three books to read, so I read them over and over: the Polish translations of Feuchtwanger's *The Pretender*, Wilder's *The Bridge of San Luis Rey*, and *War and Peace* by Tolstoy.

I preferred *The Bridge*, because it raised the question of destiny. I could quote whole chapters from that book. In addition, the princess supplied me with the official German press as well as clandestine newspapers, which kept me apprised of the Red Army's advance. Needless to say, I was comfortable staying at the princess's, but I had to leave. Her mother was due back in Warsaw. Where could I go?

In the summer the brickyards were ideal hiding places, but in fall and winter it was impossible to stay in them. I looked out at the street from behind the curtains, and on Krucza Street I saw an old beggar lying in rags and filth on a drain pipe. Passersby rarely threw coins into his hat, but that miserable man had one thing I envied him: he could roam the city without fear. I, on the other hand, hidden in a princess's salon, well fed, was condemned to death and deprived of my freedom.

One day, a uniformed German officer, a quartermaster, walked into the princess's apartment. He had come to requisition rooms for German officers. He also came into the salon, studying the elegant furniture with interest. Behind the wardrobe, I sat and held my breath. He made conversation with the princess in German; they spoke about her family, and the Czartoryskis' connections with royalty. In the end he didn't take any of the rooms in the apartment. He probably just had a weakness for the aristocracy. He stayed for twenty minutes, but to me it seemed eternal.

Just three days later, Princess Woroniecka's youngest brother, Prince Adam Czartoryski, arrived from his country estate in Lesser Poland. He was the pride of the family, because he had five sons. Princess Aniela was out when he arrived, and he was unaware that I was there. After washing up in the bathroom, he walked into the salon to shave. He was in high spirits, humming, whistling, and talking aloud to himself on various subjects, chiefly the price of rye and potatoes.

For a long time I stayed motionless behind the wardrobe. At a certain point, however, I had to sneeze. I held it back as long as I could, but Czartoryski must have heard something.

He peered behind the cupboard and saw me.

"Out!" he said. "What are you doing here? Are you a thief?" He turned pale, began to tremble all over, and fainted onto the soft rug. I sprinkled water on his face and laid him on the sofa. He came to after a moment.

Just then, Princess Woroniecka arrived and explained to her brother who I was. He reproached her bitterly. How could she take a Jew into the house? This was dangerous not just for her but her whole family, even the tenant. They could all be held responsible. After all, the Germans had carried out mass executions on more than one occasion. "We're not anti-Semitic," he said, "but what you're doing is madness. I won't stay a moment longer. It's either me or the Jew." That was his ultimatum.

But the princess knew I had no other refuge. I remained in the apartment, and Prince Adam went off to a hotel.

Shortly after that, Pola lost her job with Countess Karczo-Siedlecka. A young man had knocked on the kitchen door one day and told her how attractive he found her.

"Well, I'm not attracted to you, so leave me alone," Pola said, and slammed the door.

The man would not give up. He knocked louder, then rang the bell. Pola opened the door a crack, with the chain still on, and then the man made it clear he knew she was a Jew.

"So you owe me a good time. . . ." Pola was wise to this.

"Give me a minute. I'll be right back. I have to get dressed," she said decisively. She quickly packed up all her things and left the apartment via the front door. Meanwhile, the young man was waiting for her outside the kitchen door, in back.

She never returned to Countess Karczo-Siedlecka's. She called to say that she had had to leave unexpectedly as her child had fallen seriously ill.

The countess complained to Princess Woroniecka about how unreliable the help had become, and that was that. After all, weren't people disappearing every day from Warsaw without a trace?

We never learned how the young man found out that Pola was a Jew. Perhaps he had seen her with me that evening in the crowd on Wolska Street.

So Pola, as Pelagia Jankowska, rented a tiny room in the Wola district in the home of a streetcar driver. He was unaware of her background; it later transpired that he was a Communist. Pola came to see me often, and we would sit behind the wardrobe and speak quietly about our future. The old princess Czartoryska was due to return shortly, and I had to find a new place to hide.

By sheer chance, Pola ran into her Aunt Hania on the street. Hania was relatively fortunate. She had been working as a maid for quite a while, and had managed to leave her little daughter with a sweet elderly woman. Hania's husband, Uncle Dawid, my mother-in-law's brother, had been killed during the liquidation of the occupants of the Hotel Polski on Dluga Street in Warsaw.

The story was that the Gestapo had sold South American citizenship papers for large sums of money, and then billeted the freshly minted Jewish "foreigners" in the Hotel Polski. A first transport had been sent to Vittel in France, from where glowing letters were sent back. This encouraged many wealthy Jews to leave their hiding places for the Hotel Polski.

All the subsequent transports, however, were sent straight to the gas chambers. This was how Uncle Dawid had died.

But Hania gave Pola the secret of a good hideout for Jews at 14 Walicow Street.

A Russian man, Sergiusz, was hiding a large number of Jews there. He agreed to take us both for fifty zlotys a day, but said he would accept us even if we couldn't pay that much.

Meanwhile, Pola fell into the clutches of some blackmailers on the street, a Pole and a Volksdeutscher. They recognized her as a Jew, because they had spotted her on Wolska Street. They demanded money, but she had none. The Volksdeutscher accompanied her back to her room. After searching it, he realized that she was truly penniless. He professed to be moved by her poverty, but nevertheless took the last *grosz* from her purse, as well as her wedding ring.

"You'll be fine," he assured her before leaving. "You can go on living here and nothing will happen."

But we had learned from bitter experience about this sort of reassurance.

Pola did not return to her room in the streetcar driver's apartment, but spent that night in the princess's kitchen.

When she returned to the apartment two days later, the streetcar driver took her aside and spoke to her in a whisper. "I don't know who you are," he said, "but last night a group of Gestapo officers came here looking for you. You'd better watch out."

Pola packed up her wretched belongings and never went back. What would have happened if she had trusted the *volksdeutsche*? Luckily, we had our new hideout with Sergiusz, and I no longer had to worry about the return of old Princess Czartoryska.

In fact, forewarned by her son, Prince Adam, she returned to Warsaw earlier than planned without telling her daughter she was coming.

Aniela Woroniecka had to shut her double windows so that people on the street and in the courtyard wouldn't hear her mother's screams. "How dare you hide Jews here and put the entire household at risk? Have you lost your mind?"

We were forced to leave at once. But first I expressed our gratitude to Princess Aniela, that noble soul, the greatest woman in the world.

26

It was dark, and we were wrapped in a gray October fog that protected us from the rapacious eyes of the informers. We arrived at 14 Walicow Street, where Sergiusz the Russian lived. No one saw us enter the building or take the elevator up to the third floor of the left wing. We knocked twice, as we'd been instructed, and the door to the apartment was opened by an aged woman. She placed her finger to her lips to signal silence.

She didn't say a word as she led us into a large room. Sergiusz emerged from another room. He was a tall, lean man with a small head. He greeted us and showed us the other room, whose floor was almost entirely covered with mattresses and sheets. Then he led us into the empty kitchen. A large number of pots and pans hung on the walls.

Sergiusz made some kind of sign to the old woman, Wanda, who was deaf. She said one word: "Free!" It was barely audible, but with that strange signal, the lower part of the wall hung with the pans and kitchen implements began to rise.

From their hiding place behind the wall, seven men, three women, and two children emerged. A superb refuge that even the craftiest Gestapo agent would never have detected. We introduced ourselves to one another. Pola and I understood right away that the existing occupants were hardly thrilled to see us. Now things would be even more cramped in the room with the mattresses, as well as in the astonishing space behind the wall. And of course there was the danger of being discovered, which would be greater if more Jews were hidden there.

A smile lit up Sergiusz's face when I admired his hideout. He said good-bye, and we all went into the little room. Sergiusz reappeared a moment later and announced: "From today on, besides Wanda, Dr. Reicher's wife will also open the door. She looks perfectly Aryan, and no one will suspect her of being a Jew. Wanda is a real Aryan, but she can barely hear, which has already gotten us into a lot of trouble."

That evening our comrades in misfortune told me more about our host. Sergiusz belonged to the old Russian nobility and had received a first class education. He was a devout member of the Russian Orthodox Church. His father was a wealthy man with enormous holdings in Stolin, then part of Belorussia, and a villa on the Crimean Sea. Sergiusz's parents had dreamed that he would choose a military career, and after graduating from grammar school and the Petersburg cadets' school, Sergiusz had been accepted into the Czar's personal guard. He had often stood guard at the Winter Palace in Petersburg, protecting the ruler of the Russian Empire. He had met the czar, who chatted willingly with the young officer. Back then, he had had numerous amorous adventures, which he still loved to recount.

He used to steal women's hearts. He liked to tell how whenever he saw a beautiful, well-dressed woman driving along the Nevsky Prospect, he would leap onto the running board of her carriage; no woman had been able to resist him.

At the start of World War I, Sergiusz had been at the front. Later, he had fought on the side of the Whites against the advancing Bolsheviks. When the Bolsheviks won, he had fled to Poland. Since Stolin had been within the borders of resurrected Poland after 1918, Sergiusz had led a carefree life. His father had also settled in Poland, and owned thousands of acres of farmland and forests.

Sergiusz had married in Poland, and had a son. Between the wars he had led the pampered life of a rich gentleman, spending more time in Warsaw than in Stolin. He had sold his share of the forests, and denied himself nothing.

Then came 1939, and Stolin was occupied by the Soviet Union. Sergiusz remained in Warsaw, while his family fled to England. Sergiusz himself was a member of a Belorussian Fascist paramilitary organization that supported Germany. As a former officer of the White Guard and a fanatical opponent of Communism, he was greatly respected within that organization.

But one of Sergiusz's grandmothers was Jewish, and the rabbinate had placed a curse on her for marrying a Christian. This was the main reason why Sergiusz felt a connection to the Jews. Their persecution by the Nazis upset him.

In July 1941, Sergiusz returned to Stolin, which had been occupied by forces loyal to Hitler a few days after the outbreak of the Soviet-German war. Once again, he became a wealthy landowner. He was there the day the Jews of Stolin were rounded up and marched into his family's ancestral woods to be shot. That experience had convinced him to help the Jews.

Sergiusz had always been very religious, and now came to believe that God had given him the mission of saving the Jews, for which he would be rewarded with salvation.

When it turned out that, despite his efforts, he was powerless to help the Jews of Stolin, he returned to Warsaw, which had the largest ghetto in Europe. He advised the surviving Jews of Stolin to follow him to Warsaw, where he would save them.

As a valued member of the White Russian organization, he was allowed to have two apartments, one at 14 Walicow Street, and another on Zygmuntowska Street, in the Praga district. There were Jews in hiding in both. Sergiusz often picked up Jewish children he found begging in the streets to keep them from falling into the hands of the German or Polish police.

In time, even among the hidden Jews, incredible stories began to circulate about Sergiusz, especially after he began to save so many little children.

In fact, there were multiple reasons for his behavior. Not only his attachment to his Jewish grandmother, but also his love for his fellow human beings, and his hatred of brutality, murder, and injustice underlay his actions.

If a Jew had nowhere to spend the night, Sergiusz would never turn him away, even if he didn't have a *grosz* to his name. Sergiusz accepted money from those who had it in order to help and feed those who had nothing.

Our host was a strange man, but I was very happy to have found him.

27

We stayed at Walicow Street for half a year. Fourteen people shared the living space: the Grynberg family, including their sixteen-year-old son, Bolek; a calm, reasonable man of twenty; Abbe, a wealthy industrialist from Lodz, and his wife; another elderly couple, the Czertows, who were quite intransigent and always sought the maximum comfort for themselves, provided it was at the cost of others; Kazik, a handsome eighteen-year-old from Kielce; Kleinzingow, a well-known Warsaw bookseller; Jozio, an eleven-year-old boy with strongly Semitic features; and Michas, a seven-year-old orphan with a beautiful, Aryan face.

We lived together by necessity, not choice. Our shared misery could have brought us together, but alas, such was not the case. We waged unceasing war. There were transient, cyclical friendships, enmities, allegiances, and cliques. Petty incidents led us to quarrel constantly and without dignity. We fought not just with words but also with our fists. We had all been so profoundly shaken, and we were in such a state of anxiety, that the least problem took on absurd proportions. It was as if we were living in a room full of explosives, into which we each continually tossed lit cigarette butts.

In normal times, while staying at a guest house in the mountain resort of Zakopane, we would have been the best of friends, but before arriving here we had all witnessed too many things, lived through too many catastrophes.

The worst of it was the continuing dread that we would be discovered. We never had a single tranquil day. Even our wonderful hidden room behind the wall gave us only a paltry feeling of safety, so that at every moment of the day and night we were prepared for the worst. Everything was fodder for disagreements and disputes.

Who was going to clean the house? Over such a question, quarrels and fisticuffs could be provoked.

Who would do the shopping? Again, huge arguments.

Who's going to cook today? Shouting and fights.

The men fought much less than the women. Mrs. Grynberg was almost pathological. Old Wanda didn't let us cook during the day, so all the cooking had to be done at night. The worst thing, however, was the fact that some of our number were sick—not physically, but mentally; not entirely normal. Old Wanda, the Aryan, was devoted to us, but she was in her second childhood.

Sergiusz was clearly unbalanced, too; one never knew what to expect from him.

Kazik, the youth from Kielce, had frequent nervous attacks that resembled the mild epileptic fits known as "petit mal." These would come on whenever he argued. For a moment he would lose consciousness and have no awareness of what was happening to him; he even foamed at the mouth. The fact was that within our little community everyone got on each other's nerves, and that our life together was unbearable. The fear of being discovered was driving us mad. There were no exceptions. The calmest of the group was Bolek.

Kazik, on the other hand, fell in love with my wife, and whenever anyone said a cross word to him, he would go pale with rage, start fighting, and his unfortunate illness would surface once again.

Kazik's brother Stefan, who was able to pass and was very brave, lived openly as an Aryan, without hiding. He kept us supplied with various paying jobs: rolling cigarettes, applying glue to envelopes, filling little bags with baking powder, and mixing a stain remover for clothes. But our primary activity was making soap. We used lye, mutton bones, and resin to make a good homemade soap for which Stefan had a ready market. The Germans issued green soap through their ration cards, but no one liked it. It was known as Jewish soap, because it was rumored to be made from the fat and bones of murdered Jews. . . .

Stefan provided us with all the basic materials and sold our products in the city. Work was a great distraction from our daily grind; it had a calming effect and allowed us to forget the danger bearing down on us.

Our greatest source of concern, however, was our host Sergiusz. "Two souls live in my breast," Faust said, and so it was with Sergiusz. At times he would have given his life, as he put it, to help us. But sometimes he was a hardened narcissist for whom nothing else mattered but his own personal pleasure, and at such times he would shout, "Death to the Jews, all the same!"

Since his unforgettable days as a guardsman in Saint Petersburg, he had been a skirt chaser; he was also a glutton. Whenever he came to visit us, he was more interested in the meal he was about to have than in anything else.

"What's for dinner?" was his usual greeting. We'd offer him meat, butter, cream and other delicacies we could never afford, since we had to be content with potatoes, kasha, and noodles.

Woe to his Jews if he didn't like the meal.

"Those damned Jews. The wretches don't even know how to cook. Useless nation of thieves, usurers and turncoats!" he would scream. Then he would be overcome with remorse and go to church, beating his breast in fierce despair and banging his head against the sacred stones of the church floor. It made no difference to him whether the church was Catholic or Orthodox, so long as he could cross himself.

Sergiusz was highly gullible and took everything he heard at face value. He reacted to things in a highly emotional way, without thinking, which often led to dangerous outbursts. If Sergiusz had used his mind, he never would have taken us all in.

When he was finally suspected of harboring Jews, he was beaten mercilessly at Szucha Avenue and in Pawiak prison, but he never said a word.

Still, his mistresses were as important to him as his Jews. Two souls struggled constantly within him: good and evil were locked in endless combat.

In the end his imprudence led us to the edge of the abyss.

28

Not a day on Walicow Street went by without fear. When anyone knocked at the door, either Wanda or Pola opened it, while the rest of us slipped into our hiding place.

"Is this where Mr. Kowalski lives?"

Someone had come to the wrong place, and we breathed normally again.

There was another knock. Wanda went to the door and we jumped back into our lair.

One day, the meter reader asked, "And exactly why do you need fifty pounds of potatoes if you live here all alone? The grocer told me about you, and it sounds a little strange."

Wanda was hard of hearing, and either didn't or wouldn't understand. The meter reader repeated himself in a loud voice, but Wanda did not reply. He finally gave up and left, but that's how we found out that people knew about us, and that people in the building and the neighborhood were talking about us.

One day, the opera singer who lived above us ran her fingers through the hair of our youngest resident, Michas, when we passed her on the stairs. "Your grandson's hair is bleached," she told "Granny" Wanda. "That child is Jewish." We were in despair, but what could we do? It was obvious that we were living there, but days, weeks, and months went by and nobody denounced us, even though the entire apartment complex, which was home to several hundred people, knew of our presence. Even the Polish prostitutes who received German clients in the same building did not betray us. We considered it a miracle, since Jews were being murdered every day. It was as if we were living under divine protection.

One night there was a violent knocking at the main entrance to the building. It had to be the Germans. We woke the children and dove for our hideout to await our final hour. But this time the Gestapo was hunting not for Jews but for Polish resistance fighters. They were going through the building door to door. We were forced to spend hours in our refuge. I couldn't help but think of the terrible days of the first ghetto uprising in January 1943, when a hand grenade exploded in the cellar.

Our anxiety increased our need to urinate, but we had only one chamber pot. It had overflowed, but we were in the dark and didn't notice. A thin thread of urine began to leak through the hinged wall of our hiding place into the kitchen, forming a small puddle.

When they reached our apartment, the Germans shouted orders at Wanda in German, but they left without noticing the tell-tale puddle. There was nothing we could do to wipe it up until we were able to come out. We had escaped all right, but by sheer luck.

29

Sergiusz was madly in love with Danusia Konarzewska. She was a classic Polish beauty: medium height, seductive, beautifully shaped, blond, and about twenty-five years old, with beautiful wavy hair and blue eyes. She was an attractive woman, men were drawn to her. She was not only with Sergiusz; she was a "courtesan." She met rich men on the street and in expensive restaurants, and accompanied them either to their homes or to secluded rooms in restaurants or hotels. She stole their money, their watches, or other valuables.

One day, she brought Sergiusz a man's Longines watch and asked him to sell it for her. She was afraid to sell it herself, since she had stolen it from a one-night stand.

Sergiusz sold it to a well-known jeweler on Wierzbowa Street, where he had to provide his name and address.

The men Danusia robbed did not normally report the thefts because they wanted nothing to do with the police. Most of them were married and were afraid of complications. But this time, the man who had been robbed reported his loss, and an investigation was launched. The watch was found at the jeweler's, after which a search began for Sergiusz, who was suspected of fencing.

And so it was that police detectives knocked on our door one fine morning. Pola opened the door.

"Is Mr. Sergiusz home?"

"No."

"Where is he?"

"I'm afraid I don't know. He went out."

"Who are you?"

"I'm his cousin," Pola lied.

"Very well. Get dressed. You're coming with us."

"But why?"

"You're under suspicion of stealing a watch."

"But this is ridiculous. I know nothing."

"We'll see about that."

Pola had to go to the police station. They searched her whole body, and of course found nothing. The apartment on Walicow Street had already been cursorily checked, but again, nothing was found.

While Pola was being interrogated by an inspector named Zaron, the rest of us remained in our hiding place.

He examined her identity card, then looked her straight in the eye.

"This card is fake." Pola turned pale and was visibly upset.

"Calm down, madame. I'm inclined to believe that you're a Jew, but I need to check; I want to be sure." He left the room. Pola was in despair.

Meanwhile, worried sick for her, I completely lost all self-control. I had no idea what had happened, because I had been behind the wall in our hiding place the whole time the police were at the apartment. Wanda, who had seen Pola on the street with the policemen, told me that my wife had been arrested. I was sure she was done for. I banged my head against the wall and the floor in despair. Then I ran to Princess Woroniecka's house on Nowogrodzka Street and begged her to sell some of our jewelry so she could ransom Pola back from the police. For a price, you could get anything from the Polish police; it was another story once the victim was handed over to the Germans.

Woroniecka had no contacts with the police force, but promised to do everything she could to save Pola. Half out of my mind, I returned to Walicow Street. And found Pola waiting!

The inspector had come back after fifteen minutes and confirmed that her identification card was forged.

"But that's of no concern to me. Another department handles that, and I have no reason to harm you. I'm returning your card. But now you're going to come face to face with the man whose watch was stolen."

The handsome, elegant man was taken aback when he saw Pola.

"This woman bears a slight resemblance to the thief, but it's definitely not her."

So Pola was released.

The real thief, Danusia Konarzewska, was apprehended shortly afterward, but unfortunately for us she was soon released, because Sergiusz paid for the stolen watch and bribed the police with a still larger sum of money.

Konarzewska was beautiful, but she was not very bright. She had a friend who was cleverer than she but ugly. Do beautiful women seek out the company of those uglier than they are, so that their beauty stands out?

Sneaky, cunning, clever Jadwiga Glos made a mint fencing things from Konarzewska. Danusia told Jadwiga everything; she kept no secrets from her. This is exactly what ultimately put us in such jeopardy.

One day or night, a drunk Sergiusz told Konarzewska about his Jews. She repeated everything to Jadwiga, who immediately saw a gold mine.

Under pressure from Jadwiga, Konarzewska demanded money from Sergiusz. He was hiding Jews, and they could give him what they had.

Sergiusz came to see us. First he ate copiously. Then he told us of Danusia's demands. He played down the danger, assuring us that his friend was a good woman, incapable of doing anything to hurt him. As soon as Konarzewska received a little money, she would leave us alone. Most of us, however, had had terrible experiences with blackmailers. We knew that if we gave in to her at all, her demands would never end. We knew nothing yet of the existence of Jadwiga Glos, for Sergiusz had not mentioned her. He thought his lover's demands were terrible, but in matters of the heart he was her slave.

It was already April 1944. The Soviet army continued its advance, and the Resistance slogan "Death to blackmailers and traitors!" was gaining ground. We, too, resolved to defend ourselves. Stefan had contacts in the Polish Armia Krajowa, whose clandestine courts issued death sentences to Polish and German agents of the Gestapo along with blackmailers and traitors. They would be shot by firing squad, and news of their execution would circulate in an underground Polish newspaper.

One bright spring day, Danusia was strolling along Krakowskie Przedmiescie Street, looking every which way for a suitable client. Two young men approached her and blocked her path. They told her they were from a secret organization, and that if anything happened to the Jews on Walicow Street, she would die.

Danusia was terrified and told Sergiusz and Jadwiga what had happened. Jadwiga told her to relax. She said the threats were empty, because the Jews had no way to carry them out.

So in the end Konarzewska came to us one day and demanded a huge ransom. She wanted a hundred thousand zlotys. If she didn't receive this sum within the week, she would report us to the authorities.

Endless deliberations began among us. The two older couples, the Czertows and Abbes, who were rich, were prepared to pay. But we prevailed. If we gave her money, we would never see the end of it. We still knew nothing of the existence of Jadwiga Glos, so we assumed that if we got rid of Konarzewska, that would be that. We informed the relevant people in the Armia Krajowa, but we also decided to take matters into our own hands.

We devised a carefully constructed plan; each step had been meticulously thought through.

With the pretext of handing over the ransom, we would lure Konarzewska into our apartment, kill her, hack her body into small pieces and make soap from it. . . . Such a plan could only have been born in the time of the Nazi persecutions and methods. . . . Today it seems like the product of a madman, but we were completely serious. We were prepared to do anything to save ourselves.

Stefan obtained sixty liters of lye, which partially filled the bathtub. Sergiusz knew nothing of our plans.

We waited impatiently for the great event. At some point, the true horror of our plan became so overwheming that I was unable to sleep at all for several nights.

During Easter week, Konarzewska went to visit her parents, who had a farm in a village a few miles from Skarzysko Kamienna. Exactly what happened during her visit we learned only afterwards, from Sergiusz.

In the middle of the night between Easter Sunday and Monday, armed soldiers from the Armia Krajowa appeared on the Konarzewskis' property. They dragged Danusia from her bed and ordered her to dress. Then they hitched a horse to a cart, and drove the girl into the woods. Her parents heard a series of shots. The next day, the horse returned to the farm alone. Sergiusz learned all this from Danusia's sister, who came to Warsaw to retrieve her sister's things.

I was greatly relieved that we had not had to murder Konarzewska ourselves, since she had been executed by decree of the Resistance. At that point we still didn't know about Jadwiga Glos, who was partly responsible for the death of Sergiusz's lover.

30

Sergiusz was in despair after Danusia's death. He was inconsolable and seemed adrift. But he soon forgot about her in the arms of another woman.

An anonymous letter left beneath our door gave us a dreadful shock. "In three days' time," it read, "we will come for the one hundred thousand zlotys. If you don't pay up, you will die."

Only then did we realize that Konarzewska had not acted alone. She had an accomplice or possibly accomplices, and this meant that our days at Walicow Street were numbered.

We all began the feverish search for a new hideout. Only Bolek and the two children, who had no money, had no choice but to stay.

Pola went to see Princess Woroniecka, but she could not take us in; her mother would not consent to it under any circumstances. Meanwhile, we were still at Walicow. One day, Jadwiga Glos came around. She was between thirty-five and forty, and had a pale, emaciated face. She claimed to have been sent by a friend of Stefan's, a very honest Aryan woman thanks to whom Stefan was able to survive on the Polish side. Still, we suspected that Jadwiga Glos must have known

Konarzewska. Later on, we found out that it was indeed Glos who had written the letter demanding the ransom. She made no mention of the letter, claiming rather that she wanted to help us, even take us in herself—of course, for a large sum of money. But we were suspicious of her and unwilling to take her up on her offer.

Meanwhile, threatening letters continued to arrive and drove us to despair. We had no way to know that they were all written by Glos with the sole purpose of forcing us to move in with her and to pay the princely sum of a hundred thousand zlotys "for finding you a hiding place."

Finally, after seeing our hesitation, Jadwiga Glos decided to use a ruse. She went to the concierge of 134 Walicow and told her that the Jews living with Sergiusz were a major threat to everybody in the building. The concierge, in turn, told this to all the other tenants, and people who had tolerated us and remained silent for so long now began to threaten Sergiusz.

We expected a visit from the Gestapo at any moment.

By this point, it was the end of April 1944. At six o'clock one evening, Sergiusz came to see us, sick with worry and out of breath. He closed the door behind him. He could barely speak, and his voice was hoarse.

"The Gestapo will be here any minute. Run, or else they'll kill us all. Flee while you can!" He paced the room, gesticulating nervously, and his eyes looked as though they would jump out of their sockets.

So we hurriedly wrapped our modest possessions in some towels, and one by one we abandoned our hideout. Sergiusz sadly watched us leave. Some people went to other places they had prepared in advance. Six others, including Kazik, had no place to go, so they opted for Jadwiga Glos's apartment on Zgoda Street. Bolek and the two children stayed behind in the apartment on Walicow Street.

Pola and I decided to go to see the princess.

"I'm terribly sorry, but I simply can't take you in. My mother will never consent to it, and I'm powerless against her."

"But we have nowhere to go, nowhere. No one wants us. Are we just supposed to die?" Pola sobbed.

In the end, the princess took pity on us. Pola stayed in the kitchen, while I, without the knowledge of the older Madame Czartoryska, was placed in a wardrobe in an unused room. It was narrow and so low that I had to sit to fit inside it. If I tried to stand up, my head banged the top. The minuscule cracks let in no light. I was the plaything of dark, despair, and fear when I was in that wardrobe. I had terrifying hallucinations, and I was half mad.

In order to gain some respite from the terrible reality of that coffin-closet, I escaped into daydreams that were like waking nightmares.

After the war, I told myself, I will travel from town to town in Germany and poison the wells with cholera and typhus bacteria. I imagined laying waste to that country of murderers, exterminating everyone. I wanted to see all of Germany reduced to stones, a land as bare as a moonscape.

Strangely enough, these nightmare visions were a source of solace, but in my rare moments of lucidity I realized I could not go on like this much longer. I was on the verge of delirium.

I begged Pola to do whatever it took to find us a place with Jadwiga Glos.

"We'll be like two turtledoves at Jadwiga's. Everything will be peaceful, and we'll just wait for the war to be over. I beg you, get me out of this wardrobe."

Pola could come to see me only when Princess Czartoryska was out, which happened rarely. When the princess was at home I had to stay in the wardrobe.

Pola had promised to go see Jadwiga Glos. They met at Gogolewski's café on Marszalkowska Street.

"You won't find a better place to live than with me," Glos assured Pola. "My tenants can wait out the war without worrying about their safety." But Pola didn't like Jadwiga Glos's duplicitous eyes.

When she told me that she couldn't trust Jadwiga, and that we couldn't live there, I was overcome with despair. Unstoppable sobs shook my body. I cried and laughed by turns, and when I calmed down a little, I realized that I couldn't stay another minute in the wardrobe.

But Pola had guessed right; she had not been taken in by Jadwiga Glos. That trickster of a woman had taken in nine Jews, among them a millionaire from Lodz by the name of Bielanowski, the Abbes, and Kazik. They had given her a fortune; some of them even gave her their jewelry for safekeeping. Once she had it all in her clutches, she turned them in to the Gestapo. The murderers arrived at Zgoda Street at five o'clock one morning.

"Come out, my pets, the Gestapo is waiting for you," Jadwiga Glos said, laughing. One by one, the victims filed out of their hiding place; poor Kazik had an attack, but that was neither here nor there. After an interrogation on Szucha Avenue, they were all shot to death in Pawiak prison.

We were lucky that Jadwiga Glos didn't know that we were living with the princess. Bolek and the children survived on Walicow Street. The Gestapo never went there.

31

It was Sergiusz who saved us. He had a second apartment, on Zygmuntowska Street. The entire building was occupied by Germans; Sergiusz had obtained his apartment because he was a member of a pro-German organization.

A German military guard with a sub-machine gun that the Poles called a "vaporizer" was posted in front of the building. I learned that this apartment had once been Sergiusz's and Konarzewska's love nest. Her death offered us a pathway back to life.

Before we moved in, Sergiusz had built a magnificent hiding place with the help of Byzek, the concierge—an absolutely reliable man, and a member of the Polish underground. Part of the living room was partitioned off with a brick wall. The entrance to the hideout was through the oven. Six of us lived there: Sergiusz, Pola and I, and the Grynbergs and their sixteen-year-old son, Marek.

Marek had undergone an operation to reconstruct his foreskin. Performed by a well-known Warsaw surgeon, this graft had been successful, and the boy now felt safer in his supposed Aryan identity. The Germans would not be able to prove anything. He was bursting with pride.

In this apartment, it was Sergiusz who opened the door; Pola did the honors if he wasn't there, while the rest of us would cram ourselves into the hideout.

Sometimes the German neighbors paid a visit to our host, but we felt safe behind our wall. I began to recover my morale and started writing down my experiences present and past. I felt more alert, and life weighed less heavily on me now.

I trusted my instinct, that "evil spirit" in my chest, which had never failed me.

From our hiding place we could clearly hear the voices of Sergiusz and his German visitors. This was how we picked up the latest news about the German retreats and the advance of the Red Army.

One day, Sergiusz was chatting with a German officer, drinking vodka. At one point, Grynberg made a clumsy movement in our hideout.

"Who's that in your kitchen?" the German asked.

"The mice," Sergiusz answered without skipping a beat.

There were no more questions. After all, how could anyone suspect a member of the White Guard, and an anti-Semite to boot, of harboring five Jews?

On another occasion, a German railway worker who lived two floors above us asked Sergiusz why his living room was so much smaller.

"There's nothing strange about it; the higher the floor, the thinner the walls, and hence your room is bigger. . . ." The neighbor believed Sergiusz. . . .

Meanwhile, Allied troops had landed in Normandy, and the Russians were eight miles from Praga, the right-bank district of Warsaw where we lived. We were sure our liberation was around the corner. Alas, we were mistaken.

Sergiusz often went to visit my brother's mother-in-law, Bronia, to whom I had introduced him. Bronia had lived for many years in Odessa, and the two of them loved to reminisce about old times in czarist Russia. Bronia was unwell. She had suffered from stomach problems for years, but she was now having frequent abdominal hemorrhages, and was in much worse shape than ever before. I desperately wanted to visit her, but Sergiusz would not allow it. It was becoming harder and harder to come and go from our house; there was a thorough document check whenever anyone came through the entrance.

Bronia's condition grew worse and she had to be hospitalized. She was operated on for stomach cancer, but died shortly after the operation. She was buried in a Catholic cemetery. There was nothing to be done. The plaque read: "Here lies Bronislawa Lozinska." Only a handful of people attended her funeral: Professor Zawadzki, Sergiusz, and Tomek.

So Bronia was dead, our dear Bronia who always gave all she had and asked for nothing in return. She died of a terrible disease without living to see Liberation.

32

July 31, 1944.

We had been living with Sergiusz for three months when he came home with the news: the Polish uprising in Warsaw was about to begin. The concierge warned Sergiusz that our building had been designated as the headquarters of the insurrection, and that there could even be combat in the building. They both advised us to return to Walicow Street. Happily, we all managed to leave the house without being noticed and made it back to Walicow Street, where Bolek and the two children were still living.

That same afternoon, on July 31, Pola and Jadwiga Turek went to get Elzunia from the convent in Miedzylesie. We were afraid there might be battles in Miedzylesie between the retreating Germans and the Red Army.

"Now all the bad times are over, and you'll be with us forever," I said, as I embraced our daughter.

In the streets of Warsaw, an endless procession of people who had collaborated with the Germans and now feared revenge was moving west: Ukrainians, Latvians, Lithuanians, Cossacks, and Hungarians. They were fleeing with all their belongings piled onto horse-drawn carts, along with their livestock, swine and poultry.

On August 1, 1944, Pola and Elzunia went to lunch with Princess

Woroniecka. At five o'clock that afternoon, the Warsaw uprising began, and fierce fighting erupted all over the city. Jerozolimskie Avenue, Warsaw's main thoroughfare, split the city into north and south. I was in the north, on Walicow Street; Pola and the child were on Nowogrodzka, in the south. Jerozolimskie Avenue was under heavy German fire and I had no way to get through to my wife and child.

There was fighting everywhere. I wanted to fight the Germans too, and I reported to the command headquarters, but they wouldn't take me. The battle belonged to the young. Nobody needed my hatred of the Germans. I also thought of offering to work in a field hospital as a physician, but something held me back from revealing my identity. So I simply took part in ancillary tasks, such as antiaircraft defense, digging trenches, and building barricades.

One day, some Polish partisans appeared in our house and asked us to help with some auxiliary work. Bolek, the young Grynberg boy, and I went willingly. The boy's mother didn't want to let him go, but he said: "I want to do something for the liberation of my country, too."

We went to the next street, Ceglana, where we dug trenches and built barricades. All around us we could hear the noise of rifle fire and exploding hand grenades. Some young soldiers were standing near us and sounding off about the Jews. They were clearly anti-Semitic, but naive young Grynberg boasted to them that he was a Jew. Perhaps he had not heard them talking.

"What are you talking about? All the Jews were turned into soap!" one of the group jeered.

"I was a Jew, but now I'm an Aryan. I had an operation," the boy said proudly.

"Marek," I whispered, "how could you say that? We still can't reveal our true identity."

"But we're in independent Poland now, and I have nothing to fear. . . ." Just as he said this, two soldiers grabbed him and pulled him to one side. One of them took aim and fired. Marek fell dead into the trench. I lunged at the soldier with my shovel.

"How could you, you piece of scum?" I screamed. My heart was racked with grief and rage.

"Fuck off or I'll shoot you, too!" the murderer shouted.

I ran to find the policemen who were posted at the corner of Walicow Street and told them that a minor had just been murdered, revealing nothing of his identity. Although a search was launched at once, it was in vain. In the tumult of the insurrection, the murderers had escaped. Bolek sat by the body, tears streaming down his face. The Grynbergs were destroyed. Marek was their only child.

33

The fighting continued, but it was hopeless. The new independent state of Poland was about two miles square; all it had to its name were rifles and the enthusiasm of its young combattants, who had to stand up to the onslaught of the German army.

The fighting near Walicow Street was intense. I lay flat on my stomach in the courtyard. The walls of the buildings all around me were pitted by gunshot and grenades. Bolek, the Grynbergs, Sergiusz, and the two children had disappeared into the cellars somewhere and I couldn't find them. When dusk fell and the explosions died down, I went downstairs. Staying close to the walls of buildings, I reached Sosnowa Street. I registered with the building committee at number 12, and stayed there for three weeks.

I tried to make myself useful. I carried water from distant wells, because we no longer had running water; I helped to bury the dead; and I performed first aid, claiming to have been a paramedic in the army. Only from time to time did I receive a bit of bread for some favor or another. There was nothing left to eat, and I had no money; we had left everything at Nowogrodzka Street with the princess.

In all my life, I had never felt such hunger. I became weak, and my legs began to swell. I lost thirty-five pounds and continued to grow thinner. My only hope was to be reunited with Pola. I prepared myself to cross Jerozolimskie Avenue via the tunnel that had been dug across it.

This tunnel, which was the only link between northern and southern Warsaw, was under constant fire from machine-gun snipers on the roof and in the windows of the National Savings Bank at the corner of Jerozolimskie Avenue and Nowy Swiat. As soon as I reached it I hunched down and ran the length of the trench, whose edges were protected only by sandbags. Bullets whizzed past me from all sides. The dead lay along the trench, along with others who were gravely wounded, who moaned and babbled with fever. A man running alongside me took a fatal hit. Finally, I reached the end. I dove into a cellar, then another, and at last I reached the princess's house.

Pola, Elzunia, Jadwiga Turek, and the whole royal family were all in the cellar taking cover from the bombs. They gave me something to eat. The princess still had some foodstuff tucked away. Only after lunch was I told that the schnitzel I had just eaten was made from dog meat; I had quite enjoyed it. All the horses had been eaten, and it was said that people were eating rats. Posses had been organized to hunt stray dogs for food. Man's best friend had fallen victim to his hunger.

34

The uprising continued. In order to break the heroic resistance of the Poles, the Germans brought in aerial bombers. This was a weapon against which the insurrectionists were powerless, because they had no antiaircraft defense. The civilian population paid the highest price for this.

The German high command allowed civilians to leave the city that was being strafed. On certain days, for a few hours, the firing let up, and one could then leave Warsaw along certain prescribed routes.

The Germans had their reasons for this. It allowed them to detain the youngest, ablest men and ship them as forced labor to Germany. I begged Pola to leave Warsaw. With a small child she would not be taken, and she would escape the bombings. In the end she agreed. She cried as she left, but a few hours later she was back.

"I couldn't leave you! It will be easier for us to survive together. . . ."

The bombardment did not let up. Two days later I was wounded in the head by an exploding bomb. Pola and I went to a first aid station. They bandaged my wound and prescribed some anti-infection pills.

On our way to the pharmacy we ran into our first blackmailer, the Polish policeman to whom Zygmunt the counterfeiter had betrayed our address on Nowiniarska Street. Now he was wearing the typical uniform of the Armia Krajova, light brown with blotches of camouflage. His arm was in a sling. He recognized me at once.

"Fancy seeing you again, Jewish railwayman. I thought you were long dead," he smiled without malice.

"I only survived by a miracle, and you pushed me right to the edge of the cliff, though you swore on your son's health . . ."

"I was severely punished for that. My wife and son were killed. A bomb fell on our house and the basement where they were hiding was completely buried. My boy lived for a few hours after everybody was dug out." The police officer–insurrectionist wandered off, lost in thought.

We entered the pharmacy. Just as I was handing my prescription to the pharmacist, people came running in, shouting "Bombs! Everyone take cover!" Then there was a terrifying crash, and the ceiling caved in. I tried to pull Pola toward me, but she had vanished somewhere in the cloud of dust. I felt a violent throbbing in my head and I passed out.

When I came to, I could not make out where I was. I looked around in a stupor. I was lying on a straw mattress among rows of other makeshift hospital beds. I tried to move, but in vain. I was bandaged from head to foot, and my head ached badly. All around me the stench of disinfectant, blood, and urine hung in the air. "Pola! Pola!" I shouted at the top of my lungs.

A tidy, remarkably clean nurse appeared before me. "Take it easy, Mr. Szewczak, your friend is well."

She grew hazy, blurry, and then disappeared, losing the outlines of her body.

"My friend is alive . . ." I thought, or perhaps murmured, and fell back again into a profound faint. When I came to a second time, the nurse was standing by my bed, holding a thermometer under my arm.

"Nurse, please tell me what happened to me."

"You were buried under the rubble of a house that was bombed. You were lucky that the rescue team found you alive. Now you're in the field hospital at 71 Marszalkowska Street. The woman with whom you were found, Mrs. Pelagia Jankowska, is your friend, is she not? She's in shock, but she'll be fine, so there's nothing to worry about."

"How long will I be here?"

"There's no telling. You were admitted for an unlimited period."

The nurse had to leave. I wondered if I had been recognized as a Jew. That fear never left me.

Days passed and my pain subsided. Pola was allowed to get out of bed. We spent a lot of time talking at my bedside. The senior doctor authorized Elzunia to stay with with us, so Princess Woroniecka brought her to the hospital herself, despite the constant shooting, bombardments, and intense street fighting. The uprising was near its end, and the resistance had lost. The city was in flames. But the fact that all three of us were back together again gave us heart, and we awaited future developments with hope.

I felt strong enough by then to take a few steps. But I was uncomfortable without my railwayman's cap, which I had lost in the pharmacy during the bombardment. Without it I felt ill at ease, because it was my cap that made me look like a real Aryan and gave me a sense of security. It was like one of those magic disappearing hats in fairy tales. Without that hat, my Semitic nose was all too obvious.

So as soon as I was back on my feet I returned to the pharmacy, which had been reduced to a heap of rubble. I spent a whole day searching for the cap without success. That evening, I returned to the hospital empty-handed.

I cajoled the physician for just one more day's leave from the hospital, and early the next morning I set out once more in search of my miraculous cap. And this time I found it! I dug down to the pharmacy counter, and beneath it lay my hat—dusty, squashed, misshapen, and filled with holes. To me it was like winning the lottery. I brushed it off, and when I put it on my head I felt almost happy.

35

After the collapse of the uprising, in the first days of October, all the residents of Warsaw had to leave the capital. A million people were driven from their city, allowed to take only as much as they could carry. This was the punishment for the uprising. The city itself was set on fire.

A few field hospitals remained in Warsaw, among them ours, at 71 Marszalkowska Street. There were frequent inspections by the German military authorities. One evening, a group of drunk German soldiers kidnapped all the young nurses. The girls returned a few hours later, pale, their faces streaming with tears.

I asked to meet with the medical director of the hospital. He was a trustworthy man who reminded me of Dr. Jankowski from Żyrardów. The well-being of his patients was everything to him. I trusted him entirely, so I confided in him that I was a Jew and a physician, and asked him to perform a partial reconstruction of my foreskin, so I could claim to have had it partially removed due to a recent lesion. A fresh post-operative wound would make the story credible.

I had experienced so many horrors because of my foreskin that I wanted to end them once and for all.

At first, the doctor refused, but after I pleaded with him, he agreed.

The operation was scheduled for the following morning. I was taken to the operating room and received a local anesthetic administered by the head nurse.

The surgeon had his scalpel in his hand when a junior physician walked in and said that a German medical inspection team had just arrived. The surgeon went pale, and the scalpel trembled in his hand.

"Cover him up and take him down to the ward," he said. The operation was never performed.

On October 17, 1944, our hospital was slated to be evacuated. All of Warsaw was burning. Special divisions were dousing house after house with gasoline and setting them on fire. The flames made the nights as bright as days.

There was a fine men's clothing store next door to the hospital. It too was due to be burned down. We asked the military chaplain for permission to remove various things from it. He consented, on condition that after the war we reimburse the proprietor for the things we took.

The injured and sick broke into the store and took whatever they wanted from the stock of elegant, expensive merchandise, much of it imported. I wanted a bolt of English wool for making men's suits, but when I picked it up it was too heavy. Instead, I took several dozen neckties and hundreds of bow ties. They would prove very useful down the line . . .

The next day, we were loaded onto German military trucks and driven away in an unknown destination.

36

We headed west. Behind us, the Polish capital was in flames. The caravan stopped in Piotrkow, a small town not far from Piastow. The vast hangars of the Tuder car battery factory were being used to house the evacuated Hospital of the Holy Infant Jesus from Warsaw. It was run by Germans, but the physicians were Poles, and the nurses were Polish nuns. Our field hospital was absorbed into this hierarchy.

No one in this huge hospital complex suspected us of being Jewish. Pola passed as the wife of a Polish officer being held as a German prisoner of war, and I was the railwayman Jan Szewczak, with a huge mustache, a dirty black uniform, and a battered railwayman's cap. Officially, I was Jankowska's man friend, which people couldn't understand.

"What's such a pretty young woman doing with a down-and-out railwayman? He's a good-for-nothing, filthy bum, and you're such a beautiful woman, Mrs. Jankowska."

"That Szewczak's a good man," Pola would say. "It's true you can't expect too much of him, but he brings in the coal and does whatever he can for me. After all, I've a child to think of."

That would stop them for a while, and then they began all over again. But Mrs. Jankowska had no intention of ditching her dirty railwayman.

By now Pola had been discharged from the hospital and was working in the kitchen. I was still being treated, and I had to lie in bed when the doctors made their rounds. When they were gone, I would dress and go to the marketplace in Piastow, where I sold the ties I had taken from the store in Warsaw. "Ties, ties! Neckties and bow ties! Buy them while you can!" I became well known in the marketplaces of Piastow, Wlochy, Milanowek, and other villages, and was able to support my family on the money I earned. We had not eaten so well for a long time.

Meanwhile, the Russians were pushing forward and the front was approaching.

Blackmail became less frequent. Life was easier than before, but the Polish people continued to be anti-Semitic. Still, in my railwayman's uniform and cap I felt as safe as if I were in an underground bunker. I had become a true Aryan: courageous, proud, daring, and always ready for a drink.

The nuns in the hospital thought highly of me. I was always first at morning and evening prayers, and crossed myself assiduously throughout the day. The devout women were delighted by my religious fervor and held me up as an example to the other patients.

One day, a man came up to me in the local market. "Szewczak, I'd like to have a word with you," he said. He was a small, lean man with sunken cheeks, and his cunning eyes gleamed beneath his heavy eyelids.

Was he a blackmailer?

I now carried a knife, a real dagger, which I had bought at the market. The louder the Russian guns became, the harder it was going to be to blackmail me.

We sat in an inn on the square in Piastow. The modestly dressed man placed a bottle of brandy on the table and drew two shot glasses from of his pocket. "L'chaim!" This Hebrew word was also used by Poles. My suspected blackmailer gave me a knowing grin.

"Don't worry, Szewczak, you have nothing to fear from us."

"Who's 'us'?" I asked.

"The Party."

"Oh," I said quietly.

"You'll be given money, and you'll distribute it among your co-religionists." He slit his vest open with a pen knife and pulled out a wad of dollar bills.

"Give each Jew ten dollars a month. Don't carry information on you; keep it well hidden. If you can keep track of your accounts by memory, don't write anything down at all."

From then on, I distributed money among the Jews in the hospital in Piastow. The money came from British parachute drops.

37

There were thirty patients on my ward, among them a number of intellectuals who were still alive even though, according to Hitler's plans, they were soon to be exterminated. The Germans had broken the resistance in Warsaw, and they had torched the city and exiled its people. Even so, Polish hatred was directed mainly at the Jews. Was this because the Germans had provided such a steady flow of anti-Semitic propaganda for so long? Whatever the reason, on my ward in Piastow, the Jews were still the main topic of conversation.

The Jews were to blame for everything. From poisoning wells to committing ritual murder, nothing had changed since the Middle Ages. In the minds of many of the patients on my ward, the Jews were like evil spirits who wandered the earth with the intention of bringing misfortune on humanity. If there were no Jews, the world would be carefree and happy. There would be no murder, crime, war, or disease.

Hitler, Goebbels, and Streicher all spoke through the mouths of my fellow patients. Their slogans had filtered into popular speech. It was evident that Goebbels's propaganda had been effective.

"The Jews are Communists."

"The Jews are capitalists."

"The Jews are imperialists."

"The Jews are slave traders!"

"Jews rule the world!"

"The Jews are millionaires!"

And, repeated ad nauseam, "The streets belong to the Poles, but the houses belong to the Jews."

"The Jews caused the war!"

"That Jew Julian Tuwim dares to be the greatest Polish poet. . . ."

"Jewish capital has taken over America!"

"The Jews use the blood of Christian children to make matzoh!"

And so on, endlessly. Not everyone contributed to these conversations, but nobody protested.

I lay in bed and had to listen to all this in silence, night after night. One evening, a new arrival, Professor Szmurlo, a middle-aged man, sat down on his bed. He was the head of an ear, nose, and throat clinic in Vilnius and, as I was to learn, a valiant man.

"Permit me a word."

The talk died down.

"My good men, I would like to set certain fundamental matters straight. In every nation there are all kinds of people, all sorts of characters. That is the case among us Poles, among other nations, and also among the Jews." The professor cast a long, slow look around the ward. Nobody interrupted him, so he went on: "There are both good and bad people, decent men and scoundrels, just as there are tall men and short, fat men and thin.

"'To call a whole people evil only proves the limited intelligence of whoever says such a thing. As a physician and as a professor of medicine, I have had much contact with Jews, and I've rarely met an evil character among them. But they exist. It's only understandable, for the Jews are human beings too, and have all the qualities and faults of the human race.

"My respected Jewish colleagues were doctors of the highest level, both medically and ethically. Some Socialists were of Jewish origin; the Jews always fought for the betterment of mankind. And how much they did to advance science and art! You have no idea on whom you're passing such unreasonable judgement. You have no idea about the Jews."

Professor Szmurlo fell silent. He looked around, as if attempting to penetrate the minds of those blinkered men with his gaze. For a moment there was absolute silence, but then they started up again. They were not to be convinced by any arguments or truths. These people actually preferred to be deluded. In a sense, they needed their beliefs.

The old professor had placed himself in grave danger with his speech. There was still no shortage of informers. But I would like to think that even the traitors there recognized his courage.

38

There were many Jews hiding in the hospital in Piastow. When they were discovered, they were taken out to be shot next to the garbage heap or against a wall. In their hunt for Jews, the Nazi authorities organized an examination of all the patients. Everybody had to stay in bed, and the sentries at the entrance to the hospital were reinforced.

I had actually discovered a small gap in the outer wall, but it was impossible to escape. There were so many sentries and patrols, and besides, I had nowhere to hide in the town. So I prepared to defend myself with the story about the operation on my foreskin.

The moment of truth arrived.

A physician in a white coat entered the ward. He was of medium height, with a round face and a thick mustache. I could not believe my eyes. It was Dr. Plockier, the famous Jewish gastroenterologist from Warsaw. I knew him well; we had seen each other in the Warsaw ghetto. And he was the one assigned to inspect our Aryan credentials—he, who was surely as circumcized as I was! He went from bed to bed. He stood by my bed and smiled faintly. The corners of his lips twitched impishly, and then he moved on to the next bed. How in the world had he wound up working for the Germans as a trusted Aryan physician? In any case, that was one of the most remarkable personal encounters in my life.

After the war, Dr. Plockier became a professor of gastrology at the Warsaw Academy of Medicine, renowned throughout Europe in his field.

And so I passed my test of "Aryanness," although other surprises still awaited us. Pola was working in the hospital kitchen, and the director was pleased with her. But she began to suspect that Pola was Jewish. The worst of it was that she and her adult daughter began to openly speculate on "Jankowska's" true identity. Rumors made their way around the hospital. I boldly went to the kitchen and took them aside for a talk.

"You've been spreading rumors that Jankowska is a Jew. I am a member of the Party. We are right on the front. In a few days, everything will change. Keep in mind that if anything happens to

Jankowska, you will not survive the war." The two women turned crimson. They stammered excuses, and I knew we had nothing more to fear from them. But by this point too many people were gossiping about Pola, so I also knew I had to find a safer place for her and our child.

At the marketplace I had made the acquaintence of Grundkowski, another railwayman. I confided in him that I had a lady friend who was looking for a place to live. Grundkowski knew a policeman who slept in the stationhouse but also had a room somewhere in the city. This room was available for rent. It was a small, dirty attic room with sloping walls and a little window in the roof that let in scarcely any light or air. Aside from a narrow metal bed and a broken wardrobe, there was nothing there at all. Pola and Elzunia moved in.

39

Now, every day after the doctors' morning rounds, I would dash off to Pola's attic. Christmas was approaching, and we were invited to the Grundkowskis' for Christmas dinner. There were several other guests, and the atmosphere was festive. We exchanged good wishes over the traditional Christmas prayers, ate plentifully, laughed, and drank brandy. We sang carols and drank toasts to our homeland, and to our victory over the Germans.

Our host, a kindly, jovial man, took Pola to one side.

"Mrs. Jankowska, your friend Szewczak sways when he sings like a Jew in the synagogue. He must be Jewish."

"What nonsense, Mr. Grundkowski! I ought to know better than you whether he's a Jew or not!" Pola laughed.

The party continued, but the suspicion remained.

After Christmas, we heard a heavy artillery cannonade, which comforted us.

But even as we awaited liberation, the Germans launched a large-scale hunt for Jews, especially within the hospital, where patients' records were gone over with a fine-toothed comb.

One of the office workers, who was also a member of the resistance, filled me in on what was happening. He also tipped me off about another planned examination of the patients, this time to be performed by German doctors.

The examination began in the ward next to mine. They found a Jewish man there disguised, like me, as a railway worker. He was in hiding with his wife and six-year-old daughter. A family exactly like my own. I knew them. They were very brave. They were shot on the garbage heap on December 31, 1944. I took this as a warning and decided to flee.

It was New Year's Eve. A frigid wind blew in my face. At six o'clock in the evening I walked toward the hospital gate, which was locked. I had to go for broke. Three elderly German soldiers from the Landwehr were warming themselves by a cast iron stove in the gateway guard post.

I had once downed a bottle of brandy with one of them, a Silesian who spoke Polish.

"I'm off to get some vodka for New Year's Eve," I said, pulling two empty bottles from my coat pocket. "The New Year deserves a toast!"

The soldiers laughed.

"So long as one of those bottles is for us," the Silesian said. "But make it snappy. We need a drink too."

"Of course. One of these will be for you." They never saw their bottle. I ran through the snow straight to Pola's attic.

40

I ran up the stairs and knocked on the door. We fell into each other's arms.

"I'm sure we'll be free in just a few more days," I said.

Suddenly we heard footsteps. Then there was a knock at the door. "Who's there?"

"Szwaryszewski," came a quiet male voice. Pola opened the door. In came a tall, dark, handsome Jew, one of those to whom I delivered monthly aid. He had been a journalist in Lvov, where he wrote for the well-known daily, *Chwila* (The Moment).

"What do you want?"

"I want to stay with you. You must say yes," begged our unexpected guest with the intelligent eyes.

"But there are too many of us for this tiny room," I said.

"I know you will survive. Nothing will happen to you; you have a small child."

"Very well, you may stay, but you'll have to sleep on the floor." Now we were four.

At eight in the morning there was a knock at the door, but we didn't move. The knocking grew more insistent. Pola sat up in in bed.

"Who's there?"

"The landlord."

"What do you want?"

"I left a jacket in the wardrobe. I need it."

"I'm not dressed yet. Come back in half an hour." The footsteps receded. Szwaryniewski and I tiptoed down the rickety stairs and headed to the marketplace. We went to sit in a smoky inn, where we downed a quarter-bottle of brandy. That raised our spirits.

Just then, the worker from the hospital office who had tipped me off before came and sat down at our table. He looked around cautiously and then whispered to me that the Germans had come looking for me in the night. The soldiers at the gate who had been waiting for their vodka must have turned me in. As soon as he got up, I told Szwaryniewski that we had to get out of Piastow.

We left the inn and stepped out onto the market square. A farmer's cart with rubber tires, to which two horses were hitched, was parked in front of the pharmacy. A young lad of perhaps eighteen came out of the pharmacy and proudly surveyed the cart.

"Good horses. Go like the wind."

"Where are you from?" I asked.

"Kotorydz. I came to buy some medicine for my mother, and now I'm going back."

"We need to get to Piaseczno. We'll pay you well if you'll take us."

"You must be from Warsaw, right?" the young man asked.

"Yes. But we have our family, and some luggage. Will you take us?"

Half an hour later we drove off together into the unknown.

41

The cart rolled on in the direction of Turczyn. A low sky with streaks of clouds weighed heavily above us. It was freezing and looked as though it were going to snow.

We chatted about this and that. I mentioned that we were planning to rent a room in Piaseczno.

"Why Piaseczno? Come live with us in Kotorydz. There's plenty of space in our house And there's fresh country air."

"What will your parents say?"

"My father's dead, and my mother does what I tell her."

I accepted his offer.

Just ahead of us on the road, a uniformed German came into view. He lifted his hand as a sign that we should stop. The cart pulled to a halt. The horses were panting and their breath filled the air with white steam.

It was an SS man with a death's head on his cap. He wanted to hitch a ride. We kept our cool. The SS man scrutinized us carefully, but because of the child he suspected nothing. He traveled a few miles with us, and when we dropped him off, he thanked us politely. We drove on along a deserted road. We saw neither vehicles nor people. The fields now slumbering in snowy solitude were shortly to be plowed up by grenades and dyed with soldiers' blood.

At last we drove up to a farm. The boy offered us fresh milk and thick slices of bread. It was a relief to be somewhere so peaceful, away from the constant gaze of Germans.

Pola, the granddaughter of a Jewish peasant, knew all about farming, and she helped the boy's mother with her chores—milking the cows, feeding the chickens, and cleaning the house. We had money enough, because I sold my ties in the neighboring villages. As a last resort I had a twenty-dollar gold coin, which I had hidden in a bar of toilet soap made during our days on Walicow Street. A lot of people had washed their hands with that soap in the hospital, but it was still nice and round.

On Sundays we went to mass at the village church, and after church

I joined the merry drinking session at the inn. The roar of cannon fire drew closer by the day.

42

Nothing had changed with the Germans; there was nothing to indicate that they were in retreat. As late as January 14, 1945, they were still rounding up young men in the surrounding villages for labor in Germany. But news of the Russian advance came from every direction.

One day, I went to the village store in Kororydz for a bottle of alcohol. There were a few men drinking at the counter. I recognized one of them as Rundberg, an old friend of mine from Lodz who had taken the Aryan name Czerwinski. I had known him since childhood. He had won more than one hand in poker by my side.

I struck up a conversation with him, but he didn't recognize me. We chatted about recent events. I threw something into the conversation about Lodz, and Czerwinski took me for a informer. I teased him for another few minutes. When I finally told him who I was, we fell into each other's arms. In the excitement over our imminent liberation, we drank too much.

I dragged myself back to the farm, losing one of my boots along the way. When I got home, I told Pola and Elzunia that better times were coming. "You can both stop calling me Mr. Szewcak." Then I collapsed into a deep sleep.

That afternoon, some German soldiers walked into the house and ordered our hostess and Pola to cook them some food. They urged them to flee before the Bolsheviks arrived, but the peasant woman said she wasn't leaving her farm. I heard nothing of all that. Not even the roar of the cannons disrupted my sleep. To be on the safe side, Pola, Szwaryniewski, and the boy hid from the Germans in the barn.

I awoke early the next morning. I crawled out of my haystack toward the barn door. It was well below freezing, and the sky was a pale blue. Snow covered the fields as far as the eye could see, and not a single sound broke the silence of that winter morning. The noise of war had stopped.

Suddenly, I saw the steel hulk of a tank that was grinding its way through the snow on its chains as slowly as a snail. When I saw the Soviet star, I ran toward it. I paid no heed to the threatening mouth of its cannon. A Soviet officer was climbing out of the beast.

"Thank you, sir, with all my heart, for liberating us!" I said in Russian.

"There are no 'sirs' among us," the officer replied, drumming his chest with his two fists to keep warm.

This was the moment of my liberation, on January 17, 1945, in Kotorydz, near Turczyn.

Part IV

THE ENDLESS ROAD

1

We were free. The period of fear and disguises was over. But what exactly freedom would mean was not yet clear to us.

For the time being, we wanted to return to Lodz so we could rebuild our lives.

The Russians occupied Lodz on January 19, two days after we ourselves were liberated, but rail transportation had still not been restored. Military vehicles refused to take us, because they said they were heading straight to Berlin.

According to the soldiers, Berlin was to be occupied and Hitler captured in a matter of days. We were supposed to wait patiently in our village.

Back in Piastow, in the hospital, the tide had turned. Russian soldiers were shooting informers who just days earlier had been handing Jews over to the Nazis.

Our young host drove us back to Warsaw in his cart. The left bank of the city had been burned almost to the ground. The city was dead, filled with ruins and huge piles of rubble. Here and there, a few lone, partly destroyed houses were still standing.

But in the former ghetto, not a single residential building had survived. There wasn't even a trace of where the streets had been. It was a sea of rubble. I tried to find 42 Muranowska Street, where I last lived, but the street no longer existed. I went back downtown, to the corner of Nowogrodzka and Krucza Streets. There I saw the home of the Czartoryskis princes, which was almost intact, although everything around it had been destroyed. Could that mean that the Military Headquarters had been installed there? In any case, the Czartoryskis were not in Warsaw; they had gone to the prince's estate in Lesser Poland.

I heard military music and walked toward it. On Jerozolimskie Avenue, outside the Hotel Polonia, a group of Soviet generals were reviewing the parade of the victorious army, including the Polish Army that had been trained in Russia.

The soldiers marched in step, bundled up against the cold. They had all kind of weapons: both light and heavy artillery.

It certainly felt like a conquering army. The Germans looked the same when they streamed into Zwardow in 1939. I went up to one of the commanding officers and asked him in Russian what he could tell me about Lodz. He said it had been liberated two days earlier practically without a fight, and that it was undamaged. He advised me to try to get there in a military car.

Since my attempts to do so had failed, I sliced open the bar of soap that held my last gold dollar coin and traded it for seven five-ruble gold coins, which were known as piglets. Only a few days after the Soviets marched into Warsaw there was already a thriving black market at the intersection of Jerozolimskie and Marszalkowska Streets. A Russian army driver pounced on my coins and offered to drive us all the way to Lodz. We left in his truck at six o'clock that evening. The Russian stopped constantly along the way to ask if we were close to Berlin. He thought we had already left Poland. He wanted to be the first to arrive in Berlin so he could capture Hitler in his bunker.

2

We reached Lodz at night. Our truck pulled up on Liberty Square, where the Tadeusz Kosciuszko memorial had stood before the Germans blew it up. The night was cold and it was snowing. I had waited for five years; five years during which I had longed for this moment and lost all hope of seeing it.

I was back in the place of my birth. We said good-bye to our driver, who was so naive and in such a rush to reach Berlin, but a fine driver nonetheless. He headed west again down Piotrkowska Street, toward Pabianice.

We walked to Poludniowa Street, where I was born and where I had spent almost my whole life. My father had lived at number 4 until his marriage in 1885, when he built the house at number 28, where my older brother was born. This street was the story of my life.

At the corner of Poludniowa and Wschodnia Streets, revolutionary fighting had broken out in 1905 between Polish workers and Cossacks. Here, barricades had stood and blood had been spilled. I had witnessed those events when I was five years old. Seeking to deflect the blame, the czarist government had organized pogroms against the Jews, recruiting members of the feared Black Hundreds, who incited the locals to pillage. We closed all the shutters in our house, and our driver, Stanislaw, stood guard outside the nursery, armed with a huge iron pickax.

Here, at number 11, was the home of the Pidowicz family, famous for the exploits of their beautiful daughters-in-law, who were such interesting characters that they became the talk not only of all Lodz, but of Paris and London as well.

Number 13 was Mr. Witnoski's store. He was not just a pharmacist, but also a passionate medic and barber. People called him Doctor. He had a huge belly, bulging eyes, and a beard in the style of Napoléon III. His son had become a physician, and had been my colleague.

Number 19 was occupied in its entirety by the Society for Aid to the Indigent Sick, known as Linas Hacholim. Here, for ten years, I had treated people of limited means, and it was here that my fame as Lodz's leading dermatologist was born. It was here, in 1939, after the war began and before the ghetto, that the Jewish community organization had its offices.

Across the street, in number 20, was the famous building of Lachomonowicz, where my first love, fifteen-year-old Janka W., often spent time. I used to wait for her there; she floated before me in a cloud of purity. She suspected nothing until the day I brought her a vase of white lilacs for her birthday.

Farther down, at number 24, the old Hubel family had lived for decades. The father taught Jewish religion in the secondary schools; his son, my friend, was the man who was shot at the beginning of the war in Zwardow.

In number 25, on the second floor, lived Rabbi Segal, hunchbacked, bandy-legged, and saintly. It was he who had married us in 1935. Pola had kissed him on his hump. He was the first to be seized by the Germans, who paraded him in an open car dressed in his prayer shawl and holding his phylacteries, to be mocked and jeered at by the mob.

Further on, set in a beautiful garden, number 26 was the villa of a famous Lodz publisher and bookseller, Ludwik Fiszer. For some reason, we boys from number 28 waged a war for years with the Fiszer children, using stones as our weapons. Later, once I was already a physician, Chaim Rumkowski, the future "king of the Jews," lived there.

During our brief nighttime stroll down Poludniowa Street, my entire life flashed before my eyes, as in a kaleidoscope. Now I stood outside my family home, which looked the same as it had before the war. I rang the bell. Nobody answered. I was holding Elzunia's hand and shielding her from the cold wind. We were tired but free. We no longer had to fear the Polish police or German soldiers. There were no curfews or false papers to worry about. Freedom, that splendid word, was our most prized possession. Can anyone who has not experienced slavery know its true meaning?

I knocked so long on the door to our house that my hands hurt. An hour passed. We were standing in an empty street, with the door to my birthplace shut before us. Finally, there was a creaking sound and we heard footsteps. A man's voice muttered incomprehensible obscenities, and the door swung open. There stood Matusiak, the concierge, with a flickering kerosene lantern in his hand. He was dressed in greasy, fetid rags. His face was furrowed, his hair ruffled, and there were puffy bags under his eyes. His mouth was toothless, his lower lip drooped, and his nose bulged. He stank of alcohol and stuttered. He recognized us right away, and stared at us with evident displeasure, barring the door. He had held on to his job and escaped all the storms of history.

"Jesus! Mary! The doctor has survived, with his wife and child. And all this time I kept a close watch on this house, as if it were the apple of my eye, . . ."

"We'd like to come in," I said, unable to keep my voice from shaking.

"You can't stay here," he said, blocking our way still further.

I was overcome with rage, and pushed the drunken man aside. We crossed the yard in silence. I looked up at the window on the second floor, where I had been born forty-five years before.

"There were Germans living here all through the war, but now they've left, and the house is almost empty," Matusiak said. Then, in a shrill voice, he shouted, "And you'll have to pay me for protecting the house all that time!"

"It's not as if the Germans could have put it on their backs and carried it off," Pola said without turning around. Her voice contained all the venom she felt towards him.

Matusiak had robbed us.

He hadn't allowed my father to take everything with him, and now he was demanding a fee for his loyal service. Like all concierges, he had always lived in a small apartment next to the front door, but now he had taken over a three-room apartment on the third floor. He didn't want us to spend the night, and didn't even offer us a glass of tea. So we took the back stairs up to the fourth floor. My heart was pounding. I knew the sound of every step, just as an old violinist knows the strings on his instrument. Childhood memories swept over me. Here, on the fourth floor, had lived my inseparable friends Dyzio and Oskar Rozental. We were never apart. For Dyzio's confirmation, I had given him a beautiful collection of Mickiewicz, Pushkin, and Lermontov.

When we reached the top, we knocked at the door of a little room where we had noticed a light. The door opened, and there was Jozia. A smile lit her careworn, still beautiful face. Jozia had once been my mother's faithful maid. She did her best to make us comfortable in her tiny room. I noticed a small antique bookcase that had belonged to my father, the one that had held the work of Heinrich Heine, because of which a Nazi soldier had knocked my teeth out at the very beginning of the war. Jozia had taken it to her room for safekeeping. After the war, I left it to her as a memento.

That night at Jozia's, I was unable to sleep, and I did not sleep for many nights afterwards. My tortured thoughts would not leave me.

I had survived every disaster with a single aim: to head off catastrophe for myself and my family. So long as I had a clear, well-defined goal, that was all I saw. Despite the heartbreak and discouragement,

I had stayed on the path I needed to travel and I had kept walking straight ahead.

But now I had achieved my goal. Would I find another?

3

The naked walls of my father's house stared back at me. Nothing remained but memories. My parents' bed was still in their room. This was where my bedridden mother had spent seven years until her death. I saw it with the eyes of my soul, because this vast apartment was now cold and impersonal. I was lost in the vibrant, piercing past. The present was empty.

During the German occupation, a Hitler youth organization had been billeted there. The secret cache of silver in the pantry had been plundered; the niche in the wall was empty. My memories were so invasive that I lost all desire to stay in that building, which nonetheless belonged to me. We moved next door, to number 26. Here, after Rumkowski, a certain Poppe, an SS officer who had seized the electrical store that belonged to my brothers, had lived throughout the war. Among his papers, I found SS decorations signed by Himmler himself, and documents that testified to his participation in SS training programs and in concentration camps. God only knows what crimes that man committed.

On our second day in Lodz, I paid a visit to the Jewish Council. There, no one was willing to believe that I was Dr. Reicher, or even a Jew. All they saw before them was a typical Polish railwayman. I was forced to seek out people who had known me before the war. Of the two hundred fifty thousand Jews in the Lodz ghetto, about eight hundred Jews remained. Shortly before liberation, mass graves had been dug for them, and they were awaiting execution by firing squad when they were saved at the last minute by the arrival of the Russians.

Even tears eventually run dry. Nature protects itself. I could not keep crying.

I walked up and down the city. On Kilinski Street I ran into an old German I had known before the war. He owned a building. I engaged him by telling him certain facts about his life. I could tell that I had hooked him. He was dying of curiosity. Finally, I told him who I was. The effect was shattering. He just didn't want to believe me. My survival could not penetrate his spirit.

After that I went to the Reicher synagogue. It was piled to the rafters with sacks of salt. My father had built this synagogue to the glory of God. He died of hunger in the Lodz ghetto. But his was the only Jewish house of prayer left in Lodz; all the others had been razed by the Germans. The foundation laid by my father had survived the barbarians. My father had sensed this, repeating that his synagogue would not be battered by the coming storm.

There is a legend about the Tzadiks, the holy men who live among us, who are known as the Just. There are supposed to be thirty-six. No one knows their names, but it is they who determine the greatness and enduring value of an epoch. When I think of the Tzadiks, the deeply spiritual face of my aged father appears before my eyes. Yes, the image I have of a Tzadik is the image of my father.

Every act of worship by a devout Jew begins with bread and salt. After the ritual hand-washing, a piece of bread is broken off and dipped in salt, and then the devotions begin. And in fact it was salt that saved the synagogue.

I went to see the Jewish Committee and asked them to take back the synagogue and restore it to its former use. The new Polish authorities and the American Joint Committee pledged the necessary funds, and the synagogue became even more beautiful than before the war. A commemorative plaque in my father's honor was set into the eastern wall, in the exact place where he used to pray.

The days passed, and we tried to settle down in our new apartment. But we were unable to recover our furniture, our carpet, our silverware, our linen, and all the other things I had given people for safekeeping. Some things had vanished along with the people I had given them to, while others had been confiscated by the Germans; some people were simply dishonest. My paintings had been siezed by the German authorities. All I got back were my medical diploma and a tuxedo that Pola turned into a regular suit.

One day, as I walked along a crowded street, a sled piled high with wooden planks full of nails skidded on the sidewalk and tore my pants. My whole pant leg was ripped, and my bare leg showed through. Two Russian soldiers who had witnessed the accident hid me between them. When I told them I was a doctor they took me to their superior, a captain, who was ill. Thanks to my skill as a physician I was able to buy myself another pair of pants. In Lodz shortly after liberation, food was very scarce. We lived on rations from the Soviet military base.

I wanted to see the house in the ghetto where my father had lived and died. Depressed, I wandered down the filthy, smelly streets. There was really nothing left of the house. It had not been bombed or burned down, but it had been so thoroughly stripped by scavengers that only the bare walls remained, with no windows, doors, kitchen, or stoves. I looked for photographs or other mementos, but there was nothing.

But in the mansion on Wolborska Street where Dr. Rozowski had lived, I found his family photographs and papers, and even his medical diploma. I took them with me. The house was empty, but it had not been sacked. But when I returned ten days later I found it in the same condition as my father's. Scavengers had taken everything apart and stripped it down to its foundation.

One night we heard a hammering on the door. We were free, but the terrible times we had lived through had left an enduring mark on our psyches. Besides, the war was not yet over. I calmed Pola down and opened the door. Before me stood a tall, red-headed Soviet soldier about twenty-five years old, with a long, red face and a fearsome gaze. His face was filled with anger and cruelty.

"Are you Reicher?" he asked in German, with a Jewish accent.

"I'm Dr. Reicher." I saw the soldier's anger turn into rage.

"Good. If you're Reicher, you're going to die!" He slammed the door and stepped into the room. I drew back. He stood in front of me, his rifle aimed straight at me.

"What is this supposed to mean?" I asked, in Russian.

"You're Reicher. You're German, and I'm going to shoot you and your whole family!"

"I'm Jewish!"

"You can't fool me. You're German. You and your whole family are going to die, because you murdered my whole family. I the only one left alive." The soldier's face was full of pain and hatred.

"I'm circumcised!"

"Anybody could have had that done."

I recited the "*Shema Yisrael*," the title of a prayer and also the last words of the dying. "Anyone can learn that," the soldier insisted.

But I continued. "*Adonai Eloheinu, Adonai echad, Baruch Shem. . . .*"

The soldier's face changed, and he froze. He threw his gun on the floor.

"Forgive me," he said in Yiddish, and wrapped me in his arms.

I took this lonely, devastated young man into our living room, this boy who was the only one of a large family to have survived the war. He turned out to be the youngest son of Baruch Weiss, the owner of a large grocery store in the old market square in Lodz. The Weisses used to buy sugar from my father.

The soldier had fought as far away as Moscow. When he finally reached home, not a single member of his family remained alive. He wanted to take revenge on the Germans and thought I was to blame. We ate, drank, and told each other everything we had been through. We talked all night. Day had long since dawned, but the lamps were still burning in our house.

4

In Lodz, the city I had missed so much, and where I knew every last little lane and alleyway, I felt like a stranger. We were sometimes assailed by the most peculiar fears. We might be sitting in a café, with music playing, people dancing and having fun, when we would suddenly notice someone staring at us. It was that unmistakable gaze: they had recognized a Jew. And although we knew that the nightmare was over, and that they could no longer hurt us, we would quickly leave the café, hail a cab, and go home. This fear remained with us for many years. Even now, it is still there.

Our friends, acquaintances, and colleagues were no longer in Lodz. What had become of them? Dr. Klinger, a tall, handsome man, author of a well-known book, *Vita Sexualis*, was a close friend of mine. We used to see each other every day. On the first day of the war the Germans assigned him to hard labor: paving roads. There wasn't a moment's respite. In 1939, he fled to Grodno, which still belonged to Russia. When the Germans occupied Grodno in 1941, he and his wife took cyanide.

Dr. Trepman, a kind, honest soul, felt safe among the workers at the *Werterfassung* in the Warsaw ghetto, the institution that collected the assets left behind by Jews who were deported. Dr. Trepman believed that as physician to the workers of that official German institution, he was irreplaceable. He would stroll about in his white coat among the workers who came to see him with their medical problems. One day, during a major roundup, the Germans confronted him.

"What are you doing here?"

"I'm the doctor for the workers at the *Werterfassung*."

"We don't need a doctor here. You'll be more useful at Treblinka."

And Dr. Trepman went straight to the gas chamber.

The youngest of the three was my friend and assistant, Dr. Henrykowski. Short, lively, and gifted, he was an able physician and also the composer of several dance hall hits. Even now, on the radio, I occasionally hear one of the tangos he composed. During the war, Henrykowski married an Aryan woman, his sister's governess. They fled to Lithuania. There, in a small town, the local people tied them up and threw them alive into the Niemen River.

That is how my closest friends perished. And I survived. Life was a blessing, but also a burden. I felt the chill and emptiness of a world that seemed to me like a vast cemetery.

I rarely went back to our house at 28 Poludniowa Street. The shadows of the past tormented me too much there. The friends of my youth, the children of our tenants, all the Szpigiels, Finkelsztajns, Mondszajns, and others—where had they hiden? How did they die? Not one of them returned. I loved my native city, but I was all alone there. Sometimes I went to the movies or to the theater, but among all those thousands of people, I didn't see a single familiar face, a single friend, a single acquaintance. I might as well have been in Milan, Athens, or Oslo.

5

But fate gave me the chance to repay my debt of gratitude to those who had saved my life. One lovely day in the summer of 1946, Roza Chmielewska turned up at our door out of the blue. We received her like a princess. She was much better dressed and made a much more favorable impression than she had during the war. We sat on the balcony of our house and reminisced over old times. Roza had brought the calling card with the roses on it, which was my promissory note.

"What would you prefer, Roza? A gold wristwatch or a diamond ring?"

"I would prefer cash."

I called up a watchmaker I knew and found out the price of the best bracelet watch that could be had in Lodz at that time. A Schafhausen with a fashionable gold chain cost eighty dollars, which was a hefty sum in those days. So I presented Roza with the equivalent amount, rounded up, in Polish zlotys.

I was pleased to be able to repay her, if only partially, for what she had done for me.

"If you ever need more money, don't be shy. Just let me know," I said.

I could never have imagined what Roza would do with the money. She opened a brothel. She hired several women, although that was illegal at the time. She ran that business for a long time, greasing the palm of the local policeman in charge of her neighborhood; he would look the other way for money. But when that officer was replaced, she had to deal with his successor. Unfortunately, the new man pretended to accept one bribe, then reported her and took the money to his commissioner.

The prosecutor brought charges, and Roza was sentenced by a Warsaw court to one and a half years in jail. She appealed.

Since Warsaw was completely destroyed, the Warsaw court of appeal had been transferred to Lodz, and it was there, at 1 Kosciuszko Street, that her case was heard.

I took a day off from my job at the hospital and appeared before the judge as a witness for the defense. I testified in detail about how I had met Roza on that unforgettable night in 1943, how self-lessly she had hidden me, risking her own life, bringing me food, and even giving me money to buy shoes for my little daughter. The judges and the prosecutor were moved by my story and the court-room fell completely silent. In effect, I proved that I was to blame, because I had given Roza money without advising her how to use it wisely. Roza's attorney, one of the best in Warsaw, had little left to do. She was acquitted.

We celebrated in the Raspberry Room at the Grand Hotel, the best restaurant in Lodz. That afternoon Pola and Roza went to the hair-dresser's, and Pola bought Roza some nice clothes. Roza looked like a real lady. I ordered champagne to accompany our dinner. After-wards, the lawyer and I took turns dancing with Roza and Pola.

Roza shut down her brothel a year later. She got married. She brought her husband to meet us. He wrote to us frequently when Roza was sick, and on several occasions I sent money to Pruszkow, where they lived. I continued to help them out financially for many years.

When Roza fell seriously ill and had to be hospitalized, I contacted the head of the department and asked him to take special care of her. Soon after that she was released.

One day, Roza wrote asking me not to send any more money or parcels, because I had done enough for them in exchange for the two weeks that she had hidden me. She said that her husband had been writing to me behind her back, and was drinking away the money I was sending.

6

The Czartoryski family and Princess Aniela Woroniecka were dis-possessed by the Polish government. They were assigned one small room in their house on Nowogrodzka Street in Warsaw. Whole fami-lies were billeted in each of the other rooms. There were also prosti-tutes who received their customers in this ancient home, along with a number of rowdy children. It was a collective apartment known as a "kolkhoz," an instant hell that led to constant, serious conflicts. The tenants helped themselves to the antique furniture and stole everything they could get their hands on—linens, bedclothes, the contents of whole wardrobes, and jewelry. The three dignified women of the aristocracy put up no resistance.

The elder princess Czartoryska, who was related to various royal families, was unable to withstand this decline in their fortunes and soon died. Aniela Woroniecka remained as virtuous as ever, always ready to help others and sacrifice her own well-being. One day, she noticed a sick woman lying on the sidewalk. Despite her own limited straits, she took her into her small room and nursed her for months until the woman died.

Although she was past forty, Woroniecka resumed the medical studies she had begun before the war. She had exhausted her funds, so I helped her financially until she was finished. Today she is a respected bacteriologist. Not only did she earn a living, she also helped the rest of her family. She lived in the "kolkhoz" for nearly twenty years. In the end, she and her sister, Maria Czartoryska, were able to buy a small cooperative apartment on the outskirts of Warsaw.

In 1945, I bought a grocery store on Wschodnia Street in Lodz with an apartment behind it for Jadwiga Turek, the Czartoryski family's housekeeper who had placed Elzunia in the convent. In the immediate aftermath of the war, business was booming, because there had been nothing to buy during the war. But Jadwiga still had a hard time staying afloat.

Vodka was sold officially in state stores that were closed in the evening, exactly when demand was at its peak. Mrs. Turek started selling alcohol from her small room in the back of the store, and sometimes her customers would consume it on the premises. The police were soon onto the scent of her illegal drinking den, and during a raid, they seized two liters of pure spirits. Formal charges were filed. I saved Jadwiga Turek by issuing her a doctor's letter prescribing twice daily alcohol rubs for a chronic skin condition, and the matter was dropped.

This was somewhat dangerous for me, but how could I refuse to help a woman who had risked her life to save my child? I'm indebted to the chief of police in Lodz, whom I had treated as a patient, for not having suffered any consequences. Jadwiga Turek didn't have all her marbles, so she didn't learn her lesson. She continued to sell vodka; it was easy money. Unfortunately, she was caught again, but this time, despite my contacts in Lodz, I could do nothing to help her. Since the jails were overcrowded, she was sent to Mięlecin, near Włoclawek, a labor camp for those convicted of financial crimes. When winter came, she caught pneumonia. She recovered, but from that time on, she began to have heart trouble and developed signs of a persecution complex.

Thanks to my contact with the camp physician, I succeeded in having her exempted from hard labor, and she was transferred to the kitchen. Finally, with the help of the wife of the health minister, Sztachelski, president of the League of Women, I managed to obtain her release from the camp. Minister Sztachelski's wife was so moved by my account of how Turek had rescued my daughter that within a few days Jadwiga Turek was back on Wschodnia Street in Lodz. In the meantime, however, her premises had been broken into and someone had set up a mechanics workshop in her store. Turek instigated a court battle with them that dragged on for ten years, but she failed to have them evicted; her own criminal record worked against her. In the end, Turek set the whole place on fire, and she was sent to an institution for the mentally ill.

7

Sergiusz, our host and defender, voluntarily left Warsaw during the uprising. He was transported to the Reich to do hard labor. The work was difficult, and for the first time in his life he was doing something he would never have done otherwise. When he was liberated by the British at the age of fifty, he began to study philosophy in Innsbruck and later in Italy. He moved to England with the Polish Army.

Consumed with remorse, he would go to church just as he had in Warsaw. He banged his head on the tiled floors and crossed himself hundreds of times. But even the holy water from Lourdes that he poured on his head could not free him from his demons.

Through all the years of persecution, neutral Poles—those who neither turned Jews in to the authorities nor did anything to protect them, who were the vast majority—used to say that only a madman would try to hide a Jew. A normal man wouldn't risk his life or that of his family. This was certainly true in terms of Sergiusz, who was clearly mentally disturbed.

Sergiusz was a despot to his Jews, but he hid them at great risk to his own life. He loved to rail and rant about the Jews, but he saved us, and he paid for his good deeds by being tortured in Pawiak prison. I did everything I could to ensure that he received reparations from the Germans so he could live out his days in peace, free of financial worries.

8

After the war, Ignacy Fuks, who lost his wife and son in Falenica, filed charges against Mucha and his sons, who had betrayed his loved ones to the Gestapo. Alas, he could find no credible witnesses. There were numerous eye-witnesses to the execution of his wife and son, but there was no way to prove that the Muchas had been the ones who turned them in. Gniewkowski, to whom Mucha had complained for finding him a Jewish tenant, would have been an ideal witness, but he was dead. The Muchas denied all responsibility, even under oath; thus, they were innocent. Their crime went unpunished, and they continued to live comfortably in Falenica.

Similarly, Stefan Kotecki, the brother of poor Kazik, who died after being betrayed by Jadwiga Glos, brought charges against her. The few remaining relatives of her other victims joined his lawsuit. Stefan Kotecki was a man of great integrity and energy, and he made sure that Jadwiga Glos was arrested. As with Mucha, however, there was no way to prove her role as an informer to the Nazis. Jadwiga Glos went free.

Moreover, in 1945, immediately after the war, there were many dishonest and corruptible officers working in the Polish Security Office. Jadwiga Glos had large amounts of looted Jewish money. That may explain how she managed to escape judgment and the gallows. Besides, a number of important witnesses in the case had died, and others had moved to foreign countries.

Many Jews who survived the occupation in Poland lost the will to keep fighting and abandoned the search for those who had informed on them.

Jerzy Lewinski, a lawyer and officer with the Jewish Police, who led thousands of Jews to the Umschlagplatz, among them Korczak and his children, had the gall to join the Party and became a prosecutor in the District Court of Lodz. He handed down sentences of prison terms and death, even setting former Nazis free. How could anyone trust such a character? Several lawyers brought charges against him. The well-known pianist Władysław Szpilman* and I were the chief witnesses in the case, which was heard in Warsaw. I was approached by several of his colleagues and friends, some of whom I knew, who asked me not to accuse Lewinski, who had a ninety-year-old mother. Some of them even threatened me. Others held that after such a terrible war no one should accuse a Jew.

I told the whole truth, and Lewinski was debarred as an attorney. No criminal case was ever brought against him, however. He lay low for a few months, but then he started to climb back up. Eventually, he ran the Polish film company, Film Polski. Where is justice in all this?

Zygmunt, the counterfeiter from Jagiellonska Street, continued to drink and forge documents well into the war. One day, however, he was arrested by the Gestapo. He went crazy in jail. Going without vodka was worse for him than being locked up. He died in Pawiak. His wife told me the story when I went to visit her after the war.

9

In 1946, I was tired and sick. Only now was I beginning to feel the full effects of the horrors and persecution I'd experienced during the occupation. In order to have a rest, I went to the resort of Sopot, on the Baltic. Little had changed there. The casino was gone, but the roar of the sea was the same as before. It was a beautiful summer.

We stayed in the Grand Hotel, formerly the Hotel Casino. One evening, standing in the lobby not far from the reception desk, I was

---

* On whose memoir the movie *The Pianist* (2002) was based.

approached by a drunk. He was an English officer, a captain in the British merchant marine, as it later transpired. He was of medium height, stocky, very powerfully built, with an energetic red face. His hands closed about my neck. He screamed in English that he was going to strangle me, because I was a Jew. The hotel porter and a few other men who happened to be in the foyer at the time managed to free me from the captain's grasp.

At that time, the British were fighting the Jewish underground army, the Hagana, in Palestine. They weren't letting the few Jewish survivors of Hitler's pogrom into the country. I reported the incident to the citizens' militia in the port, Gdynia, where the British ship was berthed, but they brushed it under the carpet.

The pogrom in Kielce in 1946 came as a terrible shock to me. In liberated socialist Poland, this was a massacre of Jews who had survived the war. When I examined the wounded survivors in a Lodz hospital, and when I heard about the vicious murders and other horrors that had taken place in Kielce, I decided on the spot to leave Poland. I sold my house in Ruda Pabianicka for a fraction of what it was worth. I had spent my best years there, and during the dark days of the occupation I had dreamed of spending the rest of my life there. It was only a dream.

The persecution of Jews in resurgent Poland became more widespread. The new socialist institutions in the provinces, especially in the villages and in rural areas, had not yet consolidated their authority and were unable to protect their few Jewish residents, who were pitilessly murdered by anti-government hordes. These were Jews who had returned to their home provinces after surviving the horrors of the concentration camps, only to find death. Generally speaking, the conduct of the anti-communist resistance was essentially anti-Semitic. Armed bandits would stop cars and buses, and if they found any Jews, would shoot them on the spot. The stories so familiar from the occupation were beginning all over again: men were being forced to lower their pants. . . .

We decided to visit my wife's birthplace, Dabie, on the River Ner. A few miles from town, in Chelmno, we noticed crowds of people in the fields and woods. What was going on? Men, women and children from the nearby towns, and some from more distant villages and hamlets, were digging and sifting the earth with large sieves. There had been a death camp there under the occupation, where Jews were gassed and incinerated. Now the site had become a new El Dorado. People were panning for gold. They found gold dentures, jewelry, gold coins . . .

In my quest to leave Poland, I sought an exit visa several times. I was turned down, on the grounds that Poland had a shortage of doctors, since the Germans had murdered most of them. In 1948, Jews around the world breathed a sigh of relief: the State of Israel had been born.

I continued my attempts to emigrate, but my applications were rejected time after time. Not until twelve years later, in 1960, was I allowed to leave.

10

After the end of the war I wrote a brief account of my wartime experiences and deposited it with the Jewish Historical Institute in Warsaw. During the Eichmann trial, the activities of Hermann Höfle came under close scrutiny and my testimony was discovered. It turned out that in 1947 the Allied authorities in Austria had extradited Höfle to Poland as a war criminal, but Höfle had managed to jump off the train and for fourteen years had lived peacefully with his family in Salzburg, where he had prospered as the manager of a large food store. He was not arrested until 1961. He was jailed so late because another war criminal by the same name had been hanged in Yugoslavia, and it was thought that Hermann Höfle had already been punished.

As one of the main witnesses for the prosecution, I was sought in several countries. I was finally located in Germany, where I had settled after leaving Poland, and received an invitation to go to Austria. With my expired Polish passport it wasn't easy to obtain the necessary visa. In the meantime, one of the foreign embassies received a secret message to the effect that an attack on me was being prepared in Salzburg, where there were strong neo-Nazi organizations, so the Austrian authorities guaranteed me police protection.

On the train to Salzburg, I was unable to sleep.

In my mind's eye I was reliving my encounters with Hermann Höfle. I saw the headquarters, the strange delusional dreamer Leon, the tens of thousands of inhabitants of the Warsaw ghetto herded to the Umschlagplatz, Dr. Korczak, and his orphans. . . .

Only now had justice caught up with Höfle. . . . Only now was he being called to account for the extermination of more than three hundred thousand people. I was traveling to Salzburg as the representative of all those who had been gassed and incinerated in Treblinka, killed in the ghetto on the Umschlagplatz, or suffocated to death in the cattle cars carrying them to the concentration camps. I had become the accuser.

The prosecutor was waiting for me at the station. For reasons of security, a police officer was assigned to follow me everywhere like a shadow, and I had the use of a police vehicle.

My confrontation with Höfle took place on October 26, 1961. I had previously been shown over a dozen photographs of different people to make sure I could identify Höfle; I did so without hesitation. The prosecutor and I went together to the prison, which adjoined the Austrian district court in Salzburg. The judge warned me that Höfle had a nervous condition due to the recent death of his young twin sons.

Hermann Höfle was greatly changed. Twenty years had tarnished his elegant allure. He no longer looked so sleek and smooth-skinned. He had put on weight. His face was bloated and pale, his eyelids were puffy, and his eyes were dull. This fifty-one year old man, who looked much older still, now scrutinized me carefully and declared that he had never seen me before. I told him that I had treated him for a skin disease, and pointed to the place on his scalp where he still had a scar.

"I would never have allowed a Jewish physician to treat me, but if it was a skin disease I can't rule it out. . . ."

That was his confession.

Before coming face to face with me, Höfle had read my deposition and declared it to be false. "You had no need to hide on the roof," he said, "All you had to do was ask, and I would have issued you a safe conduct pass." Even though he knew that the discovery phase would be followed by a trial, he expressed no remorse. At no point did he ever admit his guilt.

"I would not be sitting here before you if I had done what you just said; in other words, if I had trusted your phony safe pass," I replied. Höfle looked uncomfortable.

"I never killed anybody. I never heard any gunfire in the ghetto. I never saw any bodies, and I never issued any orders to have people killed."

"I can't state that you personally killed anyone. The dirty work was carried out by your subordinates. But I do know from officers of yours who were my patients that you gave the order to kill Kohn and Heller. Besides, I was there when you ordered one of your officers to cleanse certain streets of Jews. As for shots in the ghetto, you have to have heard them, because I heard them myself from up on the roof. I also saw the bodies of those who had been murdered, even though I had a very limited field of vision, while you moved freely all over the ghetto."

Höfle grew increasingly nervous. "I did nothing wrong to the people who worked for us at headquarters. Besides," he added, "the Jews volunteered to go to Treblinka. They went willingly." He was evidently thinking of those who allowed themselves to be "bribed" with some crumbs of bread and jam. I could barely contain my fury.

"Klara is alive, and she too will tell the truth," I fired back at him.

Höfle's face went crimson, and his whole body began to shake. The prosecutor broke off the confrontation, and the prison doctor was called. Höfle drew back, and looked at me wide-eyed. I never saw him again.

According to the official accounts that appeared in the newspapers, Höfle hanged himself in prison with strips of torn sheet. This occurred seventeen years after the end of the war, and twenty years after his activities in the Warsaw ghetto. Did that coward really take his own life? Personally, I doubt it. Perhaps someone helped him, because they feared his dangerous confessions. There were plenty of Nazi criminals still at large about whom Höfle knew too much. His death would hardly have upset them.

11

I searched for Toni through any number of offices, including the Red Cross and veterans associations. This went on for a long time, with no results. Finally, thanks to the information office for Sudeten Germans, I obtained some information. But the letter I sent to an Austrian address was returned marked "Addressee Unknown." I ended up at the annual congress of Sudeten Germans.

This was a vast event that took place every year in Munich. Tens of thousands of people gathered to drink beer, sing, and dance. I approached hundreds of them, asking if anyone knew Toni, but learned nothing.

I went to see the congress organizers and was advised to broadcast a message over the public address system. I waited for hours, but Toni did not appear.

Finally, the next day, Pola and I decided to go to Klagenfurt in Carinthia where, according to the only information we had, Toni supposedly lived. We arrived at our hotel in the afternoon, and went straight to the address we had obtained from the information bureau. But none of the tenants of the two-story building had ever heard of Toni.

We had almost lost hope when we saw a thirteen-year-old girl in front of the building. She told us that Toni had once rented a room from her parents, and that he now lived in a new apartment building on the outskirts of Klagenfurt.

We knocked on the door of Toni's apartment. Nobody answered.

Wooden planks were still piled in the courtyard, so we sat down on one of the stacks and waited patiently. Hours passed.

We went to the nearest restaurant to get a bite to eat, and then returned to the house once more. Night fell, and we continued to wait. Our hearts beat faster every time a car drove past. It was a beautiful May evening. A warm breeze rustled the treetops, and a full moon illuminated the whole region. We did not return to our hotel until dawn. . . .

When we woke up it occurred to us to look in the telephone book. To our surprise and joy, we found Toni's name. He owned a music store and had become a violin maker. We saw him through the shop window, standing behind the counter. We entered the store and introduced ourselves as customers, asking him to show us several violins. But Toni recognized us right away. He was so overcome by emotion that all he could say was: "Doctor . . ."

Toni was no longer the slender, carefree policeman we had known during the war, but his laughing eyes were the same. He closed up his store and drove us in his car to Wörthrsee. We sat for hours in the garden of a restaurant in Pörtschach, where we traded memories, told stories, and gazed at the shimmering lake with its patches of silver. The past came alive once more. We spoke of Alina, of my father, of Poludniowa Street. Tears came to Toni's eyes when we told him of Alina's death. He had never married, and lived with an elderly German woman.

We stayed in Klagenfurt for two days. Toni took us all over Carinthia, showing us the sights. Again and again we evoked those distant times, the days, the hours, the misfortunes and the people who existed now only in our memory. It seems astonishing, but Toni, who had witnessed our undoing, could never bring himself to believe in Alina's death. He was convinced that she was married and that she had children. . . .

In the end, we stopped trying to convince him otherwise.

12

One year, we spent New Year's Eve in Paris. We strolled around Place Pigalle, where people from every country and of every race had gathered to welcome the New Year. It began with a deafening concert of car horns that were allowed to honk at full throttle only on this one night of the year.

Uniformed men stood outside, trying to entice people into their restaurants and cabarets. In front of one strip-tease joint I felt a tug at my sleeve. I tried to pull free, but as I did so I recognized the man.

"I've seen you somewhere before," I said, in Polish. The man looked at me in surprise and disbelief.

"Do you remember Krochmalna Street in Warsaw, and my stuffed bear lined with gold . . . in the ghetto? . . ."

The bouncer of Place Pigalle was the father of the little thief who had grabbed the precious bear from my daughter's arms during one of our moves.

"You mean you're the doctor?" he asked uncertainly.

There was no way to turn him down. My whole family had to follow him into the club.

We sat through the whole show with naked dancing girls and drank champagne at his expense. He told us the story of his life. He was the co-owner of the club. He had managed to save his family thanks to thieves who had hidden him on the Polish side. . . . If the father was to be believed, his son, the little thief, had graduated from law school and had become a sought-after attorney in Paris. His two younger children lived on a kibbutz in Israel.

He had left Poland soon after the war, because it felt to him like one big cemetery.

About the Author

Edward Reicher was born in 1900 in Lodz. He studied medicine in Warsaw and dermatology in Paris and Vienna. Both before and after the war he practiced in Lodz as a dermatologist and specialist in venereal disease. He died in Frankfurt am Main in 1975.

Translator Magda Bogin is acclaimed for her "suave" (*Publishers Weekly*) and "strikingly true" (*School Library Journal*) translation of Cervantes' *Don Quixote*, Isabel Allende's international bestseller *The House of Spirits*, and letters by children deported to Auschwitz, which appear in the landmark publication *French Children of the Holocaust*. Bogin's own novel, *Natalya, God's Messenger,* received the Harold U. Ribalow Prize. She lives in New York.